JAZZ

MASTERS

OF THE

FIFTIES

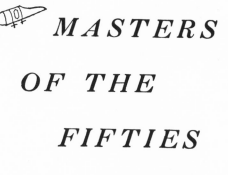

by Joe Goldberg

A DA CAPO PAPERBACK

Library of Congress Cataloging in Publication Data

Goldberg, Joe.
  Jazz masters of the fifties.

  (Da Capo paperback)
  Reprint. Originally published: New York: Macmillan,
1965 (Macmillan jazz masters series) With added photos.
  1. Jazz music. 2. Jazz musicians — Biography. I. Title.
ML3506.G64 1983   785.42′092′2 [B]   83-10141
ISBN 0-306-80197-3 (pbk.)

The author would like to thank The Atlantic Recording Corporation and World Pacific Records for permission to quote from their record liner notes.

Excerpt from Nat Hentoff's interview with Sonny Rollins and John Coltrane's article on himself used with permission of *Down Beat* magazine.

Excerpt from *Conversations with Igor Stravinsky* © 1958, 1959 by Igor Stravinsky. Used with permission of Doubleday and Company, Inc.

Excerpts from *Jazz Panorama* © 1958, 1959, 1960, 1961, 1962 by the Jazz Review Inc. Used with permission of The Macmillan Company.

Excerpt from *The Charlie Christian Story* by Ralph Ellison, published in the *Saturday Review*, May 17, 1958. Used with permission of the author and the *Saturday Review*.

This Da Capo Press paperback edition of *Jazz Masters of the Fifties* is an unabridged republication of the first edition published in New York in 1965, here supplemented with an insert of photographs. It is reprinted by arrangement with Macmillan Publishing Co., Inc.

Published by Da Capo Press, Inc.
A Subsidiary of Plenum Publishing Corporation
233 Spring Street, New York, N.Y. 10013

ACKNOWLEDGMENTS

I AM INDEBTED to many people for this book, primarily to those musicians, recording company executives, and others who gave valuable time, and, in some cases, overcame suspicion instilled by the long history of misquotation that seems indigenous to jazz journalism. There are too many to list here, but the frequency with which they are quoted is a fairly accurate index of their assistance. I am grateful for the chance of meeting with and learning from some fine artists and fascinating people.

To Martin Williams I owe the opportunity to write this book. To Nat Hentoff, whose work is referred to so often, because he is one of the few people to recognize that the way a man lives while off the stand will influence the way he plays when he is on it, I owe several instances of unusual professional generosity and encouragement.

Many of the musical insights here first belonged to Cecil Taylor, many of the nonmusical ones, to Eva Stern. Were it not for the different kinds of help offered by Nadine Martens, Sara Lownds, Billy James, Bob Levin, and Shelley Burton, this book would still remain unwritten.

Sonny Rollins will never know how much he helped, and for a casual act of friendship worth years of listening to records, I thank Miles Davis.

J.G.

CONTENTS

INTRODUCTION

WHITNEY BALLIETT, one of the most astute observers of jazz, once wrote that authors of books about the music tend to "preface their remarks with indignant statements about all the 'nonsense' written on the subject, and then sit down and write some more." He may have been defining my method.

The nonsense, I think, comes because jazz writers are in the nearly untenable position of insisting on the importance of something that most people consider as a background to drinking, dancing, conversation, and attempted seduction. As a result, writers tend to overjustify themselves; they want very much for the reader to know that they are men of intelligence, education, sensitivity, and perception, even though they write about jazz. Often, this recognition is gained at the expense of the music. A writer may unconsciously take the attitude that the music exists only so that he may make brilliant sense of it. He may base his reputation on such brilliant little treasures as the discovery that a recording by a saxophonist A, when played at the wrong speed, sounds like a recording by saxophonist B. He may indulge in the kind of wishy-washy sociology that makes an editor preface his magazine piece: "It helps put Ornette Coleman in perspective as what, at base, he is: a human being." Style, in such work, often consists of printing a man's full name (Theodore Walter Rollins); criticism, of replacing other subjective opinions with one's own; anecdote, of telling about the record on which Gene Krupa dropped his drumstick. I apologize in advance for any such instances that appear here.

Most of us probably began our appreciation of jazz knowing about some such incident as the time Gene Krupa dropped his drumsticks during a recorded *Jazz at the Philharmonic* performance of *How High the Moon*—knowing

1

that, one was immediately part of an in-group, superior to those who knew nothing more than that there were no drums for a few bars. And many people continue to use jazz for that purpose. The girl who loves to sleep with musicians is only the extreme; there is probably a bit of the "band chick" in every fan and critic.

This, too, has helped make jazz seem more than what it is: the music suffers from assuming three aspects at once; business, entertainment, and, more rarely, art. The business aspect becomes continually more grinding: the saxophonist Paul Desmond, a member of the Dave Brubeck Quartet since its formation in the early fifties, notes that Birdland is the only club in the United States still open where he played a decade ago. Because jazz is a business, many superlative musicians, such as the trumpeter Clark Terry, have settled for being craftsmen, and rarely rise above that designation to their full potential. The entertainment aspect makes clowns out of some great musicians, and has elevated to the status of jazzmen many who are only players of Negro popular music. Both aspects together run trends into the ground, so that both Sonny Rollins and the society trio at Billy Reed's Little Club could be found playing the *bossa nova* in New York shortly after it had been widely introduced into this country. On the other hand, business and entertainment have given us the LP (in jazz, an artificial means of retaining that which was never meant to be permanent), which has perpetuated many classic performances and perhaps led to the present trend toward discursiveness.

There are more pernicious aspects of the impact of business and entertainment, one of them as old as the mythology of this country. We believe in The Fastest Gun in the West; it is not enough that the new be celebrated, the old must fall before it. Thus, Ornette Coleman somehow makes Benny Carter old hat; the admission that John Coltrane or Sonny Rollins can play somehow implies that Ben Webster cannot.

In seemingly paradoxical coexistence, we find imitators of the newest style getting jobs incommensurate with their abilities. Ahmed Jamal may be remembered only as inspiration for some of Miles Davis' rhythmic ideas; the highly imitative, Ramsey Lewis, has far more LPs than the unfashionable and original Mr. Nichols. If jazz were only an art, this would not happen. Even a third-rate imitation of Miles Davis will sell records, so we hear endless recordings by muted trumpeters playing two-beat ballads. This may be good business, but it is bad jazz. If jazz is a method of self-expression, then there is a basic philosophical error in imitating another player as a profession rather than as a stepping-stone toward individuality. But business is business, and the originals only rarely record at full potential. Thus Davis, constantly burdened with thinking of something new to play may make a less polished recording than Nat Adderley imitating him.

The artists must find their music for themselves. When a listener says of a musician that he likes "the way he plays," he senses only a little of what he means. To improvise means to create—tone, melody, rhythm—so much so that someone unfamiliar with jazz might be shocked to learn that Paul Desmond and Ornette Coleman both play the alto saxophone.

This book is concerned with players who may be considered as artists. They have all come to prominence since the rise of Charlie Parker; in a sense, this book is a consideration of different uses to which Parker's discoveries have been put. To put it differently, bop, or modern jazz, is the common language of the twelve musicians discussed here, and each man speaks a different dialect. For there is, of course, a tradition involved. Too often, what seems a radical departure is that only within a jazz context; other musics have employed the startling new methods for years.

Alexander King tells a story of the hermit who went up on a mountain for twenty years and returned with a wonderful new invention that turned out to be the typewriter. The hermit had never heard of typewriters. Likewise, some of what John Coltrane plays has been known in India for centuries; some of Ornette Coleman goes back to plainsong; some of Miles Davis, to Gregorian chant; John Lewis' *Django* to a piano piece of Bartok's. What is more germane is what the painter Willem de Kooning has called "inventing the harpsicord." Harold Rosenberg has said of de Kooning that he "looked at Michelangelo's *Last Judgment* as if he were about to paint it. . . . To produce from scratch something already there is as much an act of creation as inventing something new." A parallel in jazz would be alto saxophonist Paul Desmond's use of the clarinet style of Lester Young.

Speaking of tradition, the musical shadows of two men lie over these pieces. They are the two authentic geniuses of the music, Duke Ellington and Charlie Parker, and it became necessary for me to have some knowledge of their achievements, just as, in another and far more important way, such knowledge was necessary for the musicians written about in the pages that follow. A somewhat different tradition is that of Count Basie and Lester Young, which has had a meretricious effect, too often ending in the supper-club hipness of Mel Tormé and Sammy Davis, Jr. Basie himself has begun to rely on flutes, and the West Coast fiasco of the fifties has taught us that unusual instruments begin to dominate a jazz style at the approach of the style's sterility.

That I find particular meaning in the music played by the musicians discussed herein is probably not so much a function of acute critical perception as of my age. Two friends of mine write about jazz professionally. One is about six years older than I; the other is about six years younger. The former admits to getting his greatest pleasure from Roy Eldridge, Coleman Hawkins, and Jo Jones; the latter prefers Don Cherry, Eric Dolphy, and Elvin Jones. I, in the middle, with Miles Davis, Sonny Rollins, and Philly Joe Jones, have no

1. (left to right) Bud Powell, Charlie Mingus, Max Roach, Dizzy Gillespie, and Charlie Parker in rehearsal at Massey Hall, Toronto in 1953. Photo: Frank Driggs

2. Gerry Mulligan in a still from the film *Jazz on a Summer's Day*.
Photo: Frank Driggs

3. Art Blakey in a recording studio. Photo: Frank Driggs

4. Sonny Rollins and Thelonious Monk at the Five Spot in New York, circa 1957. Photo: Frank Driggs

5. Multi-reed player Jimmy Giuffre. Photo: Frank Driggs

6. Cannonball Adderley and Miles Davis in 1959. Photo: Frank Driggs

7. Charlie Mingus in a publicity still, circa 1951. Photo: Frank Driggs

8. Ornette Coleman. Photo: Frank Driggs

ultimate recourse more meaningful than that jazz first made
its impression on me when these men were at their height.
My friends and I evolve theories and rationalize, our ages
remain.

Which perhaps only means that jazz is, after all, emotional.
I may defend Milt Jackson's romanticism only to find it become another man's sentimentality. One man sees Ella Fitzgerald as a supreme jazz singer; I find that Miss Fitzgerald
does not understand words, and has only half the answer.

I once heard two of my colleagues arguing about Lennie
Tristano. One maintained that the pianist never became a
great influence because he was rhythmically uninteresting;
the other said Tristano failed because he was white. In
this book, I have attempted to give both sides. Strict
labeling can lead to mistakes. There's also the problem of
what's new. Many of the men written about here have become the current orthodoxy even as this book was being
written. To strike out in a new direction is not of itself necessarily good. The final word on the power of what is new I
leave to Igor Stravinsky, speaking here as an old man: "Of
course, it requires greater effort to learn from one's juniors,
and their manners are not invariably good. But when you
are seventy-five and your generation has overlapped with
four younger ones, it behooves you not to decide in advance
'how far composers can go,' but to try to discover whatever
new thing it is makes the new generation new. The very
people who have done the breaking through are themselves
often the first to try to put a scab on their achievement. What
fear tells them to cry halt? What security do they seek, and
how can it be secure if it is limited? How can they forget that
they once fought against what they have become?"

That, applied to jazz, is most astute. There is also a remark
made by a gifted and learned pianist whose jazz work I
deplore, André Previn. Previn was speaking of Duke Ellington. "You know," he said, "Stan Kenton can stand in front of

a thousand fiddles and a thousand brass and make a dramatic gesture, and every studio arranger can nod his head and say, 'Oh, yes, that's done like this.' But Duke merely lifts his finger, three horns make a sound, and I don't know what it is." Similarly, the real meaning of all jazz defies explanation. But despite cries of imperfection, jazz endures, resisting all explication, while more easily categorized work is forgotten. I should like to say that it is precisely this elusive element which makes for its greatness.

Having been thus unmasked, I will add the hope that this book clears up some of the existing misunderstandings about jazz, and that it perpetuates no others.

The beginnings of the 1950's found the leadership of modern jazz somewhat demoralized. As the decade arrived, Dizzy Gillespie had to disband his big band and form a quintet which depended more on the leader's stage personality, jokes, and various musical and vocal novelties than on his brilliant trumpet or the playing of his sidemen. True, Charlie Parker was into his first public success, but he achieved it by leading a group of mushy strings, which he both embraced and disliked. Thelonious Monk's career was still obscure and esoteric except to a handful of insiders. And in 1949 and 1950, Miles Davis made, with a nine piece group, a series of recordings almost equally obscure—except to a generation of musicians who immediately marveled.

Three years later, baritone saxophonist Gerry Mulligan, who had been a contributor both as a writer and a soloist to those Davis records, was in Los Angeles. He made some records of his own with a quartet, and suddenly modern jazz had its first fad of the decade. Mulligan is certainly not responsible for the quality of some of the derivative "cool" "West Coast" music that followed, but his success seems to have triggered it.

Inevitably, the fad involved other public successes. The Dave Brubeck quartet with Paul Desmond was one. And perhaps the initial popularity of the Modern Jazz Quartet is also a part of the fad for "cool" music.

Inevitably a reaction had set in by the middle of the decade, a new fad for the "hard" and "funky" jazz that had its center in New York. And the important manifestations of it were its initial announcement by the Art Blakey group with Horace Silver; the rediscovery of Thelonious Monk; the rebirth of Miles Davis; the maturity of Sonny Rollins; the music of Charlie Mingus; and the striking, multi-faceted career of Ray Charles.

By the end of the fifties, jazz music was clearly ready to take a major step, perhaps its first truly *major* step since the mid-forties. Pianist Cecil Taylor's work was clear early evidence. The departures of John Coltrane buttressed the possibilities. And late in the decade, alto saxophonist Ornette Coleman moved from Los Angeles into the Five Spot Café in New York.

If there is any other development, fad, or style we should mention, here in the beginning, it is the so-called "third stream." The "first" stream is the European classical tradition, as it has continued there and as it has been transplanted in the United States. The second stream is the continuing evolution of jazz. The third represents efforts to combine the two, but not in the occasional borrowings of an effect—a blue note or a rhythm—by composers like Stravinsky, Milhaud, and the rest, but pieces composed for classical players and improvising jazzmen, performing together.

Jazz reached the public in the 1950's largely the way it had reached them in the previous decade—in nightclubs and on records. New styles and new fads created some new record labels and some new clubs. And as the fads passed, many of the labels and clubs also failed.

This period had seen one innovation: the jazz festival. The daddy of them all is the one at Newport, Rhode Island. Newport had the respect and enthusiasm of musicians at least at first. Later some of them came to think of it as just another job, and some journalists began to treat it as an all-star package show, spread over several days, with performers, only some of whom were worthy jazzmen. Hope lay, some felt, in the Monterey, California festival.

That briefly sketches the course of American Jazz in the fifties. To understand its real achievements, we can now take a closer look at some of the men and their music.

GERRY MULLIGAN

"IN THOSE DAYS," drummer Baby Dodds once said of early New Orleans jazz, "the instrumentation was different. When I first started out they had no piano. They mostly used bass viola, guitar, clarinet, trumpet, trombone, and drums. The guitar carried only rhythm in the bands. Actually you have a much sweeter jazz band when you have a guitar and no piano. In that way the drums couldn't outplay the other guys, because the drummer had to keep in touch with the guitars."

Since that time, jazz has evolved by adding some elements and dropping others. The classic swing rhythm section, Count Basie's, consisted of piano, guitar, bass, and drums. The bop revolution dropped the guitar, retaining it only as an occasional solo instrument.

In 1952, Gerry Mulligan, who has always had an affinity with several different eras of jazz, took the piano back out, and the result was the Gerry Mulligan Quartet, one of the most highly successful small groups of the fifties.

Mulligan, a tall, boyish, highly articulate man, knew exactly what he was doing and why: "The idea of a band without a piano is not new," he wrote in the notes to his first Pacific Jazz LP. "The very first jazz bands didn't use them (how could they? They were either marching or riding in wagons). . . To have an instrument with the tremendous capabilities of the piano reduced to the role of crutch for the solo horn was unthinkable . . . I consider the string bass to be the basis of the sound of the group, the foundation on which the solo builds his line, the main thread around which the two horns weave their contrapuntal interplay. It is possible with two voices to imply the sound or impart the feeling of any chord or series of chords as Bach shows us so thoroughly and enjoyably in his inventions.

"When a piano is used in a group it necessarily plays the

9

dominant role; the horns and bass must tune to it as it cannot tune to them, making it the dominant tonality. The
piano's accepted function of constantly stating the chords of
the progression makes the solo horn a slave to the whims of
the piano player. The soloist is forced to adapt his line to the
changes and alterations made by the pianist in the chords
of the progression.

"It is obvious that the bass does not possess as wide a
range of volume and dynamic possibilities as the drums and
horns. It is therefore necessary to keep the overall volume in
proportion to that of the bass in order to achieve an integrated
group sound."

By 1959, the pendulum of taste had swung so far that the
English critic Max Harrison could say of Mulligan's once-
revered quartet that "its instrumentation threw emphasis on
clear melodic expression and simple rhythmic construction.
The resulting lack of tension was another attraction. Whereas
artists like Tatum or Parker compel our attention with the
hectic complexity of their work, the somewhat detached relaxation of the Mulligan Quartet entertains and even in-
trigues the listener without unduly involving him. Thus,
audiences who failed to respond to the uncompromising attitude of bop or the Davis 1948 band were able, in listening to
the Quartet, to congratulate themselves on their advanced
taste while really experiencing quite straightforward music.
. . . The air of rather smart disillusionment that surrounds
interpretations like *Funny Valentine* would also be sympathetic to superficially sophisticated audiences."

In between the dates of those two quotations came a
strange era of jazz, the "cool" music of the early fifties. Not
at all strangely, now that the "cool" fad is over, those musicians who are still making a meaningful contribution are the
same ones who started the movement: Miles Davis, Gil
Evans, John Lewis, and Gerry Mulligan. The catalyst was the
nine-piece Miles Davis band of 1949 and 1950.

"Gerry wrote the easiest arrangements," Miles Davis has

said, "well, just a good sound. They were the only things that came off happy and good and quick. Gerry told me once that he was never able to get that same sound again."

Perhaps Mulligan's arrangements for the group did come off easily, but it was not because he had written something conventional and familiar. Indeed, critic André Hodeir has said that Mulligan's scoring of George Wallington's *Godchild*, along with Gil Evans' scoring of Davis' *Boplicity*, "directs jazz toward a language that seems to hold great potential riches." He further said that Mulligan's *Jeru* "boldly calls for a re-examination of form, construction, and meter."

Jazz musicians frequently borrow the so-called "song form," a European tradition actually, in which a great deal of American popular music is written. Its length is usually thirty-two measures of music delivered in four sections, each of which is eight measures long. There are usually two melodies in a "song," one called a "main strain," and the other called the "bridge" or "release." Most of us are quite familiar with the pattern, even though we may never have thought about it. For example, if we give each melody a letter, we come out with this sort of pattern for popular songs: AABA. Think of *Embraceable You*, *Body and Soul*, or hundreds of others. If a jazz musician uses such a familiar piece for improvisation, he will frequently abandon its melody, using only its outline as a basis for his improvising of new melodies. But that outline repeats regularly, over and over, as a soloist's invention flows along, much less regularly. Mulligan's scores for the Davis group not only broke down the rigidity of this song form, they broke through the usual rhythmic mold of jazz as well.

Hodeir elucidates it this way: "The exposition of *Godchild* drastically 'reconsiders' the traditional structure of this classical thirty-two-bar theme with bridge. The addition of first two beats and then four to the initial phrase makes the first period cover seventeen and a half bars instead of sixteen. The bridge, on the other hand, is half a bar shorter than customary. Only the final phrase keeps its original structure in the exposition. *Jeru* is still more revolutionary. It includes four choruses in all. The exposition begins in the traditional way with a double eight-bar phrase. The fact that the bridge has twelve bars would not be surprising in itself if five of them—from the fourth to the eighth—were not in 3/4 time. The reprise covers nine bars. Here, then, is an exposition with an uneven number of bars and beats. The same is true of the final re-exposition. Only the second chorus, which is set aside for Davis' improvisation, is brought back to the customary proportions. The third has thirty-two bars also, but two of them, the fourth and twelfth, are in 2/4."

The real origin of the Davis band's style was in the sound of the Claude Thornhill Orchestra, for which both Gil Evans and Mulligan had written arrangements. Composer-arranger George Russell says that "the most important innovator of the fifties was Gerry Mulligan. He did away with the piano and wrote some fantastic pieces." Russell described to Nat Hentoff in *The New Yorker* something of Mulligan's mood at the time: "He was very clever, witty, and saucy, the way he is now. I remember his talking about a musician who was getting a lot of attention by copying another. 'A Sammy Kaye is bad enough,' Gerry said. 'A bastard Sammy Kaye is too much.' He had more or less the same difficulties that made us all bitter and hostile. He was immensely talented, and he didn't have enough of an opportunity to exercise his talent. . . . Gerry was always interested in the way each of us felt about music, but he was impatient with anything that moved too far away from the mainstream."

With that last comment, Russell accurately isolates the reason why Mulligan, Davis, Evans, and Lewis have remained, while the West Coast movement which sprang up in their wake has largely been forgotten. It has been pointed out several times that these four men are by no means West Coast musicians to begin with, but the question involves much more than geographical accident. The prime progenitor

of West Coast jazz music was the Stan Kenton band in its
Shorty Rogers-Shelly Manne days. Many of the players who
came out of that band to become West Coast standard-
bearers were so single-minded in their pursuit of elusive
"modernity" that they often neglected to anchor their styles
in anything more fruitful than the most easily assimilated
licks of their direct predecessors. Fugues and atonal compositions were written, sometimes with a minimum of improvisation, and flutes, oboes, and cellos were employed. At the
height of the self-imposed sterility of the music, the inevitable reaction set in, and in the late fifties albums by the
better-known West Coast players began to appear that were
heavily influenced by Miles Davis, Sonny Rollins, and Horace
Silver.

None of this, however, really affected Mulligan. Very early
in the publicized stages of his career he arrived at what
was, for him, a viable concept of jazz, and all the work he
has done since has been a variation on that concept, even
some scores he did for Kenton. He has said on several occasions that he deeply admired the work of trumpeter Red
Nichols. Nichols, in an earlier era, was concerned, as it had
become necessary for Mulligan to be, with the problem of
finding what Max Harrison has termed "an ensemble style for
white jazz." Nichols sounded much like Bix Beiderbecke, and
at this point lineages begin to mesh. Beiderbecke's partner
on several occasions was Frankie Trumbauer, the C-melody
saxophonist whom Lester Young called "my idol." At a certain stage in jazz history, the names Lester Young and Basie
are virtually synonymous, Young the sideman and Basie the
pianist and leader combining to create a style of jazz that
has been a predominant influence on most jazz and certainly
many white saxophonists since. Young was a melodist, a
horizontal thinker. Mulligan found it freer to explore melody
in the absence of a piano—indeed, Young had made a few
pianoless records himself.

Music has always been Mulligan's prime concern. Born

Gerald Joseph Mulligan in Queens Village, Long Island, on April 6, 1927, he began playing such youthful instruments as the ocarina and the ukelele, and took the piano lessons that are mandatory in many families. His father was a management engineer, forced to travel to where the job was, and Mulligan spent his youth in several different towns. He told Hentoff, in possibly romanticized fashion, that the real beginnings of his career occurred one day in Marion, Ohio. "I was on my way to school, when I saw the Red Nichols bus sitting in front of a hotel. I was in the second or third grade, and that was probably when I first wanted to become a band musician and go on the road. It was a small old Greyhound bus with a canopied observation platform, and on the bus was printed 'RED NICHOLS AND HIS FIVE PENNIES.' It all symbolized travel and adventure. I was never the same after that."

His decision to become a jazz musician was greeted nowhere by shouts of joy; his first arrangement, for a school band in Michigan, was rejected because the song, *Lover*, was not thought proper material. At fourteen, he briefly decided to become a priest, but when he learned the realities of church music work, he abandoned the idea.

The first person to give him active encouragement was a former dance-band musician named Sammy Correnti, who taught Mulligan clarinet and the rudiments of arranging. In 1944, the family moved to Philadelphia, and Mulligan, now playing clarinet and tenor saxophone, organized a dance band in high school and sold two arrangements to the house band at radio station WCAU. He quit high school after his third year, because a band he had been playing with that summer was planning to go on a road tour. When the tour did not materialize, Mulligan got a thirteen-week arranging contract with Tommy Tucker, certainly no jazzman, and went on the road with him. At one point on the tour, he had an opportunity to hear the great band Billy Eckstine had at the time, and was greatly impressed with it. The experience caused Mulligan to change his arranging style to the extent that the conservative Tucker terminated their relationship at the end of the contract period. Returning to Philadelphia, Mulligan took a regular job as an arranger at WCAU, whose band was now led by Elliot Lawrence, and remained for about a year.

He began traveling back and forth between Philadelphia and New York, primarily to see a new friend, Charlie Parker, who was one of the few musicians to encourage him. By January 1946, he had settled in New York and became an arranger for Gene Krupa, who had a substantial hit with Mulligan's *Disc Jockey Jump*.

That job lasted another year, after which he got the job arranging for Thornhill. A friendship began with Thornhill's chief arranger, Gil Evans, and the result was the long sessions of talk in Evans' apartment which eventually led to the Miles Davis recordings.

It was during this time in New York that Mulligan—an occasional user of marijuana since a Tommy Tucker sideman had introduced him to it, and arrested once for possession of it while walking down a Los Angeles street with Parker—found himself a prisoner of heroin. Both because of addiction and lack of steady work, the next years were chaotic ones for Mulligan, who has little to show for them but a Prestige LP and one famous arrangement for Stan Kenton, *Young Blood*. His subsequent rehabilitation, he says, was largely due to his friend Gale Madden. It was Miss Madden, he also says, who introduced him to the possibilities of the pianoless rhythm section.

Mulligan, then living in Los Angeles, formed a quartet based on that idea. In 1952, a young man named Richard Bock, press agent for a small Los Angeles club called The Haig, hired Mulligan to play at the sessions he was producing there on the club's off-night. Bock was sufficiently impressed with the pianoless quartet to borrow enough money to record it. That was the beginning of Mulligan's success and also of Bock's company, Pacific Jazz Records.

That first Quartet, featuring trumpeter Chet Baker, was phenomenally successful. There is no telling what the group—a definite combination of right thing, right place, right time—might have achieved, but in September 1953, Mulligan was arrested on a narcotics charge, and went to prison until Christmas of that year. As one of Mulligan's friends recalls, "Chet met Gerry when he got out of jail and said, 'I want four hundred dollars a week.' This to a guy who'd just taken a bust and didn't have a job." That, of course, was the end of the Mulligan-Baker Quartet. Since then, Mulligan has led groups of various sizes and shapes, always searching carefully for sympathetic partners.

"You look for people to play with," he once wrote, "who have that same kind of attitude toward music as the older men you admired and learned from." Mulligan was committed to a style which has variously been called neo-Dixie and neo-swing, and he affirmed that counterpoint could be used in a modern jazz group without recourse to classical pastiche. "What I came back to," he has said, "is that jazz is a music to be played and not to be intellectualized on." He has also said, "Jazz music is fun to me."

It would seem to an observer that each of Mulligan's groups has stressed humor, counterpoint, and the pleasure of playing. But the players in the various Mulligan units have themselves insisted on the unique qualities of each separate group. Mulligan himself has said, "Each of my groups has had an entirely different sound and an entirely different effect on me." Some of the musicians who have been in and out of Mulligan's small units are saxophonist Zoot Sims, trombonist Bob Brookmeyer, trumpeter Jon Eardley, bassists Carson Smith and Bill Crow, and drummer Chico Hamilton.

Perhaps the Mulligan co-instrumentalist who most felt his own uniqueness was the trumpeter Art Farmer, who

joined Mulligan in 1958 after two years with Horace Silver.
"I was the first one in the Quartet not from the West Coast
group, so to speak," Farmer says. "They talked about Red
Nichols and others, and I had a whole different set of influences. It was hard for me, at first. Not so much because
there was no piano, but because the bass lines and Gerry
playing behind you can pretty much direct your solo, and
turn it in a different way than you would play it. It's easier
for the baritone to play behind the trumpet than the reverse,
because the baritone's lower, and I didn't play behind Gerry
as much as some of the other guys did. We had some great
nights with that group; we only made one record, and it doesn't
tell you what we could do. I know the group changed when I
was in it; I think maybe I changed Gerry's playing more
than he changed mine."

In 1959, Farmer, who does not consider himself a big-band
trumpet player, left the group because Mulligan was working toward the fulfillment of one of his long-cherished
dreams: still considering himself to be more arranger than
soloist, he wanted a big band for which to write.

In many ways, the Mulligan "Concert Jazz Band" which
resulted was a direct outgrowth of the Quartets; the two
major soloists were Mulligan and trombonist Bob Brookmeyer. Sometimes the band played behind the soloist the
sort of contrapuntal line one man would have executed in
the Quartet. The band also echoed the Miles Davis Capitol
recordings, and used re-scorings of some of those 1949
pieces.

"The band represents a culmination of my career thus
far," Mulligan said. "All I have learned over the years has
been applied." But a lot had happened in the ten-year
interval between the Davis and Mulligan bands, and the
best summation of it was given by Brookmeyer, in a remark
made to Martin Williams: "I was really beginning to feel that
jazz was passing me by. The newest things I have heard
in person—I go to listen to Ornette or George Russell's

group and I love them. But playing like that is not possible
for me. I feel the way I think Buck Clayton may have felt
around 1947. I put on a Joe Turner record and it gives me
a starting point, but the newer things make me feel I am
finished, and I'll have to wait out the rest of my life making
soft-drink jingles for television. This band puts me in jazz,
making jazz music I can love and respect."

Brookmeyer's comment accurately points to the fact that
not only Gerry Mulligan, but jazz itself, had become big
business in the last decade. "Jazz is a living," Brookmeyer
says, and it has become a much better living since jazzmen
have begun to be considered as candidates for work in the
major radio, television, and motion picture studio orchestras.

As Martin Williams said, reviewing one of the Mulligan
band's recordings in *Down Beat,* "This was, in effect, a
studio band. Perhaps only a studio band of the best men
could cut some of these arrangements." And so, in a sense,
Mulligan has been dependent upon a new breed of jazz
musician, new because he is able to read a difficult part in
almost any style as well as improvise with individuality.
Perhaps more than anyone else, the type is personified by
sometime Concert Jazz Band trumpeter Clark Terry.

"Every band," says Mulligan bassist Bill Crow, "needs one
or two guys like Clark or Zoot Sims, guys who can get up
and do 'that thing' at will, create excitement and get everyone swinging. Clark has a very special talent. He can fit
into any situation, play an original solo that's exactly what's
called for in the piece, and end up in just the right place,
so that it all fits in. That's why he's always in such demand."

Terry himself, a witty, urbane man in his early forties,
is sufficiently realistic and astute to know that musical
ability alone is not always enough. "You have to be something of a diplomat, too," he says. A veteran of the two
most influential jazz bands we have had, those of Count
Basie and Duke Ellington, he became an NBC–TV staff
musician, one of the first Negroes to do so. "I'm sort of like

Jackie Robinson," he says. "There could be trouble in a situation like that, and the fellows want to know not only how you play, but whether they can get along with you." Since joining NBC—he has been a member of the orchestra on both the Jack Paar and Johnny Carson versions of the *Tonight* Show—Terry has often logged as many as seven record dates a week, in situations varying from straight jazz recordings, through section work in large orchestras accompanying vocalists, to the most musically unrewarding commercial work. He is so much in demand that during any New York-based jazz recording made in the early sixties that consisted of seven or more men, the puckishly witty Terry trumpet might be heard. He is also exemplary because his reputation is largely confined to his fellow musicians and hard-core jazz fans. Since he no longer travels, many who admire his work have never seen him.

Another incident suggests the conditions in which Mulligan operates: in 1961, Terry and Brookmeyer, wishing to play jazz but unable, because of various commitments, to leave New York, formed a joint quintet to play in Manhattan clubs whenever they could; the group usually included the drummer Gus Johnson. In April 1962, the Terry-Brookmeyer Quintet played New York's Half Note for two weeks; the following Tuesday, Terry, Brookmeyer, and Johnson were all part of the Mulligan Concert Jazz Band performing at Birdland. "Bob checked Gerry's schedule before he made the booking," bassist Bill Crow adds.

That Mulligan is able to exact such loyalty is one of the reasons he was able to attempt the band at the time he did. Drummer Mel Lewis, for instance, gave up lucrative work in the Hollywood studios to travel with him. Terry points to one of the reasons: "Gerry's a real leader. He respects all the guys, and knows how much they contribute, and you feel you're part of things. He pays well, too. He's not like one leader I worked for, who used to say, 'I want you guys to remember it's *me* they're paying to see.'" And the *esprit* he was able to instill is indicated by Brookmeyer: "We didn't want to make money, we wanted to prove a point. That there could still be a great big-band."

Those who pinned their musical hopes on the Mulligan band did so primarily for one reason: they expected new Mulligan arrangements. However, Mulligan contributed few scores to the book.

Since, as his friends say, Mulligan wanted the band so that he might write for it, the question is why he did not. "Maybe it's just a long dry season," Bill Crow says. "And then, there's so much involved with this band that he didn't know about. These days, the business is so complex that you have to hire a manager to talk to your agent. And then, it takes Gerry a long time to get himself together every day to do one or two things."

Most musicians are agreed on what constitutes Mulligan's major contribution to the band. "He's a great editor," Crow says. "You should see the way he changes charts, tightens them up. He knows exactly what he wants, and he wants a quiet band. He can swing at about fifteen decibels lower than any other band."

By not writing all the scores himself, Mulligan greatly benefited the young arranger, Gary McFarland. "I asked someone if it would be possible to submit an arrangement to the band," McFarland says, "and someone said, 'Call up Bob Brookmeyer, he'll give you a straight answer.' He invited me to a rehearsal, and I took two pieces with me, *Weep*, and another piece called *Chuggin'*. Someone said, 'You better take your scissors with you when you go up there.'

"I think Gerry taught me the greatest lesson I ever had, which is simply to make your point. An arrangement is something like an essay, and somewhere in there you have to come to the point, to say whatever it is you want to say. Those two arrangements don't sound now too much like they did when I brought them in. Gerry's a great editor, but I think business keeps him from writing himself. I get a good bit of work now, but it never would have happened if Gerry hadn't been so wise, generous and open minded about those first charts."

Mulligan himself has said, "What I've done in the fifties is not really new writing; it's based on what I wrote for Miles." In recent years, his reputation has been achieved as a personality more than as a musician. Much of his energy has been devoted to proving that he can play with anyone; on records he has "met" Thelonious Monk (in a session which throws a harsh glare on Mulligan's rhythmic limitations), Paul Desmond, Johnny Hodges, Ben Webster, and even the long-standing master of Mulligan's instrument, Harry Carney. His in-person appearances have been more varied. Well-known as one of the last of the musicians who love to play at any opportunity, he shows up at all manner of jazz festivals, and plays with members of any school or era with equal effectiveness—this with the exception of the most recent innovators, whom he says he has not had time to hear. One friend has said that Mulligan's former agent, Joe Glaser, was less concerned than he might have been with the fortunes of the big band because his primary objective was to groom Mulligan as a personality, a possible replacement when another Glaser client, Louis Armstrong, eventually retired. And he might not have made a bad choice. As Bill Crow says, "He's an unusual looking guy, a good talker, playing a very unusual instrument. A lot of the interest in him doesn't have much to do with music."

And many of Mulligan's interests have little to do with jazz. Crow says, "He's become one of the golden people, and that can be strong wine," referring to the show business elite, a loose-knit international group that exists on mutual exclamations of affection.

"Jazz," Mulligan says, "is only one of many things I want to do. I'd like to make another movie. And every once in a while, you just have to get away from all of it." An honest man, he is disturbed by the world of big business he now finds himself a part of. He is disappointed with most business dealings he has had with recording companies. Pointing to

one example, he says, 'I had a group that was really hot, and I said, 'Let's make a record now.' They said, 'There's no studio available.' Three weeks later, when we hadn't played or rehearsed, they called up and said, 'Do you want to record?'"
He has fared little better with many clubs, but one man in particular remains his friend: Max Gordon, owner of New York's Village Vanguard. The Vanguard is Mulligan's unofficial home base, and he can be found there when either he or the club has an open week, playing more exuberantly than ever, his long, lean body seeming to describe his own melodic twists, still rapping out his own acerb comments to the audience: "You'll have to excuse us. We're progressives. We have to change the chords. The only chords that are popular are the ones you can hang yourself with."

Toward the end of 1962, Mulligan, who simply stops work and retreats from public life whenever he feels like it, began accepting more and more engagements. He was apparently welcome, for he began appearing in New York clubs other than the Vanguard. Once again he had a quartet, this time with Brookmeyer, Crow, and drummer Gus Johnson. Mulligan, Crow, and Brookmeyer are men ideally suited to work together: mordantly witty, often bitter men, none of them makes his living exclusively from jazz, and all are professionals more than artists. Mulligan, especially, can stand backstage at a club, enraged at something which has just occurred, and five minutes later walk out on the bandstand and play as if he were the happiest man in the world. His charming, often poignant melodic lines and personal harmonies have made him one of the great popularizers in jazz; it is no wonder that Mulligan records and the Ella Fitzgerald "song books" are side by side in many "aware" homes. Seemingly one can have, with his music, all the pleasures of being involved without paying the inevitable price of true involvement. Which is not to say that Mulligan lacks conviction; he obviously does not. Very few musicians are capable of presenting a naked emotional experience in jazz, and few listeners can take it if offered. Mulligan himself seems to come closest on the rare occasions when he plays piano, and, significantly, Art Farmer says, "He only plays piano when he's bugged."

Probably, Mulligan's ultimate reputation will be as a writer, mentor, and organizer. He is a superb catalyst: musicians love to play with him, often play better in his company, and the list of excellent musicians with great regard for him encompasses such diverse men as Miles Davis, Paul Desmond, Rex Stewart, and George Russell. He may be one of those men who, more by example than deed, helped shape the course of jazz.

In the meantime, Mulligan, still a young man, has a long career ahead of him. With his wide range of interests and accomplishments, and his dislike of specialization, it is difficult to speculate on what direction that career might take. Brookmeyer, a close friend who seems essential to Mulligan's musical and personal well-being, once said of a famous bandleader, "It must be a terrible thing, living in your own shadow." In one sense, that remark could apply to Mulligan. But he is certain to endure as a personality. He once told Nat Hentoff of his reverence for George M. Cohan: "I've always been a sucker for the debonair, big-time, old-style show business attitude," he said. Which comes close to defining the embodiment of the jazz musican-as-craftsman: debonair, big-time, old-style Gerry Mulligan.

Selected Discography

Gerry Mulligan Quartet with Chet Baker, WORLD PACIFIC 1207.
Gerry Mulligan Quartet, FANTASY 3220.
What Is There To Say?, COLUMBIA CL 1307.
Gerry Mulligan and the Concert Jazz Band at the Village Vanguard, VERVE V-8396.
Gerry Mulligan Quartet, VERVE V-8466.

THELONIOUS MONK

"HE DOESN'T GO to see people," Harry Colomby, a Long Island school teacher, says of his friend Thelonious Monk, whose career he has managed now for several years. "If I invite him over, he'll say, 'Why not come over here? It takes just as long.' He'll stand on the corner, in his neighborhood, and somehow, people wind up coming to him. Maybe he'll dance a little to get attention, but that's all. And sooner or later, they come to see him."

Colomby's remark is the best capsule commentary on Monk's career I have ever encountered. As Nat Hentoff put it (in his book, *The Jazz Life*), "Monk's final recognition seemed to occur without his active participation. The music, of course, was there to be argued about, mocked, and praised, but there were no interviews (until recently), no friendships (slight or otherwise) with the critics, no letters to trade-press editors or ghosted articles. There was no personal advocacy at all—except the playing and the writing. The music formed a recognizable entity, although a controversial one; behind it was mostly vapor in dark glasses and a goatee."

But the recognition has come. Colomby says, "Monk felt it would happen, if he waited. It wasn't arrogance, he just knew." And it has come completely on Monk's terms. Only rarely has he been someone else's sideman, either in person or on records. You will find no Monk recording of showtune scores. He has simply done what he has wanted to, and the results have happened by themselves.

In the meantime, during the years of obscurity, the New York police force participated in the making of jazz legend. For six years, 1951–57, Monk was deprived of the right to work as a musician in New York City. His cabaret card, a prerequisite for steady employment in establishments that serve liquor, was taken away by the police. He was found sitting with a friend in an automobile that had narcotics hidden in it. Monk could have cleared himself by informing on his friend, who owned the narcotics, but he refused. Neither would he leave New York to get work. "This is my city," he said. During those six years, the only money he made came from rare recording dates and an occasional weekend job. Despite the fact that he has a wife and child, it seems never to have occurred to Monk to attempt to earn his living in any other way but through music. "He has a kind of contempt for people who are artists and take day jobs," Colomby said. "The only time I ever knew him to take a job, he helped some friends move some furniture. He took one load up, and that was it."

For two years during that period, I lived around the corner from the West 63rd Street apartment Monk has occupied in Manhattan for nearly thirty years, and he looked, on the several occasions I saw him on the street, like anything but a man who was, as Colomby put it, "sharing meals, sharing sandwiches, sharing cigarettes." Monk is one of those men who would probably manage to look regal in a sweatsuit. Over six feet tall, built as massively as, say, Broderick Crawford, he wears an impressive beard, and his eyes are usually hidden behind bamboo-framed sunglasses. Whenever I saw him, he was elegantly dressed, usually wearing one of his several hats or caps. He was obviously the king of the neighborhood, and the kids playing ball in the street would pause in their game to shout, "Hey, Monk!"

"As long as I've known him," Colomby says, "and even in the hardest times, he always had an air of celebrity."

Such an air is fitting for a man who has achieved what Monk has. For, if one of the men discussed in this book endures as a major contributor of the stature of Ellington or Parker, that man will be Thelonious Monk. And perhaps, in a way, it was the extraordinary impact of Parker's music that contributed to the long neglect of Monk's work. By now, the stories of the casual jam sessions at the Harlem nightclubs,

Minton's Playhouse and Monroe's Uptown House, which included such musicians as Monk, Parker, Dizzy Gillespie, Kenny Clarke and Charlie Christian, have been romanticized as "the birth of bop" (a birth the parents probably never realized they were attending at the time). Much perspective on what actually took place has been lost. And Parker was dead and Gillespie had been lionized and ignored in turn before the public ever heard of Monk.

Monk himself has told Nat Hentoff, "I was just playing a gig, trying to play music. While I was at Minton's anybody sat in if he could play. I never bothered anybody. I had no particular feeling that anything new was being built. It's true modern jazz probably began to get popular there, but some of these histories and articles put what happened over the course of ten years into one year. They put people all together in one time in one place. I've seen practically everybody at Minton's, but they were just there playing. They weren't giving any lectures."

What has become increasingly obvious, and what is most clearly exemplified on a historically valuable Verve reunion of Monk, Parker, and Gillespie called *Bird and Diz*, is that Monk was never a bop musician. Perhaps it is this initial misunderstanding, coupled with a press that heavily overstated the mad genius aspects of his character, that kept Monk so long in obscurity.

At one time, as the recording made of a jam session with Charlie Christian at Minton's in 1941 proves, Monk sounded a good deal like Teddy Wilson. He can be heard, on that recording, blithely making runs that many writers have for years assumed were beyond his technical grasp.

But sometime between then and 1947, when he began his great series of recordings for Blue Note, Monk apparently *chose* not to do what is commonly thought of as playing the piano. "They don't understand," says Cecil Taylor, a young pianist who venerates Monk, "about technique, they don't understand about tone. These people think that if you play fast—or that you play a lot of notes—but the ability to project sound is just as much a part of it as anything else. This eliminates a whole spew of musicians who are thought to be great technicians." It does not, however, eliminate Monk. As Steve Lacy, the young soprano saxophonist who worked with Monk in the summer of 1960, says, "If technique in jazz is the art of making sense, then he's got more technique than anybody. Or if technique is not wasting any notes, then he's got more technique than anybody. And he certainly can play the piano. He can get more varied colors, sounds, rhythms and shapes out of the piano than anybody I know. He plays the whole instrument. He gets more out of one note than any other piano player, perhaps with the exception of maybe Duke or Cecil Taylor. He's got fabulous technique. They talk about him having no technique, that's absurd."

Monk was working, probably not with any conscious deliberation, but simply because of his circumstances and because he has always been a self-feeding artist, on a music that came, to a greater extent than that of any musician of his times, completely from within jazz. Most other important composer-pianists—Morton, Ellington, Waller, John Lewis, Cecil Taylor—have borrowed, with varying degrees of successful assimilation, from formal European music. This gives the listener an unconscious feeling of ease and familiarity with their work, but there is no such convenient handle for Monk.

To find Monk's antecedents, one must look within the jazz tradition. The most direct link is to Ellington, and beyond that, one looks to James P. Johnson, Willie "The Lion" Smith, and bluesmen like Jimmy Yancey. But in each case, the influence has been stripped of European accretions. As Taylor puts it, "Monk had the kernel." The result is a jagged, humorous, powerfully swinging music that always sounds like a wryly amused commentary on itself. The supposed absence of technique is due to an unusually small pair of hands for a pianist, which leads Monk to play with his fingers spread flat, rather than in the delicate arch favored by classical musicians, and occasionally to employ his elbows for support. The adverse reaction was beginning to set in as early as 1944, when Monk was accompanist to tenor saxophonist Coleman Hawkins. "One of the worst things I went through in those days," Hawkins has recalled, "was with Monk, when he was working in my group. I used to get it every night—'Why don't you get a piano player?' and 'What's that stuff he's playing?'"

All of these remarks could well have been made on no other evidence than the Blue Note recordings. For although they comprise only two LPs and a portion of a third, even with a few alternate masters included, they constitute the core of Monk's achievement. In the next several years, he wrote only a few pieces to stand beside those on the Blue Note series (and these remarks have not, as yet, touched upon Monk's towering importance as a jazz composer). His playing, while reflecting the added depth that comes with maturity, has branched off in no startling new directions. With the exception of the Charlie Christian records and four pieces recorded as accompanist to Coleman Hawkins, Monk appeared on the musical scene full-formed, and has remained intractably Monk, with little change, ever since. In a sense, all he has done in the meantime is wait for the future to catch up to him.

This is of a piece with everything Monk has done. He has given only the kernel in his music and in his extra-musical relations with the world around him. It did not bother him that the great Blue Note records, containing such compositional masterpieces as 'Round About Midnight, Ruby My Dear, Criss Cross and Straight, No Chaser, were released in the midst of the clamor about bop, and therefore were largely ignored. It seemed enough that *he* knew what he was doing.

"Everything I play is different," Monk told Frank London Brown. "Different melody, different harmony, different struc-

ture. Each piece is different from the other one. I have a
standard, and when the song tells a story, when it gets a certain *sound,* then it's through . . . completed." One of the
things about Monk's compositions, setting them apart from
the vast slew of "jazz originals," is that they are *compositions,*
in which harmony, melody, rhythm, and instrumental sound
are all part of a carefully conceived whole. One of the few
others of whom this can be said is Ellington. "If you know
the melody," Monk once told a musician who insisted on
playing the usual string of chord changes, "you can make a
better solo." Lacy absorbed this lesson while working with
Monk. "I have respect for his melodies," he says, "and I
knew enough not to just regard them as chord progressions,
but as songs to be presented. One of the things about his
music is the way that it's put together, the way things evolve
out of other things. The way he'll build a whole bridge out
of one little part of the first section. His tunes are fabulously
put together, really. Someday people will realize just how
well put together they really are." Lacy, who recorded an
entire album of Monk's music for Prestige before working
with him, rejects the notion that the pieces are hard to play.
"They're not, really. It's just that if you learn one or two of
them you don't understand them. But if you learn thirty of
them or so, they're not hard after that. You understand how
simple they really are, how logical in his own system. They're
extremely logical, they just figure, and even when some of
his tunes might have eight bars, seven bars and seven bars,
twenty-two bars altogether, yet they're the most natural
things in the world after you get used to them, and they're
just right. They couldn't be any more, or any less. There's
another tune that has a three-and-a-half bar bridge, and if
you try to figure it out and count it out you'll get lost as hell,
but if you just relax and give in to it, it's perfectly natural.
His tunes are very old-fashioned, really, in a lot of ways. He
obviously knows the popular music of the twenties and
thirties very well, because the structures of his pieces, when

you get down to what they are underneath, they're very simple and old-fashioned, and yet they're new as today."

The world of Thelonious Monk, aside from what he has given us as a pianist and composer, is little known. He was born in Rocky Mount, North Carolina, but moved when he was very young to the neighborhood of New York where he still lives. He was attracted to the piano at about six, and had some study a few years later. His youthful musical experience was varied, encompassing church organ and a stint accompanying a touring evangelist ("She preached and healed and we played"). When he returned to New York, Monk, then about seventeen, began the search for work that was not really to be successful until 1957. "I worked all over town," he has said. "Non-union jobs; $20 a week, seven nights a week; and then the boss might fire you any time and you never got your money. I've been on every kind of job you can think of." Then came the Minton's days, and brief periods with Lucky Millinder and Dizzy Gillespie's 1946 big band, but in the main, work was always hard to come by. Probably the bitter tone of one remark attributed to him stems from that time: "Most club owners think you're a traveling vaudeville routine, with a clear-cut act twenty minutes long that's ready to go on four times a night. They want every jazz musician to get a line six blocks long outside the place every night." Monk did not cause lines to form. What he did do was help younger musicians. "If I hadn't met Monk shortly after I came to New York around 1945," Miles Davis told Hentoff, "I wouldn't have advanced as quickly as some say I did. He showed me voicings and progressions, and I remember Charlie Parker would take me down to listen to Monk all the time and make me sit in with him."

Then, in 1947, came the Blue Note recordings, which established him as a major musician and cemented his affinity with such players as Art Blakey and Milt Jackson. In 1951 came the loss of the police card. "Thelonious had trouble getting work even before he lost the card," Monk's wife, Nellie, has said. "Therefore, it wasn't a sudden total calamity. People had told so many stories about his being unreliable and eccentric that it had always been hard."

Whether or not it was a total calamity, the loss of the police card made a bad financial situation worse. But, as Mrs. Monk has said, "Monk is a proud man. He doesn't suffer on the surface. He never let people know how bad off he was, even when he couldn't find work. Not even when he was sick in the hospital. He's like a rock. I think that's why people admire him. He proves that one can keep his integrity under the worst circumstances."

Nellie Monk went to work herself, so that her husband would not have to compromise. One of the few other sources of income he had in those years came from Prestige, the label he joined in 1952. He cut eight trio tracks for Prestige in 1952, including some of his best compositions, *Little Rootie Tootie*, *Trinkle Tinke*, *Bemsha Swing*, and *Reflections*. In 1953, he recorded a quintet album with Julius Watkins on French horn and Sonny Rollins, reportedly his favorite musician. ("Bird never excited me like he did the others," he has said. " 'Bird is a god,' they said. He wasn't to me! No, and no one else was, either.") If possible, these recordings attracted less attention and more ridicule than the Blue Notes.

As with so many modern musicians, one comes to the year 1954 and finds that a renaissance was being effected on Prestige. A Monk quintet, recorded on May 11, includes one of his best melodies, *We See; Locomotive*, which sounds as though it might have had its origin in speculations on Charlie Parker's *Now's the Time; Hackensack;* and the brilliant and poignant revision of *Smoke Gets In Your Eyes*.

On September 22 he recorded what is probably his best trio set, with Percy Heath and Art Blakey. It includes *Nutty, Work*, a typically hesitant version of *Just A Gigolo*, and one indisputable masterpiece, *Blue Monk*. Not a "modern" blues in structure—the fourth bar has no rest—it is close to the blues of Yancey, and Monk makes his solo into a capsule history of jazz piano.

On October 25 he accompanied Sonny Rollins on a set of three standards, and on Christmas Eve, he recorded the legendary Miles Davis-Monk-Milt Jackson date. Davis was displeased with Monk's performance. It is understandable that Davis, who likes Red Garland and Ahmad Jamal, would not approve of Monk's accompaniment, but others, among them Sonny Rollins and Steve Lacy, feel that he is the finest accompanist in jazz. Monk's main contribution to the date, aside from whatever he contributed to the tense situation that afternoon, was his classic solo on the first take of *Bags' Groove*, an extended improvisation on one small melodic fragment.

In 1955, Monk left Prestige to record for Riverside Records. Riverside recording director Orrin Keepnews has a photostatic copy of the letter releasing Monk from his Prestige contract, unusual in that Monk owed Prestige, at the time of his release, $108.27, a sum which Keepnews advanced him. Prestige president Bob Weinstock explains it this way: "At the time, the money Thelonious got for recording for me was probably his only source of income. His records didn't sell then, and I recorded him often anyway, to help. As so often happens, those records are now historical. He had overdrawn that amount, and when he asked for his release, I was happy for him, and hoped that it would be good for him."

The first set Monk recorded for Riverside was a collection of Ellington pieces; the second was made up of standards by various composers. Both were trio dates, and both were deliberate attempts to dispel, through the use of familiar material, the myth of Monk as a nearly unapproachable musician. Keepnews states that Monk was happy with both ideas. "He told me," Lacy adds, "he never does anything unless he wants to do it, and he's the only man I've ever met who really does do exactly what he want to, with no jive at all, just exactly what he wants to do."

Two things then happened almost simultaneously to Monk which changed the course of his career and made him into the unassailable artist that much of the jazz world finds him today.

The first was the release in 1957 of an album recorded in December 1956, *Brilliant Corners.* It was the first Riverside record devoted to Monk originals, and he wrote three new pieces for it: the title tune, *Pannonica,* and *Ba-lue Bolivar Balues-are.* (Pannonica is the complete first name of the lady usually known as Nica, the Baroness de Koenigswarter, who has befriended most of the better-known East Coast jazz musicians, and has been a particular help to Monk and his family during their years of hardship. The latter tune, a phonetic spelling of Monk's pronunciation of what would ordinarily be *Blue Bolivar Blues,* takes its name from the hotel where the Baroness was staying at the time Monk composed the piece.)

Nat Hentoff gave the album five stars in *Down Beat,* and Monk moved into what Keepnews calls, with considerable accuracy, "the automatic five-star category"—indeed, all three of his albums reviewed in the magazine that year received that rating. "Before that," Keepnews adds, "Monk was small, and so were we."

The second occurrence was of far greater importance. In 1957, Monk, with the assistance of the Baroness, regained his cabaret card. That summer, he brought a quartet into the Five Spot Café in New York, and the man who had threatened to become a dim legend was again on view before the public. In a sense, it is fitting that one of the musicians who has gained the most from Monk, Cecil Taylor, should have been indirectly responsible. The Five Spot, in Cooper Square, had been a hangout for the abstract-expressionist painters who live in the neighborhood, and since many of the painters have an affinity for modern jazz, young musicians found it a pleasant place to jam, and there were even semi-regular sessions. Taylor brought a quartet in on a regular basis, and his

engagement was so successful that owner Joe Termini decided on a permanent jazz policy. Soon afterward, Termini
installed Monk, now available to play, and a minimum. It was
the making of both Monk and the club, which soon became
the most "in" place in town.

Most of the public then knew Monk only as a highly eccentric man with a highly unusual name (the full name is
Thelonious Sphere Monk; it was his father's name and his
son now carries it) who had written *'Round About Midnight*.
Aside from neighborhood people and hard-core jazz fans,
those first audiences were mostly composed of college kids,
people who considered jazz *chic*, and curiosity seekers.
Monk, who seems to thrive on challenge, proved to be almost
as good a showman as he is a musician.

The original quartet included John Coltrane, tenor saxophone; Wilbur Ware, bass; and (after a brief period with
Philly Joe Jones) Shadow Wilson, drums. Together a regret-
tably short time before Coltrane rejoined Miles Davis, the
quartet nonetheless remains, in the memory of those who
heard it, one of the classic small groups of modern jazz.

At the club, their impact was enormous. Monk, at the time,
was greatly given to "laying out"—letting his hornmen play
for long stretches with only bass and drum accompaniment.
While not playing, Monk was usually doing something he has
since become famous for—dancing. A kind of shuffle-step
with churning elbows, slightly reminiscent of a dancing bear,
Monk bemused some Five Spot patrons with it and enchanted
others, but aside from its showmanship and the fact that it
gave him something to do when not playing—a problem few
musicians but Miles Davis, who simply leaves the stand, have
ever solved—it was a way for him to express the obvious fact
that he was just as entranced by the music as anyone else in
the room, and, as with most things he does, it had a sound
musical reason. Keepnews says that Monk dances while listening to playbacks, as a way of determining whether or not
the performance swings to suit him. And Lacy adds, "He's a

wonderful dancer. He'll dance anywhere, at any time, whenever he feels like it. It works wonders at keeping everybody
feeling good. When he starts dancing, you got to feel good,
some alchemy he performs. His dancing is full of little surprises, just like his music, and full of little rhymes, too. Things
that repeat in a slightly different way. One of the things
about his music is the way that it rhymes."

Monk also showed detractors, during that engagement,
that he could, when he wanted to, communicate verbally on
any level. He was in the habit of starting most sets with a
solo piano piece, often a little-known favorite of his from the
twenties or thirties, and it seemed to surprise people who had
read about Monk more than they had listened to him that he
knew such pieces. One night, he played the entire first set
solo, and then started off the stand, when someone yelled,
"We wanna hear Coltrane!" "Coltrane bust up his horn,"
Monk replied, continuing his way toward the back. After the
intermission he came back out alone, and sat down to play.
"We wanna hear Coltrane!" came the voice again, and again
the reply, "Coltrane bust up his horn." Then the voice turned
mean: "What do you mean, 'he bust up his horn'?" At that
point, Monk stood up and gave a short speech: "Mr. Coltrane
plays a wind instrument. The sound is produced by blowing
into it and opening different holes to let air out. Over some of
these holes is a felt pad. One of Mr. Coltrane's felt pads has
fallen off, and in order for him to get the sound he wants, so
that we can make better music for you, he is in the back
making a new one." Then he fixed his interrogator with a
look of blasting contempt: "You dig?"

It was an exacting job for the sidemen. As Miles Davis has
remarked, "The thing that Monk must realize is that he can't
get everybody to play his songs right. Coltrane, Milt Jackson,
and maybe Lucky Thompson are the only ones I know that
can get that feeling out of his songs that he can. And he needs
drummers like Denzil Best, Blakey, Shadow, Roy Haynes,
and Philly." Monk himself apparently knows this, for he has,

reportedly, consistently looked more for knowledge of his tunes than solo ability in a prospective sideman. "A lot of people used to ask us," Coltrane recalls, "how we remembered all that stuff but we weren't remembering so much. Just the basic changes and everybody tried anything they wanted to. Monk's always doing something back there that sounds so mysterious, but it's not at all when you know what he's doing. Just like simple truths. He might take a minor chord and leave the third out. Yet when he plays the thing it will be in just the right place and voiced the right way to have a minor feel, but it's still not a minor chord. I learned a lot with him. If you work with a guy that watches the finer points, it kind of helps you to do the same. In music it's the little things that count. Like the way you build a house. You get all the little important things together and the whole thing will stand up. You goof them and you got nothing." Lacy adds, "A lot of tunes, you can get away with murder on. But those tunes, you got to know those tunes, and you got to come leaping right out immediately, because they're gonna go right on without you."

To some, the most exciting part of the Monk quartet was watching the leader at the piano. Miles Davis has said, "I like to listen to Monk play and watch his feet. The beat that you'd ordinarily hear on top of the piano, Monk plays down there." And Monk does indeed play with his whole body, continuing his dance as he plays. He pounces on the key he wants, his mouth open in a perpetual "O" of seeming astonishment at his music. "You have to go down to hear him," Davis summed up, "to really appreciate what he's doing."

Until 1961, it was thought that the quartet had not recorded, due to contractual difficulties (Monk refused to appear on Prestige as Coltrane's sideman, the only basis on which Bob Weinstock would agree to trade). But Riverside's subsidiary label Jazzland finally released three tracks by the group: *Ruby, My Dear*; *Trinkle Tinkle*; and *Nutty*. It is, however, a studio recording, and only the frighteningly difficult

Trinkle Tinkle approximates the great excitement the group was able to generate in person, but it is good that some document exists of the greatest of Monk's groups.

Another facet of the Monk legend received additional impetus during this and subsequent stays at the Five Spot, and later at another club Termini opened, The Jazz Gallery. Sometimes he would come late, sometimes he would play extremely short sets, sometimes he would not come at all. Harry Colomby believes that this, when it happens, is largely due to his client's sense of show business. "He seems to think it's better to come a little late than a little early, although not so late that people are inconvenienced. He plays short solos so that at the end of the set, people want more. He's really quite a showman." Lacy adds, "People talk about him not playing or caring, that's ridiculous. Out of the sixteen weeks we were at The Jazz Gallery, there were maybe one or two nights out of the whole time that he was a little sleepy and sort of noncommittal in his playing. And one night he didn't show up altogether, because he was ill. If someone happens to catch him on that particular night when he doesn't show up, or that particular night when he's tired, they put that together with his reputation, which is kind of funny, and the reputation grows a hundred-fold in that night."

As often happens with exceptional and neglected talents, when notoriety finally comes, they are ready. Monk prepared for his with two brilliant LPs, recorded just before the Five Spot engagement but released later. The first, *Thelonious Himself*, was, with the exception of one track with Coltrane and Ware, a solo piano set. Monk played such old pieces as *All Alone* in brilliantly sardonic fashion, as well as some of his own compositions. It was an opportunity to hear Monk completely unadorned. On some pieces he relied too heavily on his favorite runs, but the depth of his tradition was brought out startlingly by his brilliant *Functional*, well over eight minutes of unaccompanied blues piano (later released in a quite different, almost equally successful alternate version to

fill out the set made with Coltrane). It is, again, a complete
conjugation of the blues, and a task which few other pianists
would dare attempt. And how many could successfully bring
off a solo album? One must be one's own rhythm section, and
with a rhythmic concept as unique as Monk's, this afforded
the listener an excellent opportuniy to "see Monk plain."

The other set was *Monk's Music,* with a septet including
Blakey, Ware, Coltrane, Ray Copeland, Gigi Gryce, and
Coleman Hawkins. The set contains what I consider to be
Monk's finest composition, *Crepescule With Nellie.* Written
while Mrs. Monk was gravely ill in the hospital, it is a tender,
haunting piece, always suggestive of blues while not actually
using that structure. "He'd be in and out of the house twenty
times a day," Colomby recalls, "each time he'd work on a
little bit, change something, and go out again. It started as
an entirely different piece, but it was all changed by the time
he'd worked it out." Monk has never improvised on the piece.
When he first began to play it at the Five Spot, he would
play the melody through once, then Coltrane would join him
for a second chorus—again without improvisation. "It's not an
improvisation piece," says Lacy. "It's his little symphony. He
just plays it, and then that's it."

These two albums and the three pieces with Coltrane, also
recorded in 1957, were great Monk recordings. But Riverside
later had certain problems in presenting Monk. He recorded
with great frequency, and each album was called upon to
be different in some way. Much of Monk's time was therefore
spent in recasting previously recorded compositions for new
combinations of instrumentalists, many of whom were of such
quality that one had to wade through great stretches of indifferent music before getting to Monk. The work, though, is
often repaid. In spots on some of the many records released
since 1957 are to be found some of the finest solos Monk has
ever played: simple, clean, and concise, some of them filled
with a rare and refreshing joy and exuberance, often employing the simplest chromatic runs and harmonies to startling

dramatic effect, little models of form based on the purest thematic variations. If a glib phrase will stand for a long dissertation, Monk plays without adjectives. He has repeatedly been giving more and more of the unadorned "kernel," only pure music.

Two albums stand out in this mass of indifferent material. One is a recording made by trumpeter Clark Terry—a rare instance in which Monk, who likes Terry's work, consented to be a sideman. Monk, who has reason to know how it feels, is much concerned with the problems of musicians whom he feels to be underrated, and perhaps this was his way of rectifying one such situation while doing a favor for a friend. Keepnews says he has never seen Monk happier or more cooperative than he was on the Terry date, and the music reflects both that and the fact that, for once, the pressure was not on Monk to be the leader and organizer. There has seldom been more joyous Monk on records. The second set, *Thelonious Alone in San Francisco*, has, in contrast, a dark, brooding atmosphere, and eliminates most of the faults of his previous solo piano venture.

Monk himself may have recognized an increasingly arid quality in his albums, or else he wanted to be free to join a major company, as so many other jazzmen were doing. At any rate, after June, 1959, Riverside was unable to get Thelonious into a studio. But by late 1962, he had obtained his release and was going to Columbia Records.

Still, he goes on his own unique way, getting in difficulties with record companies and club owners, but always remaining intractably himself. Nothing, apparently, matters to him but his family and his music. According to Harry Colomby, during the long months when he has not worked, he will stay close to home and to the neighborhood, watching television if someone else turns it on, composing when the urge strikes him, and doing little else. He is anything but a social person. "Sometimes," Colomby has said, "I feel like I'm breaking into his world. He never engages in any kind of conversation he doesn't like . . . He disconnects sometimes—then all of a sudden he comes up with a statement that is so profound it scares you . . . Nothing else in the world seems to matter to him but his music . . . Nothing can distract him . . . When he walks into a room he dominates it. The force of Monk's personality intimidates you." And Lacy adds, "He's the world's greatest naturalist. He doesn't lie at all. Most people lie in some little ways, but he just doesn't bother doing that. He's a thoroughly natural man." More often, Monk will simply say nothing. One of the things he will not do, in public, is run down the talent of any musician, although he is reported to be caustically accurate in private. A typical answer for the record in such matters is, "Everybody sounds good. Everybody that's playing sounds a 'bitch.' I hear something in everybody's playing."

To most outward appearances, Monk has not been changed by the relative success that came to him so late. The few changes he does recognize, as Lacy outlines them, are important ones. "It makes a great deal of difference to him. The polls not so much, but the fact that he can command a decent salary, more than decent, really, and that he can pay his sidemen a good salary, and work in clubs where he wants to, and have people dig it. That's success, and that he certainly has achieved. He's not too concerned about publicity and what not. I don't think he ever reads the magazines unless they're thrust in front of him and certain things are pointed out. I don't think he calculates publicity values except maybe as a joke on himself. He's very fond of playing jokes on himself. His music is that way a lot, the way he dances is that way, and some of what he wears is just designed to amuse himself."

Whether Monk has been as calmly assured of the eventual coming of this success as some would have us believe is another matter. One writer, coming across Monk standing on his street corner *querencia*, attempted to tell him how much his music had meant to him. Monk seemed unwilling to believe that anyone would be so fond of his work, and kept questioning the honesty of the praise. He can, however, be quite pleased and gracious about compliments. One night in the Five Spot, I went up to Monk at the bar between sets and told him how beautiful I thought *Crepescule With Nellie* was. It had not yet been recorded, and its title had never been announced, so I did not know what it was. I told him I thought it was his piece, and asked its name. He explained the title to me, seemed quite pleased that I had liked it, and asked if I would like to hear it played again during the next set. Slightly taken aback at the offer—this was not the Monk of the columns—I told him I would appreciate it very much. He thanked me, and, as he had promised, played *Crepescule* again.

But this is rare. Monk's natural tendency is to trust and talk to no one. To see that his privacy and well-being are looked after, Harry Colomby's brother Jules often accompanies him on the road. Even so, his idiosyncracies are likely to erupt at any time. One afternoon at the Village Vanguard, crowded to the walls for Miles Davis, an attendant Monk began dancing to the music with bassist Paul Chambers' three-year-old son, stepping on feet and knocking over tables, oblivious to the presence of anyone but himself.

The reasons for strange conduct and lack of trust are not hard to seek. Monk does not require much to live on, but even that has been denied him, if not by the loss of his cabaret card, then by the fires which have twice ravaged his apartment and forced him to move in with relatives. A fiercely proud man, he nevertheless watched while his wife worked to support him.

Those who wish to help are often rejected; interviews are, because of a long history of misquotation, no longer permitted. His few friends are likely to be musicians; his saxophonist of long standing, Charlie Rouse, remains in the quartet as much because he is Monk's friend as because of his talent. In extreme cases, Monk will keep an inferior musician in his group because he cannot bring himself to fire the man.

One of the few people to know Monk well and appreciate him completely is soprano saxophonist Steve Lacy. Lacy, who got his job with Monk because of his recorded version of *Work* ("He told me it was 'correct.' It pleased him, and he introduced me to a lot of people as 'the guy who played *Work* right.'") is an invaluable source of information about his former employer's methods of getting what he wants. "He let me alone the first few days of the job"—Lacy had started work with two days' notice and no rehearsal—"but after that, he started telling me a few things I was doing wrong, not in the tunes, but just in my general soloing. If I was going in the wrong direction, doing something wrong, he'd let me know about it in no uncertain terms. He'd just stop me cold and tell me where it was at, and he'd always be right. That's one of his hobbies, is always being right. Very blunt, but very correct. He'll say, 'Stop playing all that bullshit, man,' and 'Swing. If you can't play anything else, play the melody. Don't play a whole lot of weird stuff that don't mean anything. Keep the beat all the time. Just 'cause you're not a drummer doesn't mean you don't have to swing. Don't make the rhythm section work too hard.' I was nervous every night, frantic that I wasn't making it, and that was keeping me from making it, and I *was* playing a whole lot of weird things that didn't mean anything." But Monk does not tell his sidemen specific ways to solo. "He don't mess with you, he leaves you alone, generally."

Lacy also reports that there were very few rehearsals. "Toward the end of the summer we started rehearsing a little, but on the job when the place was empty. One time we went out to Nica's house for a rehearsal, but we wound up playing pingpong. There were no rehearsals, but every night was quite an education. By the end of the job it had really turned into a good group. It seems that chemistry will out every time. There's just no substitute for playing together a certain number of weeks. Certain things just don't happen before that. But afterward, if the guys are good enough, they do happen, and it's wondrous. Everybody's sounds coalesced, and chemistry took place. We were all friends, and the sounds had sort of mingled, as it were . . . we had a beautiful blend. But that's the way it is with Monk's groups. Toward the end of the job, they're really wailin'. He's used to the piano by then, the horns are really into the songs, the rhythm section is tight. He's marvelous with a rhythm section anyway. He can make any rhythm section sound much better than they really are, just by the way he can control them from the piano. He makes everybody play good, makes everybody feel good."

Lacy also gives an insight into the way Monk works on a new piece. In the matter of composition, "Monk's system is to go to sleep, and he wakes up with the answer." But Lacy recalls one instance of the way Monk approaches a new tune. "You ought to hear him play *Body and Soul*. He started playing that around the middle of the summer, as a solo piece. I remember the first time he played it. It was kind of fumbly, and he played it every night after that. Each night it would get a little more complex and a little surer, and harmonies would change into his own harmonies, until by the end of the summer he had quite a good piece, but it was Monk. I heard him play it again a few months ago, and by then it had really evolved into something multicolored and wondrous to behold. He changed all the harmonies, and it worked out beautiful."

Lacy sums up his experience: "I hadn't played with him, and it's playing with those bells behind you that really changes you. I learned an awful lot that summer, in fact it took me the whole next winter to realize how much I'd learned that summer. I went in and sat in with him at the Gallery, and I'd improved a lot in the eight months or so since I'd played with him, and he told me so, too, and it meant a lot to me. Of course, he took credit for a lot of it, and he was right. He said, 'I see you've been listening to what I told you,' and it meant a lot to me for him to say that. Because it was true, I *had* been listening to what he told me. And he was glad to see that I had improved. Things like that keep his faith up."

There has been little enough to keep Monk's faith up in the past several years, and there may never be more than there is now: a *Time* cover, a concert at Lincoln Center, and semi-residency at the new Five Spot. He will probably never become a popular artist in the way that Erroll Garner or George Shearing have. But he is one of the greats, and that knowledge, if he has it, will have to be enough. What he thinks about it himself was best said to Robert Kotlowitz, in *Harper's:* "When I was a kid, I felt something had to be done about all that jazz. So I've been doing it for twenty years. Maybe I've turned jazz another way. Maybe I'm a major influence. I don't know. Anyway, my music is my music, on my piano, too. That's a criterion of something. Jazz is my adventure. I'm after new chords, new ways of syncopating, new figurations, new runs. How to use notes differently. That's it. Just how to use notes differently."

Selected Discography

Thelonious Monk, Genius of Modern Music, Vols. 1 & 2, BLUE NOTE 1510–11.
Thelonious Monk and Milt Jackson, BLUE NOTE 1509.
Thelonious Monk, PRESTIGE 7027.
Brilliant Corners, RIVERSIDE 12–226.
Monk's Music, RIVERSIDE 12–242.
Thelonious Monk with John Coltrane, JAZZLAND 46.
Monk's Dream, COLUMBIA CS 8765, CL 1965.

ART BLAKEY

SINCE THE EARLY 1950's, one major strain has become dominant in all American music, and it began, like most movements, as a reaction to something else. Bop, the jazz movement begun in the early forties by Charlie Parker and Dizzy Gillespie, frightened many musicians who were unable, either technically or emotionally, to play it. Some of these men were involved with what has become known as the "West Coast" movement. This had started in the Stan Kenton band with such men as Shorty Rogers and Shelly Manne, and grew to include Chet Baker, Bud Shank, Chico Hamilton, and others. Eventually, the movement became so involved in classically derived arrangements and unusual instrumentation that, many felt, the emotional center of jazz was being lost in pretense. The college students and young executives whose affluent taste makes jazz a saleable commodity found in this music a greater similarity to other musics more familiar to them, found it more comfortable than, say, the work of Charlie Parker, and for a time it was the most popular form of jazz.

What West Coast musicians were doing, however, went largely unnoticed by musicians in the East, except as an irritant. By 1954, the players centered in New York had solidified bop; had systematized some elements, discarded others, added more, and emerged with a somewhat different music. In 1955, a quintet called the Jazz Messengers (Hank Mobley, tenor; Kenny Dorham, trumpet; Horace Silver, piano; Doug Watkins, bass; and Art Blakey, drums) recorded *The Preacher*. The reaction to the reaction had taken place. Instead of complex scores, they offered what has been variously called funk, hard bop, and post-bop: a music with roots in the blues and the gospel music of the Sanctified Churches as well as in modern jazz. Many seemingly discon-

45

nected manifestations of the trend were occurring simultaneously. Sonny Rollins began to compose and play jazz waltzes, and those who called this a startling innovation were forgetting that church music had always been able to swing in 6/8 time. The rise to enormous popularity of Ray Charles, some of whose best numbers are simply gospel songs set with extremely secular lyrics, began in this period; the gospel singer Mahalia Jackson became a TV and concert star. Everywhere one turned, there was increasing evidence that the single most important element in American jazz and popular music was Negro folk and religious material. Rock-and-roll began its rise, and by the early sixties the modified rock-and-roll style of the tenor-and-organ combos of small Negro neighborhood clubs had become also a major commercial commodity. Performers such as the blues singer "Lightnin' " Hopkins, whose style is almost archaic, and the gospel singer Clara Ward became nationally known and played in clubs which would not have considered booking them a few years previously. By early 1962, young Negro entertainers were peddling the lowest common denominator of it all, the teasing, antiseptic dance called the Twist, in some of the most exclusive rooms in the country. Even the West Coast musicians finally recognized a lost cause and climbed aboard the gospel train.

But the watered-down versions and imitators were to come later. Although the catchword "soul," which has characterized most of this music, was to become corrupted, it did indeed serve as an accurate description of some of the original objectives. Technical brilliance, as the term is applied to classical musicians, was secondary. What counted was emotion. Ability to play the blues well became more the mark of a musician's stature than ever before.

Through all the permutations of this funky-hard bop-soul music, the unit which has hewed most closely to the original line and which has furnished the movement with most of its important musicians is the one which announced it to begin with, the Jazz Messengers. Now, as then, the leader of the group is drummer Art Blakey. And in him, the new leadership of one decade has by now become the elder statesman of the next decade's conservatives.

Art Blakey was born October 11, 1919, in the steel town of Pittsburgh, Pennsylvania, and he went to work in the mills as his father had done. Somewhere along the line he learned to play piano, because "I always wanted to." He worked as a pianist after mill hours in various clubs around Pittsburgh until he felt that the young group he was leading needed a change of personnel. He found a young piano player named Errol Garner and switched to drums, the only other spot he could decently fill.

By 1939 Blakey's reputation had spread to the extent that he was asked to join Fletcher Henderson's band. The year following, he left to play drums for the semilegendary pianist Mary Lou Williams. Leaving her, he tried his own group again for a while, but things didn't work out too well, and in 1941 he rejoined Henderson for a Southern tour.

The band was in Albany, Georgia, when Blakey was arrested by a local policeman and brought to the jail house.

"I got me a nigger," Blakey recalls the arresting officer as saying.

"What's he done?" the cop on duty wanted to know.

"Nothing," the policeman replied. Blakey was tossed into a cell and beaten, one well-placed kick in the forehead necessitating a silver plate which still remains. In another version of the story, Robert Reisner reports Blakey as having told him, "I received a concussion from a vicious blow made with a small truncheon. This later required an operation and numerous stitches."

After the outbreak of World War II, Blakey was called up for selective service. "They asked me how I got the plate in my head," he says. "I told them and they decided it'd be dangerous for me to join the army, so I didn't go in." He stayed at home and worked at his profession until 1944, the turning point in his career.

The big band business is erratic even under optimum circumstances, and during the war, when there were fewer men available to take girls to dances, and fewer men to play for them, even the best of the bands were foundering. One of the more notable had been the band led by pianist Earl Hines. One of Hines' commercial assets was his vocalist and sometime trombonist, Billy Eckstine. Eckstine was sympathetic to the ideas of the modernists like Dizzy Gillespie and Charlie Parker, with whom he was associated in Hines' later band, and he used them when he formed his own orchestra. Unfortunately, the two years of Eckstine's best organization, 1944–46, largely coincided with a ban on recordings declared by the American Federation of Musicians' president James C. Petrillo in an effort to obtain more royalties from recording sales for the membership.

At one time or another, the Eckstine band included trumpeters Dizzy Gillespie, Miles Davis, Fats Navarro, and Kenny Dorham; saxophonists Charlie Parker, Gene Ammons, Lucky Thompson, Dexter Gordon, and Leo Parker; bassist Tommy Potter; pianist and arranger Tadd Dameron; vocalist Sarah Vaughan; and drummer Art Blakey. Eventually, the band broke up, leaving a few recordings on the National and Deluxe labels. Gillespie recalls, "That was a radical band. It was the forerunner of all the big modern bands. But a lot of ballroom operators didn't dig it. They just thought it was weird. But it was a very fine band, very advanced."

Ironically, Blakey's membership in that band is indirectly related to the Georgia incident. "I had no drummer," Eckstine has said of his orchestra, "and I was waiting on Shadow Wilson . . . and the army had grabbed him. At that time Art Blakey was with Henderson. Art's out of my home town and I've known him a long time. So I wired him to come in the band, and Art left Henderson and joined me at the Club Plantation in St. Louis."

The next few years of Blakey's life have given rise to some confusion. Robert Reisner has written that "With some money saved from his stint with the Eckstine band Art went to Africa. He spent several months in Nigeria and Ghana, seeking for roots and philosophies that would make some sense out of this chaotic world. (He'd had his share of personal tragedy. His first wife, Clarice, died suddenly and very young on the threshold of a promising career as a lawyer.) Of this trip, he said, 'I went there to live with the people. For the first time I experienced something like brotherhood. They sang at night of the things they did during the day. New songs every night. I slept with them, ate with them, dressed as they did.' He picked up African musical ideas, too. 'In Africa the drummers hold their sticks in no set way except that which is comfortable for them. Every man searches for his own sounds, makes his own music, creates his own style.'"

This story is indirectly questioned in Leonard Feather's *Encyclopedia of Jazz,* which says that Blakey was: "With Billy Eckstine for duration of band 1944–7, then around NYC w. own groups and others. Lucky Millinder in 1949 . . ." But interviews with Blakey contain constant references to the African trip.

By 1949, Blakey had acquired a Moslem name, Abdullah Ibn Buhaina. (The first name means servant of God; the second "son of," and Buhaina was a follower of Jesus. His sidemen usually address him as Buhaina.) Although he is very much involved in the Moslem religion, he is not a member of the Black Muslims and he is not orthodox. When asked if he keeps a strict Moslem household, he laughs and answers, "This house is nothing."

By this time, Blakey had also acquired the narcotics habit. "I started it because I liked it," he says. "There isn't any other reason. It makes you feel good. I used to go back to my hotel room and think about what happened in Georgia and the plate in my head and I needed something to make me feel good. Nobody ever found out about it because I had a lot of money. Money can cover up almost anything. Today I meet young musicians who say to me, 'It's all right, Mr. Blakey, I'll stop when I want to." And I say to them, 'You'll stop when you have the guts or when they bury you.' Even today, it's a fight for me. It's something your body gets used to and you miss it. Look at it this way—if they put me in jail for a year and let me loose in a room full of naked women I'd have a hard time walking out of the room.

"In those days, though, I had a lot of money. I was being taken care of. We'd go to Chicago and I'd put everyone in the band up in his own suite at the hotel. We weren't getting that much money from the job, but that didn't make any difference. I met my wife, Diana, in Chicago. My other wife died, you know.

"I probably wouldn't have gotten straightened out if it hadn't been for her. There wasn't any more money. That happened when we got married. We lived in a little flat in Harlem, but I started working again and started the Messengers, and soon we moved down here and things have been all right since then. Even if I wanted to go back, I wouldn't. There are a lot of people that I'm responsible for. All Diana's sisters look to me as if I were their father, and then I have seven children of my own. We have a place up in Vermont where we go skiing. Diana's sisters live up there and I get up there as often as I can. The most important thing to me now, even more than music, is to keep their respect."

That appears to be the statement of a man secure in the knowledge of what he has contributed, as Blakey should be. The French critic André Hodeir sees his contribution as a desire to synthesize the various elements of modern jazz, and goes on to an assessment of Blakey's style and achievement: "Blakey is responsible for a trimming down and rationalization of the modern conception of accompaniment. By giving more of his notes the same length (his division of the beat is almost always based on the eighth note), he simplified the vocabulary of rhythmic figures created by Clarke and Roach. This simplification did not result, as might have been feared, in an impoverishment of the rhythmic foundation; it made possible a large number of figures that are simple but, from the accompanist's point of view, very effective. Moreover, Blakey plays the after-beat on the high-hat cymbal with a violent, even crushing ferocity, thus restoring to this beat a rhythmic and expressive importance that tends to place his style in a fairly traditional perspective. There is nothing surprising in the fact that, as he himself has stated, Art Blakey likes best to play with Clifford Brown and Horace Silver. The inspiration they have in common is evident."

Hodeir, in mentioning Blakey's desire to play with Brown and Silver, listed only musical reasons. There are others. Blakey, a man in his early forties, finds himself in the position of an elder statesman. A jazzman, like an athlete, may be considered old when he is still in his thirties, and often a jazzman of Blakey's age has already been forgotten or even dismissed. Perhaps the rigorous life required by both professions has something to do with the phenomenon; notwithstanding, it is interesting to note that athletics and show business, of which jazz is a part, have until recently been the only areas in which an American Negro could hope to distinguish himself.

This may have something to do with Blakey's continual shift of personnel in the Jazz Messengers. He has made of his group something of a mobile parallel to the Actor's Studio, a unit in which young musicians can practice their growing skills before audiences until they are ready to go out on their own. Some of the many soloists who have worked for Blakey are Jackie McLean, alto saxophone; Benny Golson, tenor saxophone; Johnny Griffin, tenor saxophone; Lee Morgan, trumpet; Freddie Hubbard, trumpet; Donald Byrd, trumpet; Ira Sullivan, trumpet and tenor saxo-

phone; Wayne Shorter, tenor saxophone; Curtis Fuller, trombone; and Bobby Timmons, piano. Blakey feels that a man
will find his own way in the group, and operates on the
principle by which children are thrown into the water to
see if they can swim. Some of the criticism which has been
leveled at him is really a matter of the immaturity of his
soloists. He has been called loud, which he often is, but he
has also been accused of dictating to, rather than accompanying, his soloists, overshadowing them and forcing them
into his patterns. Of this, Blakey says, "I play the way I
feel and try to get my message across. If the horn man
knows who he is and has something to say, he'll make
himself heard."

Naturally, some musicians have been at odds with this
theory, one of them being Benny Golson. At the time when
Golson was musical director of the Messengers the group
was quite highly regarded, but Golson's conception was not
entirely to Blakey's taste. "He'd come in with an arrangement
and it was a good one, but he'd tell me when to use sticks
and when to use brushes and what cymbal to play and I just
couldn't do that." Golson has since gone elsewhere, and
presumably both he and Blakey are now freer to express
themselves. The fact that Golson did leave, and amicably,
is indicative of Blakey's philosophy: he does not expect his
men to stay with him forever, but rather looks forward to
the time when they feel ready to go out on their own. He
does, however, stop short of what one might expect to be
the natural outcome of this attitude: firing someone if he
thought it necessary for the furtherance of the man's career.
"He'll either know himself or else the agencies will start
calling him and asking him to start his own group. It isn't
necessary for me to say anything."

Some men have been in and out of the Messengers on
several occasions and for various reasons. One such is a
musician whom Blakey would still like to use, but since
the man is a drug addict he is understandably dangerous

company on tour. Another ex-Messenger is pianist Bobby Timmons, who made such a success with *Moanin'*, a composition he wrote for Blakey, that he received several lucrative offers. One was from altoist Julian "Cannonball" Adderley, who, when he left Miles Davis in 1959, raided most of the existing bands on the East Coast to form his own. While with Adderley, Timmons wrote a gospel-styled piece, *This Here*, that became the biggest jazz hit in several years, and gave Timmons much wider recognition than he had previously enjoyed. In spite of the new notoriety, he began to feel out of touch with Adderley's music, and rejoined Blakey. "There's no band to go with after that one," he says.

When, in 1961, it was felt that Timmons could profitably lead his own trio, Blakey saw that the pianist signed with his own astute manager, Jack Whittemore. "That's Art's thing," Timmons says. "He builds leaders. He's a leader who builds other leaders. Not many men are really leaders, it has to do with a lot more than music. Miles is one, and Art's another. You learn decorum with him, and how to be a man. That little speech he gives at the end of his sets, about how jazz is our native cultural contribution to the world. Who else could get away with that speech? Some people laugh at him when he gives it, but he stands up there with dignity.

"He knows how to handle people. One fellow was bringing in arrangements that Art didn't think were quite right. He made the guy musical director, and the guy was happy, but when we got on the stand, we played what we wanted to, anyway. He believes that jazz is feeling, the same as I do. But he knows about music. He's the one who taught me to build a solo to a climax.

"He has an act, of course, and there's a lot of nonsense, but he knows where he *is*."

Blakey also knows where he is in his private life. He lives an extremely comfortable existence with his wife Diana, their young daughter Sakeena, and their younger son Gamal, in a Central Park West apartment which reflects the deep impression made on Blakey by a tour of Japan. Upon entering the Blakey home, one is politely asked to take one's shoes off and is offered instead a pair of *tabi* socks. Aside from a few Japanese prints on the wall the apartment reveals nothing more personal than that the family living in it has made money and spent it tastefully. The grand piano in the living room could belong to any well-to-do family. The one indication that the home is a musician's is the solid wall of framed photographs by the telephone: they are all of Thelonious Monk. Blakey and Monk hold one another in very high regard, perhaps for the reason noted by Whitney Balliett: "Monk has his own devious, irrepressible, built-in rhythm section, and Blakey is the only drummer around who knows how to supplement it without getting in its way."

One of Blakey's prime concerns is Art, Jr., a son by an earlier marriage, who lives on another floor of the building in an apartment of his own. In his middle twenties, the boy divides his time between studying for a CPA certificate, learning to play the drums—he has led his own group—and functioning as road manager for the Jazz Messengers.

"He's a good guy," Blakey says of his son. "I like him. We get along like friends more than anything else. He's a good road manager, too. I hope things work out for him. He doesn't have some of the advantages I had."

An unusual remark, if one considers that Blakey is much more secure financially than his own father was. But he explains: "If you become a famous writer, your son has the advantages of that. But what happens to my son if he's not a good drummer?" Again, we return to what seems to be Blakey's constant preoccupation with the difficulties involved in being a Negro in the United States. When the conversation turns to white jazz musicians, Blakey is quick to point out the obvious talents of musicians like Stan Getz, whom he once called his favorite tenor saxophonist. Among drummers, he is an admirer of the late Dave Tough. And on the subject of Negro musicians who do not think whites can play, he told a *Down Beat* reporter, "I don't see how they can play jazz if they feel that way."

But still, the accounts of bitterness reappear. One such is his story of an incident that happened in Philadelphia in 1956. "We played a concert there and afterwards we were driving back to New York. In the car with me were my valet, Horace Silver, and the daughter of Baroness Nica Rothschild de Koenigswarter." The baroness has been a friend for years of many of the most important jazz musicians of our time. The best published attempt to tell her fascinating story has been made by Nat Hentoff in an *Esquire* article called "The Jazz Baroness."

"We noticed," Blakey continues, "that a cop on a motorcycle was following us for about fifteen blocks and finally he asked us to pull over. When we did, I saw that he was one of the policemen who had been assigned to the concert. He was off duty and he knew who we were. I think he was just bothered at seeing me driving a Cadillac with a white girl in it. I asked him what we had done and he said, 'Come down to the station and we'll talk about it.' He pulled a gun on me. I had a gun, too. I have a permit to carry one and I took it out of the glove compartment and got out of the car. I asked him again what we had done and he saw that I had a gun. I think I would have shot him if I'd had to. He asked us again to come down to the station and we did. At the station house he slapped Nica's daughter in the face and called her a Jew bitch. This girl is a Rothschild, you know, one of the richest families in the world, and this cop slapped her in the face. He was going to hit Horace, but I said, 'This man has a spinal injury,' and so he didn't. He put my valet and myself in a cell and tied us up with our hands over our heads so that our feet were off the ground. He kept hitting us and then throwing cold water on us when we passed out. In the morning Nica had a lawyer there and that cop isn't on the police force any more, but there are a lot of other cops like that, and lots of people don't have the kind of help I did. You know the story about Miles Davis being hit over the head in front of Birdland. That cop was at Birdland, every night. That was his beat. He knew who Miles was and what he was doing there."

Although Blakey has been deeply embittered by such experiences, he is still suspicious of extreme Negro racist groups such as the Black Muslims. "They're a disgrace to a great religion. They're just as bad as the Klan. I don't think you can answer hate with hate or answer anything with force. The only answer to an idea is a better idea and a lot of people are afraid of the truth. My wife and I get stopped a lot of times by police because they think she's white. When they ask what we're doing together she tells them she's my wife. When they look surprised and ask her if she's white she always says the same thing: "My mother was, and my father is the biggest, handsomest black man you ever saw in your life."

It is not difficult to understand why Blakey is impressed with the reception he has received in other countries: "When I go to Paris I can stay in any hotel I want because I'm Art Blakey, the *musician*. Those people over there have such an appreciation of jazz. They've studied some of our records like they were symphony scores and can tell me things about them that I didn't even know we were doing."

"Bud Powell's in Paris, you know," he says, speaking of the great modern jazz pianist, "and he's playing better than he ever was before. I think he's all right now and I don't know if he'll ever come back. You have to come back, though, because as far as jazz is concerned, New York is the center of the world. I wish that people understood that and realized that jazz is our music. For instance, when the Russians send ballet troupes over here, what do we do? We send ballet troupes back over there. We're sending that to them and they invented it and they're so much better at it than we are. I think that if people heard our music they'd like it and understand it and appreciate it. We proved that in Japan. We were on the cover of every Japanese magazine and in all their newspapers and on their television shows just like we were movie stars. When we got off the plane there was a representative of every Embassy there to greet us—all except the United States Ambassador. I don't know. Maybe he had something more important to do."

All of these remarks, coupled with Blakey's instant and gracious ability to make a stranger completely welcome in his home, add up to the picture of him as a strong, decent man of great warmth and anger, aware of his position in his world and determined to keep that position with the dignity that should accompany it. But when one spends time in the vicious, hothouse world that is the New York jazz scene, one hears other stories. Blakey lies. Blakey is a racist. Blakey caused the breakup of the original Jazz Messengers by playing Iago, telling each member that the other men did not wish to play with him. One knows that such ugly rumors start about anyone in the public eye. But one does remember that he has remarked, "Stan Getz is Jewish, so he's known oppression too," and that he took delight in a television performance by Black Muslim leader Malcolm X. And one senses his pleasure when the white doorman says, "Good evening, Mr. Blakey, and how are you this evening, sir?" So one inquires further.

"The paradox of Art Blakey," Bobby Timmons says, "is that he's so simple, and he's watched by complex people. He's done some fantastic things, some of the best and worst of anyone I know, but he knows where he's at, and he's a *man*."

One tells the story of a delightful time spent with Blakey at a club between sets, when one was greeted like a long-lost friend, became Blakey's guest, and was offered a business opportunity. Blakey was to call the next day, to confirm arrangements, and did not.

"That's Art," Timmon says. "That happens every night. He promises 2500 things to 2500 people and forgets the next morning. But he means it all when he says it."

"You're writing a *chapter* about Art Blakey?", tenor saxophonist Johnny Griffin asks incredulously. "It'll have to be an awful long chapter. You ought to write a *book* about Art Blakey. He's a rascal. He's liable to do anything, if it's business. I remember, he was having trouble with a trumpet player. He had Ira Sullivan in the band, playing tenor. Ira plays trumpet too, you know. They were supposed to go to Chicago. When this trumpet player got to the airport and saw me there too, he knew what was up, and just turned around and left.

"No one's ever treated me as good as Art. When I first came to New York, I stayed at his house and ate his food."

Timmons adds, of the Blakey household, "They're like my family."

"We may not have been the best band in the world," Griffin says, "but we had more fun than anybody. A ball every night, putting each other on, playing whatever we wanted. Art doesn't read music, you know, but if he hears something once, he knows it, and he knows what he wants."

One of Blakey's major problems in the band is the constant turnover of personnel. Part of this, of course, is by design, but the growing publicity machinery of jazz has made many young musicians feel they are stars before they are fully matured performers.

There have been such problems since the first edition of the Jazz Messengers. Horace Silver, now the successful leader of his own quintet, still mourns, in a way, the passing of the original group. "I sure take my hat off to the MJQ," he says. "They've stayed together for over ten years as a cooperative unit. That's the way we started out. I guess I was the musical director, although I didn't have the title. But we had personality clashes, personal matters, and we just couldn't do it."

Silver remembers that there almost was no Jazz Messengers as we know the group. As he recalls it, on the original recording date, Alfred Lion of Blue Note was willing to use all his compositions except *The Preacher*. "He said it was too old-timey, that no one would go for it." It *was* old-timey, of course, having its origins in *Show Me The Way To Go Home*, which Silver was then playing as his final number of the evening. "It had nice changes, and we found it was good to play on." It is now hard to believe that Lion took such an attitude, since most of his company's subsequent output has consisted of a furtherance of the aims of that one record, which remains the best aural definition of the Messengers.

When the co-operative group with Silver disbanded, Blakey kept the title Jazz Messengers, but the various groups Silver has led since have sometimes stayed closer to the original ideals of that organization. The Blakey band of today has grafted some of the advanced ideas of Miles Davis and John Coltrane onto the root of hard bop. The Jazz Messengers of the early sixties, perhaps the finest of all Blakey bands (Freddie Hubbard, trumpet; Wayne Shorter, tenor saxophone; Curtis Fuller, trombone; Cedar Walton, piano; Jymie Merritt, bass; Blakey, drums) became the leading repository of the new mainstream style, the band in which the styles of the fifties were being codified, as new steps continue to be taken by others.

The personnel problem still remains, and is best exemplified by one young Messenger who, feeling constricted by the limited outlook of the group, and secure in his *Down Beat* "New Star" status, says, "Between working for Art and recording for Blue Note, I never get to play anything pretty."

Pianist Cecil Taylor comments, "Doesn't he realize what a privilege it is to play with Art Blakey? He's a historical figure. Jazz drums wouldn't be the same if it weren't for him."

One night, this young man was playing a difficult cadenza,

and not playing it well. Blakey summarily stopped the music. "We're not going to play," he said to the audience, "until ——— gets mad!"

"Art'll do that," Timmons recalls. "He'll bawl you out right there, and he'll make you play better."

After the incident, someone remarked that in a few years, the young man might be the best on his instrument. The remark enraged Blakey. "He's playing his ass off right now," he said with a father's pride.

"Art's thing," Griffin says, "is that he's a father. Some people say that he has a young band because it's easier for him to be a leader, but that's not so. He'd be the leader anywhere. He'll give advice to anybody." Even another great drummer, apparently. Griffin continues: "He was playing opposite Max Roach one night, and after one of Max's sets, he walked right up and said, 'Max, you ought to do so-and-so.' He's even a father to Monk. I've seen him bawl Monk out, and Monk just stands there and takes it."

He takes the opposite position, though, in his attitude toward the audience: "If you're selling something to people, and we're selling music, you have to make them want it. You're not doing them a favor by playing for them. You're asking people to like you and your music and if you have to get down on your knees to them, then you do that. We believe in what we're playing and we'll do anything necessary to make other people believe in it."

Eventually, every conversation returns to Blakey's basic concern: drums and rhythm. Anyone who has seen him play, often with a huge towel draped over him to stop the perspiration, knows the power and conviction he can achieve. "They always say you can tell a story on the drums, but I didn't know that was true until I went to Africa. They can sit down at the drums and tell someone in the next village that you walked by and what your name is and how tall you are and what color suit you're wearing."

Rhythm, he feels, is what is lacking in many jazz groups.

"Our young musicians are so busy studying melody and harmony that they neglect rhythm, the third element of music. Have you ever noticed how jazz groups play arrangements in all sorts of intricate rhythms, but as soon as it comes time for the solos they go back to straight 4/4 time? It's because they can't play rhythms more complicated than that. If you'll notice, our three great modern musicians— Charlie Parker, Dizzy Gillespie, and Thelonious Monk—all made significant developments in rhythm and maybe that's why they were great."

As a man who is financially secure and whose greatest musical innovations are perhaps behind him, Blakey can relax and survey the musical situation with a certain amount of detachment. He leaves his professional life almost completely in the hands of Jack Whittemore, whom he trusts implicitly, and professes to be uninterested in the material aspects as such. "I want to play the kind of music I like and see young guys come up through the band and make a reputation for themselves, and when the time comes, I want to get out of the business gracefully."

Until that time comes, there will probably be a steady stream of talented new musicians beginning their careers under the banner of the Jazz Messengers. For, as Bobby Timmons sums it up, "Art's a builder who doesn't like to live in finished houses."

Selected Discography

Horace Silver and the Jazz Messengers, BLUE NOTE 1518.
Art Blakey's Jazz Messengers with Thelonious Monk, ATLANTIC 1278.
Paris Concert, EPIC LA 16009.
3 Blind Mice, UNITED ARTISTS UAJ 14002.

MILES DAVIS

ONE NIGHT during the summer of 1957, the wonderful but short-lived Thelonious Monk Quartet with John Coltrane, Wilbur Ware, and Philly Joe Jones was playing at New York's Five Spot Café. Monk is an imposing figure, and a unique showman, but that night only one person was watching him. A small, slim, graceful man, impeccably dressed in the continental style that was then a few years ahead of its time, leaned casually against the bar smoking a cigarette and listening to the music that Monk was making with two of his former employees. Everyone else in the audience—which was made up of collegians who at the time probably did not know who he was—was busy watching Miles Davis watch Monk.

In acting classes, it is called "presence." In Hollywood, it is called "star quality." The Madison Avenue expression is "projecting an image." Whatever the term, Miles Davis has it.

Today, it is nearly more appropriate to speak of Miles Davis as a showbusiness phenomenon than as a musician. A percentage of his audience feels it has gotten full value for its money if he appears in one of his famous suits.

The striking cover of one Columbia album shows Miles' lovely wife Frances, seated alone at a table. At the opposite side is Miles, trenchcoat worn cape style, head bent to light a cigarette from the match held in his cupped hands. Photographed in black and white, it is strongly reminiscent of a still from the Humphrey Bogart-Ingrid Bergman movie *Casablanca* ("Don't go to the session tonight, Miles"). The most photographed jazz musician in the world, Davis has captured the imagination of a section of the public to which he appeals in much the same way Bogart did, or better yet, Bogart's successor, Frank Sinatra.

Recently, Davis concluded an engagement at the Village Vanguard, the New York nightclub at which he most often appears. At the Sunday afternoon performance which took place on the last day of his booking, the room was packed, and there were standees along the walls. The girl singer who appeared first was no more than tolerated, reminding one of the ballroom dancers and stand-up comics who, in other days, had the thankless task of filling out Sinatra's stage shows at the Paramount. Ex-Davis sidemen Cannonball Adderley and Philly Joe Jones chatted in the dressing room. The singer's set finished and the lights went up, but no one left. From various parts of the room, the members of the group walked casually toward the bandstand. Davis materialized from a dark corner of the room where he had been talking with the small son of his bassist, Paul Chambers. Resplendent in a tight white suit and green sportshirt, he strolled to the piano and, cigarette in mouth, played a few chords. A waiter handed him his trumpet. He stepped to the microphone, without any perceptible word to the other musicians, assumed the familiar introvert stance, horn pointed toward the floor, and began to play *Some Day My Prince Will Come*. The tight sound that prompted British theater critic Kenneth Tynan to refer to him as a musical lonely-hearts club was heard briefly (the cliché expression "filled the room" would be entirely inaccurate) and the audience applauded wildly. By the time the applause had subsided, Davis was off the stand.

He has become famous for that sort of action. When the Davis group played England, a writer complained that Davis himself was visible for no more than fifteen minutes during the evening—"stage presence" describes what Miles has, but not what he does. He is often not there, and when he is, he does not speak. Those hoping to hear Davis say, "And now, we'd like to play an old favorite of ours, featuring our bass player, Paul Chambers," or something of the sort, will have a long, long wait.

Davis has given reasons for his stage attitude, and they are, on the face of it, excellent ones: "I get off the stand during a set because when I'm not playing, there's nothing for me to do. It's ridiculous for me to just stand there and make the other guys nervous looking at them while they solo. And if I don't look at them, what's the point of my standing up there and looking at the audience? They're not interested in me when somebody else is taking a solo. I don't announce the numbers because I figure the people who come to hear us know everything we play. We have a new record about every three months, and they sell, so the audience must know what's on them."

The owner of a club where Miles works frequently has another reason: "Your jazz fan doesn't care what the tune is." And the manager of that club says, "I think Miles is afraid of the audience." Psychoanalyzing Miles Davis has, in certain circles, assumed the status of a party game. It is likely, though, that his unwillingness to remain onstand could be construed as an act of courtesy, because, contrary to what he says, the audience probably *would* be interested in him to the detriment of the soloist, as if Marlon Brando were scratching his head in a corner while, center stage, a competent actor were vainly trying to arrest the attention of the audience with a recitation.

It could also be argued that Miles Davis is, consciously or not, one of the great public relations men of our times. Audiences obviously love his treatment of them, and return for more. His fierce insistence on privacy is a challenge which many people feel they must break down. Many of them are young ladies, as might be expected. But there are others.

That afternoon at the Vanguard, a middle-aged businessman was standing against the wall with his teenage son before the band appeared, obviously resigned to an unpleasant afternoon.

"What's the name of the musician you want to hear?"

"Miles Davis."

"Does he wear a beard?" the man asked about the clean-shaven Miles.

"I think so."

The father then turned to the man standing beside him. "Mr. Davis, my son Jeff, here, is in high school, and admires your music very much. He'd like to shake your hand."

Having seen Davis bluntly refuse such overtures before, I looked around to see what would happen this time. But Thelonious Monk, whom the man had been speaking to, just walked away.

Anyone who can attract Thelonious Monk and "my son Jeff" to the same nightclub obviously has more than "star quality" going for him. And the leading symbol of the avant-garde, Ornette Coleman, was there listening, too. Most musicians have, at one time or another, listened to Miles, and what many of them have heard has shown up in their own work. Most of them admit that he is one of greatest and most influential musicians of our time. He has achieved that stature without compromise, by refining to its ultimate limits what originally seemed to be a better-than-average talent hampered by severe technical limitations.

Miles Davis' career was unique, even in its beginnings. To many young Negroes, as we have said, music and sports represent the only ways to recognition and a decent amount of money. Davis, who some qualified people think could have been as good a boxer as he is a trumpet player, did not have that need. He was born in Alton, Illinois, on May 25, 1926. His father, Miles II (trumpeter Davis' full name is Miles Dewey Davis III) was a successful dentist and dental surgeon. When the family moved to East St. Louis shortly after Miles' birth, his father began to breed hogs, and the present worth of that venture is estimated at about a quarter of a million dollars. Miles became a jazz musician almost under parental protest, a situation which is more likely to occur if the family is white (there is even a standard movie plot in which the son of the upper middle class family "runs away to become a musician"). Some observers feel that parts of Davis' public aspect stem from the fact that he could, if he wished, have retired whenever he chose without economic difficulty; or indeed, never had to start.

But he did start, at an early age. On his thirteenth birth-day he was given a trumpet by his father. His mother had wanted him to receive a violin but his father gave him the trumpet because "he loved my mother so much." Miles played in the school band, and received private instruction from a man who was highly impressed with Harold "Shorty" Baker. Miles himself was impressed with Clark Terry, who was playing in St. Louis at the time. Both Baker and Terry have worked extensively with Duke Ellington ("I think all the musicians should get together on one certain day and get down on their knees and thank Duke," Davis has said), and both influenced Davis to play the way he preferred: "Fast and light—and no vibrato."

By the time he was sixteen, Miles was playing with a local band called the Blue Devils. Tiny Bradshaw came through town, and Sonny Stitt, who was playing tenor with the band, offered Miles a trumpet chair at "sixty whole dol-lars a week." As Davis later told the story in a taped interview conducted by Columbia Records' publicity de-partment, "I went home and asked my mother if I could go with them. She said no, I had to finish my last year of high school. I didn't talk to her for two weeks. And I didn't go with the band, either."

But he got another chance, and this time he took it. The Billy Eckstine band played St. Louis and in it were two musicians who were to have a profound effect on Miles, Dizzy Gillespie and Charlie Parker. "I knew about Charlie Parker in St. Louis," Miles told Columbia's tape recorder. "I even played with him there, while I was still in high school. We always used to try to play like Diz and Charlie Parker. When we heard that they were coming to town, my friend and I were the first people in the hall, me with a trumpet under my arm. Diz walked up to me and said, 'Kid, do you have a union card?' I said, 'Sure.' So I sat in with the band that night. I couldn't read a thing from listening to Diz and Bird. Then the third trumpet man got sick. I knew the book because I loved the music so much I knew the third part by heart. So I played with the band for a couple of weeks. I had to go to New York then."

When Davis graduated from high school, the problem arose, as it does in so many families, of what college he should attend. His mother's choice was Fisk University, because "they had a good music department and the Fisk Jubilee Singers." But Miles, whose choice was dictated by that year's *Esquire Jazz Book*, saw no mention of Fisk. His father gave him permission to enroll in Juilliard, so Miles went to New York. "I spent my first week in New York and my first month's allowance looking for Charlie Parker."

He found Parker, and became his roommate. It was probably the most important association, musically and personally, that he ever had. Some feel today that Miles' public manner stems from the laying-on-of-hands feeling he has about having worked with Bird, but, if we believe what he once told a lady interviewer, he paid his dues for that: "Bird was a friend of mine. I used to put him to bed sometimes with the needle still in his arm and him bleeding all over the place. He used to pawn my suitcase and take all my money. You going to put that in your article?"

But Parker helped him musically, and some of that help has rubbed off in ways not so obvious. He has said of Parker, "He never did talk about music," and years later, Davis sideman Bill Evans told Nat Hentoff, "We never had a rehearsal. Everything was done on the job. On the record dates, half or all of the material might be all new and had never been rehearsed before."

Miles left Juilliard to play with Parker because, as he says, "I realized I wasn't going to get in any symphony orchestra." And he began to learn. Such people as Thelonious

Monk, Tadd Dameron, Freddie Webster, and Dizzy Gillespie added to his knowledge, which up to that time, he is pleased to say, consisted of what he had learned from a book called *Georgia Gibbs Chord Analysis.* But mostly, he learned from Parker. There is a widely reprinted quotation from Davis about how the challenge of Parker's improvising in that band was so great that he quit every night, and one can understand how that could be. For not only was he playing with the man generally credited with being the greatest genius of modern jazz, but he was, at the same time, attempting to find his own style.

One of the most concise statements of his problem at the time comes from arranger Gil Evans, in an interview with Nat Hentoff: "Miles couldn't play like Louis because the sound would interfere with his thoughts. Miles had to start with almost no sound and then develop one as he went along, a sound suitable for the ideas he wanted to express. He couldn't afford to trust those thoughts to an old means of expression. If you remember, his sound now is much more highly developed than it was at first."

At first, on the evidence of extant recordings, he did emulate Dizzy Gillespie, but there was an important difference. Many writers have said that Davis is by no means Gillespie's technical equal, and Davis himself has admitted as much: "I asked Dizzy, 'Why can't I play high like you?' 'Because you don't hear up there,' he said. 'You hear in the middle register.' And that's true. There are times when I can't even tell what chords Dizzy is working on when he's up high; and yet he'll tell me what he's playing is just an octave above what I do." But there is more to it than technique. Unlike musicians who are content to imitate their idols, Davis had picked Gillespie as one model for his own style, a much different matter. At least half of what any artist is to become depends on the wisdom with which he chooses his model.

Miles is obviously unable to execute some of Gillespie's

incredibly fast upper-register runs, still it is questionable whether or not Miles' solos, which are distinguishable from Gillespie's in their use of fewer notes, a greater dependency on lyricism, a tendency to remain in the middle register, and a number of fluffs are entirely due to technical limitations. "What comes out of his horn," Whitney Balliett has said of Davis, "seems the result of the instantaneous editing of a far more diffuse melodic line being carried on in his head." On the one hand, it is interesting that Gillespie has, in the last few years, made his own style occasionally more spare; on the other, it is possible that Davis was undergoing the stylistic birthpangs most accurately described by Ernest Hemingway: ". . . a style is usually only the unavoidable awkwardness in first trying to make something that has not heretofore been made . . . At first people can only see the awkwardness . . . people think these awkwardnesses are the style and copy them . . ."

Davis' trumpet style, apparent awkwardness and all, has since been the most widely imitated in jazz. The first intimation that it might truly be original came in 1949. This was the famous nine-piece band which Miles led for two weeks at the Royal Roost in New York, and which made records for Capitol that have been called the Genesis of the "cool" movement.

Gil Evans, who had been the arranger for Claude Thornhill was, with Gerry Mulligan and others, one of the prime shapers of that band, whose origin he traced as follows: "The idea of Miles' little band for the Capitol session came, I think, from Claude's band in the sound sense. Miles had liked some of what Gerry and I had written for Claude. The instrumentation for the Miles session was caused by the fact that this was the smallest number of instruments that could get the sound and still express all the harmonies the Thornhill band used. Miles wanted to play his idiom with that kind of sound. Miles, by the way, was the complete leader for those Capitol sides. He organized the band, sold it for the record contract, and for the Royal Roost where we played."

Bob Weinstock of Prestige Records, with whom Miles was associated during the formative part of his recording career, adds, "Gil Evans had a tremendous influence on Miles' musical thinking. Miles always spoke of Gil Evans, and he kept telling me, when nobody knew of him, 'Get Gil Evans, get him to do an album. He's beautiful.' I think that Miles found his true element there, at *that* time. Here was a chance for all his sensitivity, compared to Bird's savageness and deep fire and emotion, which was overpowering Miles every time Bird would play on the same stand; here was an outlet for Miles Davis to let out the sensitivity that he had as a musician."

Apparently, the calm, placid cast of the nine-piece band was not completely satisfying to Davis. What he did about this dissatisfaction is recalled by Weinstock: "Miles sort of disappeared from the scene, and I was on a business trip out to St. Louis, and I knew Miles lived around there. I made some calls, there were a few Davises in the phone book, and I reached his home. They told me he was in Chicago. I said, 'Please, if you should hear from Miles, ask him to call me in New York. I want to record him.' Finally he got in touch with me, and he came back East. Miles, at that time, although he still dug the cool music of Mulligan and Evans, some of the primitiveness in him started to come out. I say primitiveness, because to me the music of the bop masters is primitive music, like the original New Orleans music of King Oliver and Louis. He sort of drifted back into that element, and he liked Sonny Rollins, as crude as Sonny was at that time, and John Lewis. On his first date, you can hear a very different Miles Davis than on the Capitols."

The session Weinstock refers to took place in 1951, and he disposes of the time lag in his account by saying, "In those days, a lot of guys used to disappear from the scene for months at a time." Davis himself has been more explicit: "I got hooked after I came back from the Paris Jazz Festival in 1949. I got bored and was around cats that were hung. So I wound up with a habit that took me over four years to break."

Perhaps that is the explanation for the surge of great Miles Davis recordings which began to be issued in 1954, after a prolonged absence. Before that he had made recordings for Prestige with various men: John Lewis, Al Cohn, Zoot Sims, Sonny Rollins, Lee Konitz, as well as some for Blue Note with J. J. Johnson and Jackie McLean. But 1954 was Miles' year. As he told Marc Crawford in *Ebony*, "I made up my mind I was getting off dope. I was sick and tired of it. You know you can get tired of anything. You can even get tired of being scared. I laid down and stared at the ceiling for twelve days and I cursed everybody I didn't like. I was kicking it the hard way. It was like having a bad case of flu, only worse. I lay in a cold sweat. My nose and eyes ran. I threw up everything I tried to eat. My pores opened up and I smelled like chicken soup. Then it was over."

Missing from his account is the pain and extraordinary self-discipline that such a task requires; such an action inevitably changes a man. His daily workouts in the gym probably stem from that time, and perhaps the impenetrable shell does, too. But he has not become a moralist about it, and has none of the holier-than-thou attitude that, for instance, some teetotaling ex-alcoholics have. His approach, as he told Nat Hentoff, is an extremely practical one: "I just tell them if they work for me to regulate their habit. When they're tired of the trouble it takes to support a habit, they'll stop it if they have the strength. You can't *talk* a man out of a habit until he really *wants* to stop."

Davis's return was marked by a series of brilliant recordings, starting with two quartet sessions, one for Prestige and one for Blue Note, recorded within four days of one another, with a rhythm section consisting of Horace Silver, Art Blakey, and Percy Heath. Included are his composition *Four,* and

Blue Haze, which started the fashion of opening slow blues with bass introductions.

On April 29, 1954, he made a record which was to have an extraordinarily pervasive influence: *Walkin'*. Recorded with a rhythm section made up of Silver, Heath, and Kenny Clarke (forceful piano and light drums, a Weinstock idea which Davis was later to change for the opposite effect of light piano and forceful drums), trombonists Jay Jay Johnson and Lucky Thompson, it is the best example of the "hard bop" influence that was just beginning to pervade the work of the modernists. Excellent as it is, it is not really Miles' approach. What he was working toward came off better on his next session.

While *Walkin'* was the beginning of Silver's reputation, the next date began the rise of Sonny Rollins. The record, which contains *Airegin, Oleo, Doxy*—all Rollins compositions—and the standard *But Not For Me*, was a perfect instance of what can happen on a day when the elements mix properly, and a classic example of the style of the early fifties.

In 1954, Prestige had under contract some of the most important contemporary musicians. Besides Davis, the list included Thelonious Monk and the Modern Jazz Quartet. Weinstock had the idea of using three MJQ members—vibraphonist Milt Jackson, bassist Percy Heath, and drummer Kenny Clarke—Monk, and Miles, for an "all-star" session on December 24. At least one member of the group was obviously Weinstock's choice rather than Davis'; as Miles once told Hentoff, "I love the way Monk plays and writes, but I can't stand him behind me. He doesn't give you any support." Because of that attitude, he asked Monk not to play behind his solos. Monk became intractably stubborn under these circumstances, and got up from the piano in the middle of one number to head for the bathroom.

The music reveals some of the personal tensions at work that day, but Davis is magnificent. On four tunes, one by each of the three principal soloists (Miles' *Swing Spring*,

Jackson's *Bags' Groove,* Monk's *Bemsha Swing*) and the standard *The Man I Love,* he contributed his most flowing, lyrical open horn work in years. By this time, the technical limitations that had marred his playing had been assimilated into a style that could contain them. The ballad, in particular, includes some of Miles' most technically assured work. *Bags' Groove* is almost a definitive statement of his approach to the blues. It is a style unique with him, with less of a pervasive blue-note feel than anyone's, and he has never played it better.

But the real beginning of the Miles Davis legend occurred one night at the Newport Jazz Festival in 1955, when he played a brief solo on *'Round Midnight,* and the critics began talking about his "resurgence." His reply to the adulation was, "What are they talking about? I just played the way I always play." But an old adage had come true again. Miles was the right man at the right time, and all his preparation paid off in one night.

His own personal view of music was first tentatively announced in an LP called *The Musings of Miles* (now retitled, *The Beginning*), a quartet date with pianist Red Garland, bassist Oscar Pettiford, and drummer Philly Joe Jones, recorded a month before the Newport festival. The personnel and musical approach of that LP formed the basis for a quintet which Davis led from late 1955 until the spring of 1957. It has been called the most important and influential group of its time. But when the first record by that quintet, *Miles,* was released, few thought so. It retained Garland and Jones from the *Musings* record, replaced Pettiford with Paul Chambers, and added the tenor saxophone of John Coltrane. Except for later work with Gil Evans and the later "modal" pieces, all of Davis' music since that time has been an extension and further exploration of ideas set down on *The Beginning* and *Miles.*

It is impossible to see, on the face of it, how the group could have succeeded. Coltrane, at the time, was groping and unformed; Garland played many seeming cocktail clichés; Chambers was scarcely out of his teens; and Jones played so loud that sometimes he overpowered the others. And there was Davis himself, playing in simple contrast to the others. The band's book consisted of tunes by men like Parker and Gillespie, and standards, a large number of which came from the repertoire of Ahmad Jamal (Davis has said, "All my inspiration today comes from the Chicago pianist, Ahmad Jamal"). When dealing with such disparate elements, one needs a unique personal chemistry, largely intangible, to mold a group. And if the control slackens ever so slightly, the divergent elements return to their original state, five rather ill-assorted men who happen to be playing together. On occasion, to be sure, that is exactly what happened, but Davis welded his men into a magnificent musical unit.

A large number of the group's tunes were based on concepts originated by Jamal: his two-beat rhythm and ideas, his use of musical space, and his tag endings. These were most often employed on tunes out of Jamal's book (*Gal in Calico, Billy Boy, Surrey With The Fringe on Top*) and others which lent themselves to the same treatment, such as *Bye-Bye Blackbird* and *All of You*. Miles' adulation of Jamal ("Red Garland knew I liked Ahmad and at times I used to ask him to play like that. Red was at his best when he did") has led many others to praise the pianist. But if Davis is able to derive valuable ideas from Jamal's music, that does not make Jamal Davis' musical equal. Most artists borrow, often from unlikely sources, and if they are good enough they invariably enrich what they borrow. At least part of the unique quality of the quintet performances lay in a particular principle which Davis grasped, a principle so simple that it apparently eluded everyone else. To put it in terms of this particular group, a quintet is not always a quintet. It could also be a quartet featuring Miles, and, at different times on the same tune, it could be a quartet featuring Coltrane, or a trio featuring either Garland or Chambers. The Davis rhythm section, Jones in particular, was well aware of this, and gave each of the three principal soloists his own best backing. Behind Davis, the rhythm was full of space, with few chords; behind Coltrane, it was compulsive; and with Garland, it lapsed into an easy, Jamal-like feeling.

Hentoff, refuting the idea that Miles is an over-delicate musician, wrote, "The essence of Miles Davis can be determined by listening to the men he has surrounded himself with on his regular jobs." Hentoff quotes Davis as saying of Jones, for instance, "I wouldn't care if he came up on the bandstand in his B.V.D.'s and with one arm, just so long as he was there. He's got the fire I want. There's nothing more terrible than playing with a dull rhythm section. Jazz has got to have *that thing*. You have to be born with it. You can't even buy it. If you could buy it, they'd have it at the next Newport festival."

It may also be true that Miles surrounds himself with fiery players like Jones, Coltrane, and others partly as contrast. He delights in setting off his oblique style against that of a searing, forceful saxophonist, and sometimes, by doing so, makes himself appear the only pretty girl at the party. This gentle, lyric quality appeared with the quintet most notably on ballads, and Coltrane often did not play on the ballads. These quartet performances first enabled Davis to reach the vast audience he now has; an audience that, in several cases, has little affinity with any other jazz. When Davis plays ballads, mute tight against the microphone (he seems to play microphone as much as trumpet), he reveals an area of tenderness and sensitivity which is rarely visible in his public aspect. These performances, in the emotion they evoke, are comparable to nothing else in jazz.

The culmination of the quintet's recorded work came with two legendary marathon sessions held late in 1956, which produced four albums (*Cookin'*, *Relaxin'*, *Workin'* and *Steamin'*), and a spare version of *'Round About Midnight,* included on a fifth. The group simply came into the studio on two different days, played their book as they would in a club, and there were no second takes. J. J. Johnson has said, "I've recorded with Miles and I know how he operates. Most of the time he goes into the studio and one take is it! Goofs or not, there's no second or third take. That's his philosophy on the recording bit."

There are magnificent things on the records, and few men could have been successful at the marathon this quintet attempted. But it was not done for completely altruistic reasons. Jazz is big business, and "the Louis Armstrong Hot Five of the modern era," as Weinstock called the quintet, is a valuable economic property. The major recording companies have a disconcerting habit of offering lucrative contracts to jazzmen after small independents have built them up. Columbia, who had the biggest-selling jazz LP in history with Fantasy's former contractee, Dave Brubeck, had its eye on Miles after the Newport triumph, and came to talk to him. He wanted to sign; but his contract with Prestige had a year to go, and he owed four LPs. Negotiations were made, and the result was that Miles could leave Prestige as soon as the LPs were made; hence, the marathon sessions. At the same time, Columbia recorded its first quintet record, *'Round About Midnight,* while the Prestige contract was still in force, promising not to release it until the expiration date. Weinstock salvaged what he could by the expedient of releasing one quintet album a year. The last one was finally on the market in July 1961.

But things other than money were involved. Miles had once written to a recording company about a coming date, "If you can't do it that way, please recommend me to a company that can." One of the things that Weinstock would have found financially difficult to do "that way" was the second Columbia release, *Miles Ahead.*

The four Columbia albums Davis has recorded with arranger Gil Evans, of which *Miles Ahead* is the first, represent another aspect of his music, and one that, except for a single occasion in 1961, he has confined to the recording studio.

"I haven't heard anything that knocks me out as consistently as he does since I first heard Charlie Parker," Davis has said of Evans. *Miles Ahead,* which Evans scored for an orchestra of nineteen pieces, with Miles on flugelhorn as the only soloist, represented an extension of the nine-piece Capitol band.

In this and the next joint effort, a setting of *Porgy and Bess,* despite their lush, unique arrangements, the problem seemed to be the same. Evans once described the Claude Thornhill band, from which he took his inspiration, in this way, to Hentoff: "The sound had become a little too somber for my taste, generally speaking, a little too bleak in character. It began to have a hypnotic effect at times. The band could put you to sleep. An example in the variation in our thinking was the tuba. He liked the static sound of the tuba on chords. I wanted the tuba to play flexible, moving jazz passages. He liked a stationary effect so much, in fact, that if he could have had his way, I think he would have had the band hold a chord for one hundred bars with him compensating ably for the static effect with the activity of his piano. You see, the static sound of the orchestra put the demand for activity on him." In these albums Evans, similarly, had left the activity up to Miles. The result: Davis was asked to do what, in his quintet, he had left up to the other players, and the effect is often one of all relaxation with no compensating tension.

These two albums led to a resurgence of interest in Evans, who had been largely inactive since the Capitol sessions. Some critics greeted him as a kind of messiah, which somewhat disturbs him. Older than most active jazzmen (he was born in 1912), he is uncomfortable as an "elder statesman," and does not speak of himself as a composer, except to say that "it helps me get record dates."

Of working with Miles as opposed to working alone, he says, "the only difference is what you hear on the records, the addition of another artist and his ideas." But on the records he has made without relying on a major soloist to carry the brunt of the burden, he has shown that his main concern is with pure sound. His main achievement is in the field of tone color, the playing off of instrument against instrument for often exquisite effects. Almost by its nature, this talent can work best at slow tempos where the ear can savor more completely what is being done. It is a talent leading toward ecstasy in much the same way as does the music of the Russian composer Scriabin.

Evans' next collaboration with Davis was the album *Sketches of Spain.* The longest track is a rearrangement of the second movement of Joaquin Rodrigo's *Concierto de Aranjuez* for guitar and orchestra with the solo guitar part played by Davis. (It must have been while this record was being made that a cab-driver friend of mine began to fear that Miles had gone over to the gospel-funk boys. He picked up Davis in his cab one evening, and overheard him discussing with his wife the trouble he had had in the studio that afternoon with a tambourine player.) On the face of it, this kind of rearrangement can produce the worst kind of "jazzing the classics" music. But it was done here with love and respect for the original, a minimum of improvisation, and a deep involvement by Davis that elicits his best playing (Evans seems to bring out hidden emotional and technical resources in the trumpeter). Perhaps this piece only proves that there are no rules that will stand against a good enough exception. Davis' immersion in the Spanish idiom on this and the other selections is nothing short of amazing until one stops to consider the great similarities between the music of the Spaniards and of jazz and its progenitors. The work is much more successful than the so-called "Third Stream" attempts at the same sort of fusion from the opposite direction, pieces written for classical orchestras and jazz improvisers.

Stimulating as the association with Evans has been for Davis, it is sporadic ("I never know when I'm going to do a date with Gil until it's over"), and has remained outside the main body of Davis' work. His main achievement is to be found in the music he plays with the group he leads in night clubs. After the original quintet broke up in 1957, the personnel was in a fairly constant state of flux. Sonny Rollins, Coltrane, Jones, and Garland variously rejoined, only to leave again. At one point, the addition of Julian Adderley made the group a sextet. Pianist Bill Evans and tenor saxophonist Sonny Stitt were both members for brief periods. After four years, the unit resettled into permanence, with tenor saxophonist Hank Mobley, trombonist J. J. Johnson, pianist Wynton Kelly, drummer Jimmy Cobb, and the man who had remained throughout the various manifestations, Paul Chambers. It remained that way until late 1963, when changes began again.

No matter whom Davis picks for his sidemen, they all become stylistically subservient to the leader's musical ideas. Some of them have, like Red Garland, rebelled against being told what to play on occasion, but all of them have benefited. Some, like Stitt, object to the intransigent Davis manner and leave. Some of them have been awed by the prospect ("I felt the group to be composed of superhumans," Bill Evans has said). Whatever they got out of it, they got largely by themselves, through osmosis. "As for rehearsals," Adderley wrote in *The Jazz Review*, "we had maybe five in the two years I was there, two of them when I first joined the band. And the rehearsals were quite direct, like, 'Coltrane, show Cannonball how you do this. All right, now let's do it.' Occasionally, Miles would tell us something on the stand. 'Cannonball, you don't have to play *all* those notes. Just stay close to the sound of the melody. Those substitute chords sound funny.'"

By such methods, any group Davis leads sooner or later becomes an all-star group. The musicians who stay with Miles long enough will find themselves climbing to higher positions on the popularity polls, as the greater exposure and the force of the leader's personality make the fans more aware of them at the same time that they are becoming better musicians.

According to one observer, Miles delights in his talent-scout activities—he is the best in jazz—at least in part because of his contempt for critics. Davis loves to find musicians whom the critics dislike—Coltrane, for the most outstanding example—and watch, five or six years later, while his discoveries become jazz heroes.

At the same time, there are pressures his sidemen must put up with. Jimmy Cobb spent years listening to Miles tell everyone that Philly Joe Jones is Miles' favorite drummer; and one night, during a Mobley solo, Miles said, "Any night Sonny Rollins shows up with his horn, he's got a job."

The results, however, are worth the pressures. With each group, Davis has been busy refining his concepts. His own playing recalls the remark of pianist Cecil Taylor that "as Miles Davis' European technical facility becomes sparser, his comment from the Negro folk tradition becomes more incisive." This can be seen most clearly in his blues recordings. Essentially, he makes variations on solos that he has been playing since the middle fifties, sometimes so spare that he sounds as though every grudging note were as valuable as the money he gets for playing it. He has begun to echo traditional jazz more overtly, playing with the element of choice that an actor would employ: just that note, just that pause, just that tone. Seemingly casual, seemingly maladroit technically, Davis nevertheless hits exactly the right note, the one no one else would have thought of, meaningful both in itself and as a comment on the written note for which he is substituting his own.

Stimulating as it must be to play with him, his ultimate achievement may lie more as a leader than as a soloist. It is no accident that his men win polls and eventually become leaders themselves. That is what happened to such Parker sidemen as Bud Powell, Max Roach, and Davis himself. In the sixties, it has happened with the sidemen of Ornette Coleman, who are hired away into other bands as other leaders want to learn about Coleman's music. And as Parker's was the musical language of the forties, and Coleman's is the language of the sixties, it is now obvious that Miles Davis shaped the jazz of the fifties.

Davis has said, "I think a movement in jazz is beginning away from the conventional string of chords, and a return to emphasis on melodic rather than harmonic variation. There will be fewer chords but infinite possibilities as to what to do with them . . . we got to talking about letting the melodies and scales carry the tune . . . The music has gotten thick. Guys give me tunes and they're full of chords. I can't play them."

When Bill Evans replaced Red Garland with Davis in 1958, the leader began to include more "modal" pieces in his repertoire, music based on scales rather than chords. Davis had earlier recorded a similar, highly influential piece, *Milestones,* but the *Kind of Blue* album which he made in 1958 had an impact on subsequent jazz so great that this music, coupled with the earlier style of the 1955–57 quintet, gave impetus to a new language. Essentially, the album transformed Davis' one-take philosophy into an album idea: no one saw the music before the session, and only one complete performance of each piece was recorded. Echoes of this music turn up on almost every jazz LP to be released since; it has formed the new mainstream from which the players of the "new thing" are attempting to depart.

Davis records an obscure movie theme, *On Green Dolphin Street;* fifty new versions appear. Everywhere, one hears modal pieces, saxophonists playing like Rollins or Coltrane, muted trumpets playing standards in a medium two-beat.

Davis, at the peak of his career, is in an unassailable position. "Miles could spit into his horn," one A & R man said, "and get five stars in *Down Beat.*" Such remarks usually come before the fall from public grace that most jazzmen eventually suffer, but Davis may never suffer such a fall. He has escaped most of the traditional stigmata: he works, although he is a former narcotics user; his popularity has not been gained at the cost of critical acceptance. On the contrary, he has gotten where he has on his own bluntly uncompromising terms. Part of this is due to his public personality. Novelist James Baldwin, who has referred to him as a "miraculously tough and tender man," wrote, "Miles' disguise would certainly never fool anybody with sense, but it keeps a lot of people away, and that's the point." One of the very few it didn't keep away was an interviewer for *Playboy* who, in the September 1962 issue, recorded a remarkably revealing interview with the usually unapproachable Davis. Significantly, the interviewer was colored, and Davis speaks in the piece with rare candor of his own situation as a Negro, making that fact his prime motivation. As for music, he said simply that he had "worked all my life to play myself and then to get a band worth people paying to hear."

He has accomplished that to the extent that he is among the most well-to-do of jazz musicians; his money has been wisely invested in stocks that have made him financially secure. Still, his public demeanor and immense popularity is a thorn in the side of less successful musicians, who do not think that success can come without compromise. "He's going to go to Hollywood," says one disillusioned pianist.

Hollywood might not be such a bad place for him, at that. The only thing that could possibly hold him back is his curious, rasping voice. Miles had a throat operation ("He has throat cancer and he's gonna die, that's why he doesn't give a damn," say overly romantic fans), after which he was supposed to remain silent for weeks. He had a conversation with an agent a few days later—always a difficult situation in which to keep one's temper—and had to shout the man down. His hoarse voice is the result. Perhaps it is because he is sensitive about his voice that he won't make announcements. One night outside a club, he made a rueful remark, when asked how he felt playing in such a noisy room. "They aren't louder than those horns," he said. "It would be different if I was a singer, but of course I can't sing." He has, as I have said, the actor's presence of a Sinatra, with whom he shares many characteristics. Both men are pace-setters in fashion. Miles, whose taste runs to continental suits, was recently on George Frazier's *Esquire* list of the forty best-dressed men in America. Both Davis and Sinatra delight in indulging a passion for speed. Miles has a magnificent white Ferrari, which he drives as fast as the law allows, or faster. One night on New York's West Side highway, a friend cautioned him not to go so fast. Miles' pointed reply was, "I'm in here too." Both have an acute, private sense of the fitness of things. One night not long ago, Lena Horne came to the Vanguard to hear Miles. Davis, informed of her impending arrival, called the club in advance to make sure that someone would meet his friend Miss Horne's cab at the street, escort her past the waiting line of people, and show her to her table. Both men have a fierce insistence on personal privacy, although nearly anything either of them does is news. A Negro pianist, thinking of the similarities between the two, remarked that if they ever met, the trumpeter would not substitute, among Sinatra's friends, for his namesake—Sammy Davis, Jr., "Two kings," he said, "and only one throne."

Davis, like Sinatra, has had several public battles. One of them involved a concert entrepreneur whom he knocked flat backstage in a Chicago theater. What had happened was this: the night before, another band in the concert package had failed to arrive, and Miles had offered to open the show; the worst possible position on the bill, and one he was not required to take. The next night, Miles arrived late, although still long before he was scheduled to perform. The entrepreneur came up to him, announcing that he was going to fine Miles one hundred dollars for tardiness. As Sinatra once said about a similar incident, "He became punched."

The most famous public incident involving Davis occurred late in 1959. While working at Birdland, he went upstairs to the street outside the basement club for a smoke. A policeman passing by asked him to move along. Said Miles: "I work here." No completely accurate report of what happened has ever been pieced together, but Miles was badly beaten about the head by two policemen with billies. Some have speculated on what he might have said to the policemen as they became insistent, but the incident smacks heavily of police brutality. Davis' cabaret card was taken from him for a time, and his lawyer and personal manager, Harold Lovett, instituted a suit against the city of New York for half a million dollars.

Lovett is probably Miles' best friend and most constant companion. He is one of the few people who stuck by Miles during the bad years, and Miles apparently remembers such things. One person remarked of Lovett, "he makes Miles look like a choirboy," and another person says that he has heard Miles talk about Lovett admiringly on several occasions, as though Lovett's "coolness" were the ultimate in behavior. Asked about this, one club owner said, "I think Miles is much cooler than Harold. Harold tends to worry about Miles, but Miles never worries about Harold."

Davis still remembers the incident at Birdland with considerable bitterness. One night, after several attempts to reach him for an interview, I saw him standing on the street outside the Village Vanguard. It was a hot night, and I invited him to walk around the block for some air. "The last time I did that," he said, "I got hit in the head." About the interview, "It's nothing personal, but I don't give stories. If Jesus Christ himself came down from the cross and asked for a story, I'd say, 'I'm sorry, I don't have the time.' You have to write it, that's your business, so just write about the music, whether you like it or not. Write what you know, or write what you don't know, like everybody else."

It is not difficult to understand why he takes the attitude he does. When *Sketches of Spain* came out, he agreed to a press conference on behalf of the album. The first question was asked by a reporter who hadn't heard the record.

It must also be said that magazine stories titled "The Enigma of Miles Davis," or "Miles Davis: Evil Genius of Jazz," haven't hurt him at all. Probably as many people go to the clubs in expectation of watching his extra-musical behavior as come to hear him play. And in that respect, he never disappoints his audience.

As far as his extremely private life is concerned, it seems, from without, to be almost ideal. He lives in a beautiful reconditioned brownstone in the West Seventies with two children by a former marriage and his beautiful, gracious wife, Frances, a former dancer who keeps herself far removed from Davis' professional life. A lovely, gentle person, she has probably been a stabilizing influence on her husband. She, and the boxing that is his passion, account for much of his time. Guests in his home report that one of his main pleasures is watching old fight films or scenes of jungle animals in combat on a home movie projector.

Speculation on the Miles Davis character probably will go on endlessly, and countless apocryphal stories will continue to spring up. One may wonder what a man in his position has to be so angry about, unless it is simply a matter of it finally being *his* turn. But if approached with friendliness, the beatific child's smile will flash, and he can be the most charming of men. The total impression he gives is that of a wise child, impatient with any circumlocutions, always getting bluntly through to the core of a situation. (Once the advertising manager of a magazine in which he had won a poll wrote Miles a letter suggesting he take a "thank you" ad. The letter was returned, and the phrase scrawled upon it was not "thank you.")

He says that he may retire, that he plays music only for pleasure, or that "I'm retired now because I don't do nothing unless I want to."

But whatever he does, if the legend continues, perhaps someday, like Bix Beiderbecke, Miles Davis, with his genius, his presence, his lovely wife, and his white Ferrari, will be the subject of a novel that begins, "I don't know what the hell that kid thinks a trumpet will do . . ." Such a novel (he has been the prototype in more than one) would only add to his anger. "Why is it that people just have to have so much to say about me?" he asks. "It bugs me because I'm not that important."

Selected Discography

Birth of the Cool, CAPITOL T-762.
Bags' Groove, PRESTIGE 7109.
Modern Jazz Giants, PRESTIGE 7150.
Relaxin' with the Miles Davis Quintet, PRESTIGE 7129.
Steamin' with the Miles Davis Quintet, PRESTIGE 7200.
'Round About Midnight, COLUMBIA CL-949.
Kind of Blue, COLUMBIA CL-1355.
Sketches of Spain, COLUMBIA CL-1480.

SONNY ROLLINS

"YOU WON'T BE SURPRISED when you hear me," Sonny Rollins said in the summer of 1961. "I'm playing just about the way I did before, only I think much better. I have more control over myself and over my instrument and I think you'll be able to hear that, but nothing else is changed."

Nearly two years before, in August 1959, at the height of a notable career, Rollins, who many considered to be the finest tenor saxophonist in contemporary jazz, had abruptly and inexplicably stopped performing in public. To guarantee privacy, he had had his telephone removed. Like Garbo, Rollins became more famous in retirement than before. Stories grew up around him: he was a day laborer; he was a bank teller; he would never again play publicly. *Down Beat*, the most widely-read fan magazine dealing with jazz, announced that Rollins had accepted an engagement at a Chicago club. After weeks of considerable speculation among the jazz fraternity, the same magazine reported that Rollins had not appeared to fulfill the engagement. It developed later that neither the club nor *Down Beat* had contacted the saxophonist. A story also appeared in print to the effect that Rollins once visited a New York club where his friend Thelonious Monk was working. Monk, according to the story, was happy to see that Sonny was "not nuts." If Monk actually feared for his friend's sanity, his concern might have been aroused by another printed story, which stated that Rollins had been seen practicing at 3 A.M. on the Brooklyn Bridge. Jazz fans being notorious romanticizers, gossip had even stranger explanations for the disappearing act.

In 1960, Rollins himself attempted to dispel the rumors, by means of a rather painfully phrased message to *Down Beat*: "I am at present engaged in numerous pursuits, the most pressing of which are my writing and composing. These endeavors are demanding of the greater portion of my time, concentration, and energies. They will best be brought to fruition by my maintaining a certain amount of seclusion and divorcing myself as much as possible from my professional career during this period."

Apparently, no one believed him. There had been no press releases, no announcement. Rollins was simply no longer around. But anyone who had paid careful attention to an interview which Rollins gave *Down Beat* in 1958, at the height of his popularity, would have seen that the saxophonist was not acting on a whim. "Right now," he said then, "I feel I just want to get away for awhile. I think I need a lot of things. One of them is time . . . time to study and finish some things I started a long time ago. . . . I never seem to have time to work, practice, and write. Everything becomes secondary to going to work every night and wondering how the band sounds and whether our appearances are okay." About a year later, Rollins found a way to give himself that time.

He also, of course, perpetrated the greatest possible publicity stunt. To a fan, the only thing more exciting than talent is talent that rejects the public rewards of its fulfillment. But Rollins does not think in those terms. The time in self-imposed retirement, from August 1959 to November 1961, was spent on himself: practicing, thinking, contemplating. Any rewards the listener may receive as a result of that time are only indirect rewards. Rollins was not then consciously working out a "new thing" with which to return and startle those fans who have made the jazz business more subject to built-in obsolescence than the motor factories of Detroit. While the saxophonist was absent, Alfred Lion of Blue Note Records, who had recorded several albums with him, said, "I think Sonny's working on a new style. I think he was worried about some of the young tenor players coming up, but he better come back soon because it's been two years and people forget fast in this business." But as Rollins later told Whitney Balliett in a *New Yorker* interview, "When I quit working, I tried to revise the way I played the horn. Completely. But then I amended that. Instead, I have made an exploration of the horn." And on his return, some of his audience was quite vocal in expressing its disappointment at learning that he had done no more than perfect his previous style.

There is another aspect of the saxophonist's sabbatical to be considered. If a Rollins retires, that is news. But many musicians less talented than he have gone without work for periods even longer than two years, and that, sometimes unfortunately, has not always been news. Rollins had created something in the years prior to his retirement which made his presence missed. Fashion and publicity being what they are, there may be many who are his staunch advocates now who were never fully aware of what that first contribution was. Perhaps an attempt to indicate its nature is the best place to begin.

"The saxophone, after all," Rollins has said, "is still a very young instrument, and people are still finding criteria by which to judge its players." In the middle fifties, Rollins himself created a new criterion, and drastically revised the ways of thinking about and playing his instrument. The evolution of the jazz tenor saxophone, prior to Rollins, had been along two lines, one stemming from Lester Young, the other, a bit older, from Coleman Hawkins. Young had a small, breathy sound, a lazy, seemingly casual swing, and a gift for long melodic phrases which took precedence over bar lines and chord changes. In contrast to that basically horizontal approach, Hawkins was a vertical player, examining the possibilities of each chord with arpeggios as he came to it, using a rich, almost harsh tone, with a strong vibrato. In the late forties and early fifties, many tenor players, enchanted to varying degrees with the Basie tradition, based their styles on Young. Some of the best of them—Stan Getz, Zoot Sims,

Herbie Steward, Al Cohn, Jimmy Giuffre—played at one time or another with the Woody Herman band, but there were Wardell Gray, Paul Quinichette, and others who did not. Still, the Herman band made popular the distinctive "Four Brothers" sound that was derived from Lester Young, and set the acceptable style of playing the tenor.

Rollins played differently. "Coleman Hawkins," he says, "is my idol." There was also Charlie Parker, who, Rollins says, "Had a profound effect on my life, musically as well as personally." Earlier saxophonists such as Dexter Gordon and Gene Ammons had effected a merger between the tone of Hawkins and the lyricism of Young, and Rollins also modeled himself on them. "No one," he says, "is original. Everyone is derivative."

Strangely, for a man so committed to his instrument and who has wrought such changes on it, Rollins came near to never playing the saxophone at all. He was born Theodore Walter Rollins in Manhattan on September 7, 1930 (a date he has variously given as 1929, so as to seem old enough to get working papers in order to play clubs, and as 1931, at a time when he responded to jazz's obsession with youth by representing himself as younger), and he originally wanted to draw. A brother and sister both played instruments, and his parents gave him piano lessons when he was eight or nine, but he soon became bored and quit. Later, when Rollins saw a picture a friend had had taken with a tenor saxophone, he decided to get a horn for himself. Fond of the music of Louis Jordan ("He had the first of the little blues bands, like what Ray Charles has now"), he bought an alto, because Jordan played one. He then heard Coleman Hawkins, who lived in the neighborhood, and would wait on the great tenorman's doorstep just to see him. At that point, he started playing his alto with a tenor reed, and later switched to the larger instrument. Still, he did not take music very seriously, and even today gives the impression of having fallen into the profession almost by chance. "The guys in the neighborhood," he says, "seemed to like what I did, and gave me encouragement." Two of "the guys in the neighborhood" were Thelonious Monk and Bud Powell. Rollins often went to their homes to play and rehearse with them, learned much from them both, and considers them among his closest personal friends. (When asked about Powell's legendary eccentricities, he says somewhat cryptically, "I think Bud was putting on an act. He knew what he was doing all the time. He had his reasons. I think I know him well enough to say that.")

By 1947, he had graduated from high school and was working sporadically around New York. In 1948, he made his first record, an unimpressive version of the *St. Louis Blues* for Capitol with vocalist Babs Gonzales. In 1949, he recorded with Powell and the trumpeter Fats Navarro. He left New York in 1950 to work in Chicago with Ike Day, an unrecorded musician whom Rollins considers one of the great drummers of all time.

He returned to play with a small group in a Harlem club. His was the house band, working opposite whatever big names came in to head the bill. Many top musicians played the club, and many others came by to hear them. They heard Rollins, too, and his reputation began to spread. Perhaps the first major turning point in Rollins' career came the night Miles Davis walked in. "Miles already had a considerable reputation by that time," Rollins says. "He'd heard a few of my records, and of course I'd heard him, so you could really say that we already knew each other." When Davis, who has an unerring ability to discover musicians who will later be generally accepted as top men, asked Rollins to join his group, Rollins accepted gladly: "He's a starmaker."

Their first recordings were made for Prestige on January 17, 1951, and contain little indication of what Rollins was to become. But by December 17, when he walked into a studio to record his first LP as a leader, disheveled and with his horn held around his neck by a rope, many of the factors that were to shape his unique style were already in evidence.

Rollins, beset with personal difficulties, worked and recorded infrequently after that session. There were other Davis record dates with Rollins, one on which Charlie Parker also played tenor, one with Thelonious Monk, and four short tunes recorded with the newly-formed Modern Jazz Quartet in 1953. His life at the time was that of a good, but unknown, musician trying to make a living and a reputation in the fiercely competitive New York jazz world. Fittingly enough, the breakthrough came because of Miles Davis.

Davis and Rollins recorded together on June 29, 1954, the first time they had done so since late 1951, with a rhythm section consisting of pianist Horace Silver, and the bassist and drummer then with the Modern Jazz Quartet, Percy Heath and Kenny Clarke. It was one of those rare occasions when all the elements blended to perfection. Three of the four recorded tunes, *Oleo, Doxy,* and *Airegin,* were Rollins compositions; all three are now firmly entrenched in the standard jazz repertoire. Everyone played his best, and news of the recording spread quickly among musicians. In the inner circle, at least, Rollins had arrived, as player and composer.

By the end of October, he had recorded twice more; at the head of a quintet, and on an excellent quartet session with Monk. And then, on the brink of his first general success, Rollins disappeared, suddenly and inexplicably.

The official word was that Sonny was in Chicago, "woodshedding." Like most jazz argot, that word can mean several different things: rehearsing, thinking about music, or just thinking. Applied to Rollins, it meant that he was re-examining his entire life. As he prefers to have it stated, "I have seen and indulged in many things." Charlie Parker, whose personal life has become a legend, had had perhaps too great an influence on young Rollins. Sonny now began to reassess himself, particularly in the light of his friends Ike Day and Lowell Lewis (the latter a trumpeter still spoken of highly by those who heard him), two potentially great careers ruined by indulgence. He placed himself under doctor's care, and at the conclusion of that period, found work in Chicago as a janitor.

The greatest influence on this decision was also Charlie Parker, who had come to feel responsible not only for the music Sonny played, but for the life Sonny was living. When he felt that Sonny's actions were becoming dangerous, Parker recommended medical attention.

Speaking of Parker in *Down Beat*, Rollins later said, "I got to know him, not as well as I would have liked to. We'd talk about music, and he'd always encourage me quite a bit . . . Bird befriended quite a few guys. Sonny Stitt before me. With us and a few other cats, especially saxophone players, it was like a father thing. When we were hung up personally, we went just to talk to him, just to see him . . . At that time, I was going through a mixed-up personal period. A lot of things I was doing because I figured they were the things to be done because a lot of my idols did them. But Bird never encouraged me to do anything that would prove wrong for myself. And on that record date (Prestige 7044), he really told me what to do so far as music and my life were concerned.

"He asked me how I had been doing because he knew I was a young wild kid running around and not knowing what was happening. That day he showed me the thing he wanted me to do and the thing he stood for. The purpose of his whole existence was music and he showed me that music was the paramount thing and anything that interfered with it I should stay away from. Later on I was able to take advantage of his advice but he died before I had a chance to see him and tell him I had." The deep impression Parker made on him is evident, in the sense of responsibility he now feels to the young people who look up to him with the same sort of awe.

"I'm not ashamed of having been a janitor," Rollins says today, "I like hard physical work. My job was at a small office and factory, and I would sweep out, and mop the floors, and clean the toilets. I did it very well, and conscientiously, and I enjoyed it for a while. When I left, my employer was very sorry to see me go."

Rollins left for a job loading trucks, which interested him because of the opportunities it offered for exercise, but there were too many chances in such a job that he might injure his hands, so he left that, too.

He had been practicing during that time, but not playing professionally. Miles Davis, who was forming a new quintet, had made it known in print that he wanted Sonny to join him. Since Rollins did not feel that he was yet ready to return, the tenor spot went to a then little-known Philadelphia musician, John Coltrane. In November of 1955, however, the highly successful Max Roach-Clifford Brown Quintet was appearing in Chicago. For personal reasons, the Brown-Roach tenor player, Harold Land, decided to return home to California, and Rollins was induced to substitute for him during the engagement. At the end of the engagement, when the group returned to New York, Rollins went with them.

For Rollins, the experience was a personal revelation. "Clifford," he says, "was a profound influence on my personal life. He showed me that it was possible to live a good, clean life, and still be a good jazz musician."

Back in New York, and having, in his phrase, "gotten myself together," Rollins again felt that he was ready to record. There was no great audience awaiting the album Rollins made on December 2, 1955, as there was on his 1961 return. The Young-*via*-Getz tenor style was in great vogue, and Rollins, and the Brown-Roach Quintet of which he was a member, were playing against the fashion. Prior to the December recording, Rollins' talent was either taken for granted or ignored. The attitude of the few who were interested is best exemplified by the remark of one young trumpet player who bought the album, *Worktime*, on the first day of its release: "I don't know how he's playing now, but I can learn from him, because he's Sonny Rollins." Others who

chanced to hear the record were astonished, and many, including his close friend, the soprano saxophonist Steve Lacy,
still feel that it is the best record Rollins ever made. Working
with a rhythm section made up of Roach, Brown-Roach
bassist George Morrow, and pianist Ray Bryant, Rollins
turned such an unlikely tune as *There's No Business Like
Show Business*, a nearly forgotten ballad called *There Are
Such Things*, a breakneck-tempo *It's All Right With Me* and
two other songs into a powerful, moving statement of purpose. Possibly the most impressive thing about the performance was its authority. Playing with a deliberately "harsh"
tone, but with little vibrato, Rollins was obviously in command of his instrument. There was, with the release of *Worktime*, a major new jazz voice.

But Rollins, who had begun his career as one of the better
bop tenor players, was not going to remain stagnant, as he
proved definitively with his next release as a leader, *Sonny
Rollins Plus 4*. The album, recorded by the personnel of the
Brown-Roach group, is most notable for the inclusion of a
Rollins composition, *Valse Hot*. As Roach told Nat Hentoff,
"We used to talk about the idea of a jazz waltz quite a bit,
and then Sonny brought this in." Of course, the idea of
swinging in 6/8 goes back to gospels, but the only successful
prior attempt at a modern jazz waltz (and that was actually
6/4) had been Thelonious Monk's version of *Carolina Moon*.
The piece is unusual not only because it is a waltz, but because the melody itself, in contrast to many jazz originals, is
light, airy, and charming. It started something of a fad for
jazz waltzes, and served notice, for those willing to listen,
that Rollins was not going to remain in the "hard bop" category in which he had been placed. He had other things on his
mind, and would shortly be attending to them.

In the meantime, Rollins had recorded a few excellent
numbers with his old friend Miles Davis, the only time, to
date, that they have been reunited in a studio. He was doing
better work than ever, he was happy in the Brown-Roach

Quintet, and it seemed as though he had everything in hand. But on June 26, 1956, an automobile crashed on the Pennsylvania Turnpike, killing all the passengers. They were Nancy Powell, who was driving, her husband Richie (Bud's brother and also a pianist), and Clifford Brown. The quintet was never the same again; perhaps Rollins was not, either. The spring before, Parker had died, and now one of his dearest friends had been killed. Donald Byrd briefly took the trumpet spot, and was followed by Kenny Dorham, but Rollins was restless and dissatisfied. He remained with the group until May of the following year, when he left "to go out on my own."

Sometime during the eleven month period between Clifford Brown's death and the time he left Roach, Rollins recorded some of his best work, embarking upon one of the most brilliant and erratic careers in modern jazz. In one month, three Rollins LPs were released—two under his own name, and one with Roach. His friend Miles Davis told him that he was recording too much, but Rollins did not feel that way. Steve Lacy now says, "The first time you're offered a record date that isn't ideal, you have a decision to make. Sonny made his, and stuck with it." Today, Rollins feels, "I didn't do as much as I could have on record dates. I'll never be satisfied with what I do, but I mean more than that. I didn't give as much as I could have to them. I don't play them much any more, it causes me a great deal of anguish to listen to them. Some of them are good, though, I know that. I'm no dope." He has expressed a particular liking for *Sonny Rollins Plus 4* and, under Roach's name, *Jazz in 3/4 Time*.

Some of them are more than good. Two blues recorded with Thelonious Monk, *Misterioso* and *Ba-lue Bolivar Balues-are*, show that Rollins has a greater affinity for the pianist's rhythmic and harmonic ideas than any other hornman with the possible exception of Coltrane. Rollins recorded with Coltrane that year, an historically interesting tenor battle entitled *Tenor Madness*.

After continuing familiarity with the work of both tenor-men, it is difficult to recall that when this record was released many listeners had trouble telling them apart. Miles Davis' unknown tenorman would soon challenge Rollins' new pre-eminence, and Sonny was beginning to be worried by the possible threat Coltrane represented. When he says, "I was beginning to be hostile and jealous of other musicians," Rollins leaves the impression that the reference is to Coltrane.

Just as Rollins was able to play superbly with Davis and Monk, he was able to infuse new spirit into the Roach group, contributing solos of the stunning virility that, at the time, was his trademark. But all of this seemed, to some listeners, mostly elaboration on the basic ideas of others. They were waiting for what could be considered a definitive statement from Rollins.

With the release of *Saxophone Colossus,* they thought they had it. This LP, recorded with Roach, bassist Doug Watkins, and pianist Tommy Flanagan, is notable for two tracks, *Moritat* and *Blue 7.* With the latter piece, serious criticism of Rollins' work began. In the first issue of the highly influential *Jazz Review,* Gunther Schuller called *Blue 7* "an example of a real variation technique. The improvisation is based not only on a harmonic sequence but on a melodic idea as well . . . what Sonny Rollins has added conclusively to the scope of jazz improvisation is the idea of developing and varying a main theme, and not just a secondary motive or phrase which the player happens to hit upon in the course of his improvisation and which in itself is unrelated to the 'head' of the composition." Writing about the same record in *The New Yorker,* Whitney Balliett called Rollins "possibly the most incisive and influential jazz instrumentalist since Charlie Parker," crediting him with "a tumultuous and brilliant musical imagination that probably equals Parker's." At about the same time, the subject of these encomiums had told Nat Hentoff, "I've just started. I've just scratched the surface.

That's an honest appraisal of myself, so I don't dig this being an influence."

Another Rollins record from this period is one of his most remarkable. In March 1957, while the Roach group was in Los Angeles, the saxophonist recorded *Way Out West* for that city's Contemporary label. He had long wanted to record without a piano, and since Contemporary had two superb musicians available, bassist Ray Brown and drummer Shelly Manne, he formed a recording trio with them. For forty-two minutes and fifty-eight seconds, Rollins is as nakedly exposed as any musician has ever been. Characteristically, the finest moments are on the most unlikely tune, *Wagon Wheels*, which contains over ten minutes of beautifully cohesive improvisation. Balliett said of the record, "Rollins fashions choruses that are—regardless of his persistently goatlike tone and his abrupt, cantankerous phrasing—a clear indication of a striving toward an improvisational approach that is revolutionary, for it is based on a remarkable use of polyrhythm and it wrestles continually with a new, elastic phrasing that completely reshapes the accepted measure-by-measure patterns of the thirty-two bar chorus, which Charlie Parker and Lester Young were the first to break down."

Rollins' greatest fame, and some of his greatest problems, were yet to come. In May 1957, he left Roach, and for a short time during the summer of that year, he was reunited with Miles Davis. Davis' superb quintet had broken up. Coltrane was on the verge of becoming a star attraction, and when Thelonious Monk went into the Five Spot Cafe that summer, for his first New York appearance in several years, Coltrane went with him. Rollins joined Davis at the now-defunct Bohemia, but left shortly thereafter to form his own group.

Several pressures were operating on Rollins at that time. He was married, as he puts it, "promiscuously." It did not work out. "I just wanted to get married," he says, "so I looked around, and found somebody, and I did." "Promiscuous" is also the word he uses to describe his recording activities. He wanted and needed money, and recording was the quickest way to get it, so he recorded for anyone and everyone who asked him. His contract with Prestige had come to an end, and he found it more lucrative to free-lance. Some idea of his promiscuity can be gotten by a listing of labels: Riverside, Atlantic, Blue Note, Period, Verve, Contemporary—all soon had Rollins records. Sonny was for hire, and almost everyone was interested. When he finally signed with MGM records, it was almost an anticlimax.

At the same time, he was attempting to form a band that would meet his specifications. Many of the qualifications necessary for a leader are not musical, and perhaps Sonny did not have them all. The problems he had in that area were magnified by his new fame and notoriety. He was in the spotlight, anything he did was news; he felt the need to accept all the work he was offered. All of this resulted in a goldfish bowl existence at exactly the time he most could have used privacy. It was his choice, but it seems to have been the wrong one. He went into New York's Village Vanguard with a quintet including Donald Byrd. A week later, Byrd was gone, and there was a new rhythm section. A succession of piano players came and went, and finally he wound up with a trio—tenor, bass, and drums—because, "I just couldn't find any piano players I liked."

His style, during this period, was changing almost constantly. More and more unusual tunes cropped up on his records: *If You Were the Only Girl, Limehouse Blues, Rock-a-bye Your Baby With A Dixie Melody, Shadow Waltz.* The sardonic humor that had begun to creep into his music became almost standard practice, until it seemed that he saw no point in recording a tune unless he could satirize it. His tone became flat and breathy. With his deep jazz feeling and oblique sense of humor, he apparently took a delight in transforming the most banal material into the high points of his records. The strong feeling of dance music was always present, and he had developed a lazy, impudent swing. Using an unusual number of inflected notes, he would irreverently reshape melodic lines in seemingly casual but actually extremely well-organized solos that depended, to a great extent, on abrupt, supposedly "corny" phrasings that he was able to make seem completely fresh. The most delightful recorded example of this trend is *Shadow Waltz,* made for Riverside. Although there is something of value on almost everything released at this time, the records were extremely erratic, and he would allow himself to be recorded in any context deemed fit by an A & R man.

He is somewhat bitter about the records from this period, but a good deal of the bitterness is directed against himself. "I can't do anything about those records anymore," he says, "all I can do is try to make good ones now."

One session from this time which requires special attention is the *Freedom Suite,* recorded for Riverside in February 1958. Nineteen minutes and seventeen seconds long, its only performers are Rollins, Roach, and bassist Oscar Pettiford. Its form is unusual: the opening and closing sections are very fast, the latter seemingly based on the chord sequence of *Lover Come Back To Me.* The central section is a lovely Ellington-styled ballad which is enclosed at either end by a brief, powerful minor theme in 3/4, ending both times with a cadenza. Much has been made of the great problems inherent in sustaining nineteen minutes of such free improvisation.

Orrin Keepnews, who partly supervised and annotated the sessions for Riverside, recalls, "Sonny presented the idea as a trio date for himself, Roach, and Pettiford, and naturally we were delighted. At the first session, we cut the four standards that appear on the other side of the record, and what I thought was a Rollins original. If he had any idea at that time of an entire suite, he was keeping it a secret from us. The second session was about a week later. There have been a lot of stories about trouble at the session, and there was some, but that's not important to the story. What is important is that the idea of a suite apparently grew in Sonny's mind in the time between the two sessions. I don't think he thought of it that way to begin with. When we went into the studio the second time, we cut the rest of it. It happened pretty spontaneously, that afternoon."

Meanwhile, Coltrane, after his time spent with Monk, had improved so much that some were starting to say that he was better than Rollins. At the same time others were calling Sonny "the new Bird." Dozens of Rollins imitators were springing up, playing phrases, ideas, and even entire solos of his. Several musicians had settled on one or another of the several styles Rollins had discarded, and used his techniques to make small reputations. The critics, whom Rollins read incessantly, were beginning to prey on his mind. He had not been successful as a leader, in his own eyes. His marriage had failed; he was drinking heavily. And perhaps most painful of all, he saw that the kids who inevitably idolize musicians of his stature were beginning to imitate more than his way of playing the saxophone. In the summer of 1959, his old friend Thelonious Monk, playing at the Five Spot, was without a saxophonist for two weeks. As a favor, Rollins filled in. It was the last job he worked for over two years.

By the summer of 1961, rumors and speculation about Rollins had reached a point that made it nearly impossible to separate truth from fabrication. Deciding the best source of information would be the saxophonist himself, I wrote to him, telling him of my plans to write about him, and included a phone number where I asked that he call me. And that, I supposed, was that.

About two weeks later, Sonny called. He had, he said, called several times before, and had not found me at home. He wanted to know which musicians were to be included in the book. "You want to put me in the same book with those men?" I did. "That's good company," he said, and invited me to his home.

Rollins lived at the time in a small, spotless apartment on Manhattan's lower east side. I was met at the door by his charming second wife, Lucille, and a small German Shepherd pup named Major ("He's not very big, but he has a crazy personality"). "Sonny will be with you in a moment," Mrs. Rollins said.

Rollins walked into the room, wearing slacks and a T-shirt. He is powerfully built, well over six feet tall, with a long, oval face, prominent nose, a shaved head, and a square-cut goatee. A commanding but gentle presence, he speaks in a deep, considered voice with a slight stammer which, he admits, appears when he has difficulty explaining something of importance to him. Largely self-taught and an omnivorous reader, Rollins alternates polysyllables and musician's slang in a mixture as jarringly appropriate as a sudden "corny" quote in one of his solos.

"You understand," he said, "I won't read whatever you write. I'll help you in any way I can and tell you whatever you want to know, but I won't read it. I read all the magazines when they were writing about me. I began to worry about things I shouldn't have. People said that I did a certain kind of thing and I began to believe them, and by the time I figured out how I did it, I was unable to achieve the effect any more. I understand about writers and critics. They're very necessary and they have a job to do, but they're writing for the fans. I believe that it's very dangerous for a musician to read criticism of his work. I don't think, for instance, that there should have been a competition built up between John Coltrane and myself. It's an interesting thing for the fans, but it can only hurt musicians. They become jealous of one another and don't play their best."

He took me into the room set aside for his exclusive use. Spartan and immaculate, it contained his saxophone (an auxiliary cloth case hung on the wall next to a photograph of Rollins with his horn), a piano, a copy of the Rosicrucian Creed, a mountain of sheet music, and a set of bar bells.

Along with Lucille, these things represent what Rollins had retained from a life and career that he had decided, after much conscious deliberation, he would change.

He had, literally, reinvented himself. How much of the change in him was due to his wife is difficult to say, but although Rollins admits he can be difficult to live with, he seems as happy in his second marriage as he was unhappy in his first. It gives him great pleasure to enumerate the many interests he shares with his wife. She worked during his retirement, which gave him the necessary time alone to write and practice, and the two kept, for the most part, to themselves. Perhaps significantly, Rollins was married one month after his retirement, but had apparently been contemplating both moves for quite a while. He made his decision with characteristic deliberation. "I've read several studies," he said, "which prove that people who have had an unhappy first marriage are much more likely to be happy in their second one. You know more and your feet are on the ground. It seems to have worked out for me."

"I quit for several reasons," he said, in response to the inevitable question. "In spite of what was being written about me, I don't feel that I was playing my best. I've only done a small part of what I want to do and I felt that the first thing I had to do was get myself together. I had a lot of bad habits and I've stopped them. I don't drink any more and I don't smoke. I know that might sound extreme, but when you play a saxophone your physical condition and particularly your wind is very important. I know there's been a lot of speculation about why I quit, but it's only been two years. If I don't feel that two years is such a long time in my life, I don't see why it should be such a long time in the history of jazz."

"Jazz," he continued, "is a part of show business. You have to accept that, and if you become famous in any part of show business there are going to be young kids looking up to you and imitating you. I've taken a few students and I'm trying to teach them about more than the tenor saxophone. I think most people have a greater sense of right and wrong than they are given credit for, but it all depends on who they choose for a model. There are important kinds of emulation and unimportant and if kids want to grow a beard or wear the kind of shoes I do, I don't mind, as long as they do some of the other things, too.

"I haven't kept completely to myself down here. I've met several people recently, several important people, and they seem to be impressed with my deportment, so I think I'll be ready to play again soon."

"The one thing that I wish is that so many kids wouldn't try to play like me. Everyone has to start out imitating someone. I did it and Miles did it when he used to sound exactly like Dizzy Gillespie, but of course Miles only used that as a starting point from which he was able to develop his own style. I don't think there's enough depth or meat in the way I play to give someone a good starting point. There's a lot of better people they could choose. What they should really do is go back to the roots of music—rhythm, melody, and harmony—and start from there, instead of just playing notes."

Some of Rollins' time had been spent going to clubs and listening to the playing of younger men, as well as hearing their records. Even in two years, he found that the business had changed: "There is so much jazz around now and so many clubs that two things have happened—it's not that the young musicians are not as good as the guys I played with, but they don't have to play as well as they could to get jobs or record dates. When there were only a few clubs all of us had to play together. Monk was even my sideman once for a couple of weeks, did you know that? But it's not like that any more. Miles is here, J. J. Johnson's there, Monk is someplace else. They can all get their own jobs and be leaders and it didn't used to be that way. But I think that very soon you'll see those guys getting together again in the same band and if anyone does it, it will be Miles. Everyone likes and admires him and respects the way he plays."

Since Rollins had been away, there had been two developments of possible significance, the "third stream" and "new thing." Did he have an opinion? "Jazz," he said, "is not limited, as people think it is. That's why I played some of the songs that people thought were strange. I like all of the Jolson songs, for instance. But so many guys keep playing the same few songs over and over again. There's so much music in the world that it's silly to stick with just a small part of it.

"I think eventually that there won't be jazz any more or classical music, but just one big music, in which everyone can play what he feels. What they call the third stream is a beginning at that, but the writers haven't left these people alone to work their problems out for themselves. They aren't ready to be analyzed yet. Of course, the real beginning of that attempt is Duke Ellington. Monk is an extension of Duke, I think, and Duke is the unsung giant of American music. I spoke to someone recently who had seen Ellington and Duke said that he had heard some of my records and liked the way I played. Can you imagine how I felt about Ellington saying something like that? I've recorded as many of his songs as I could. Perhaps he heard one of those."

Naturally, much of Rollins' time was spent alone, practicing. "There's a rehearsal room I go to on 48th Street," he said. "They've given me a key and I go there whenever I want. I can only play the tenor until about eleven at night, but there's a piano there and I can use that all night long. There's a friend of mine who works at the Henry Street Settlement who's been teaching me piano. I don't think I'll ever be able to play it professionally, but I've learned a lot about harmony and fingering from it that I can use in my saxophone work. Of course at home I can practice just by fingering the instrument without blowing into it. We have four cats out back and the sound bothers them—maybe they're critics."

Much of his rehearsing was done with soprano saxophonist Steve Lacy, of whom Rollins says, "Steve listened to me in the right way. He found a few things he could use and he plays like himself." Lacy joined Rollins for practice sessions on the Williamsburg Bridge that, to Rollins' annoyance, had become semilegendary ("What I was doing," he later said, "was just plain work"). At the time Lacy spoke, he and Rollins were trying to keep their open-air studio a secret.

"I wish you had asked me about Sonny before I met him," Lacy said. "When I only knew him and admired him because of his work I could have talked about him all night, but now that he's a friend it's very difficult. Monk introduced us at the Five Spot when they were working together. Sonny said that he'd heard of me and invited me over to his house to rehearse with him. It was a matter of chemistry, I guess. We've been friends ever since. We do rehearse on a bridge, you know. It's not the Brooklyn Bridge, but I'd rather not say which one it is, because it's such a wonderful rehearsal spot that everyone would want to go there. There are two levels—a pedestrian level and an automobile level—and you can stand there late at night and look at the skyline and watch the tugboats go by and no one bothers you. It's very hard to get a sound there, with the wind whipping by, so if you can play well there it would be the simplest thing in the world to play in a club. We don't have any particular material that we're rehearsing, just whatever comes to mind. We're just trying to find out about ourselves musically. We practice fingering, intonation, tone, scales, intervals, everything. I've never seen anyone in love with the tenor saxophone the way Sonny is. He really loves that horn and understands it. He knows everything about it. He's the best player of that instrument I've ever seen. He won't have any trouble when he decides he wants to work again. You know how the club owners think. THE RETURN OF SONNY ROLLINS—can you imagine that?"

Rollins could imagine it, and his speculations took the form of wondering what good he could do, for he feels deeply that jazz can be a definite moral force in the world. It is for this reason that he is so greatly concerned with the pitfalls of the jazz life and so determined to overcome them himself. "You always hear," he says, "about musicians who have become addicted to harmful drugs, but you never hear about those who have been able to throw off the habit. It's supposed to be impossible to do, but many men have done it. There are ways to get around all the problems that a jazzman is confronted with. It's not inimical to live well and play good music. The problems of a club, for instance, are difficult, but they are not insurmountable. It's hard to know what to do when you're off the stand for half an hour. There's no real time to go anywhere, but there are other things to be done besides picking up a customer's girl or getting juiced. Billy Higgins, for instance, when he was Ornette Coleman's drummer, would sit in the back of the club and practice on a rubber pad. I can practice fingering in a dressing room or read or do any number of things."

The return for which he had been preparing came somewhat sooner than he had anticipated. He had been living comfortably, if not extravagantly, on record royalties and a handsome advance given him by the composer's association, B.M.I. But extensive and expensive dental work made working necessary. Late in 1961, he felt he was ready. As it became known that Rollins would soon play again, interviewers began to find out how he had spent his time. They learned about his new attitude, and about his intense preoccupation with physical fitness, which led to a predilection for health foods, constant workouts with his bar bells, and whatever other exercise he could work into a busy schedule. He believes so firmly in the necessity of a healthy body, perhaps as a reaction to earlier dissipation, that friends are always receiving embarrassed, paternal lectures about smoking and drinking. "I did do more than just practice," he told one interviewer. "I did a lot of physical exercise, and I took some courses, mostly philosophy, and I became a Rosicrucian. Did you know Benjamin Franklin was a Rosicrucian? It's a science, not a religion, and it's given me a lot of strengths, maybe developed them, that I didn't know I had before. You know, if you're looking for a difference in me, those are the differences."

Rollins, apparently, was the only person with doubts about what kind of reception awaited him on his return. "If no one comes to the opening," he told Balliett, "if they don't like me, if they rush out—I'm prepared for all those contingencies, and they would not influence me adversely."

He needn't have worried. His first public performance took place at New York's Jazz Gallery, at a benefit for the family of the late trumpeter Booker Little, which coincided with Rollins' return and the reopening of the club under new management. Wearing a white dinner jacket, leading a quartet consisting of guitarist Jim Hall, bassist Bob Cranshaw, and drummer Walter Perkins, Rollins played two numbers that were nearly drowned out by the applause that began on his arrival on the stand. The next night he began a regular Gallery engagement. "The benefit broke the ice," he said later. "At my own opening, I wasn't scared."

Rollins had returned to a peculiar situation, one dramatically underlined at the benefit by the fact that he was the only one of over a dozen tenor players present who did not sound as though he were imitating John Coltrane. Two years before, they would all have sounded like Rollins. Jazz fashion operates on somewhat the same principle as the myth of The Fastest Gun in the West. In only two years, Rollins imitators had become Coltrane imitators, and soon the two models themselves had begun to use elements of the music of Ornette Coleman. But that first night, to observers who felt Rollins owed it to them to return with a completely new style, the saxophonist sounded expert, but perhaps old-fashioned.

The basic Rollins style—initially an amalgamation of elements of Hawkins, Gordon, and Parker that had, as he concentrated more fully on thematic improvisation, added outstanding elements of Young—was now superbly in hand. Often faltering at the start of his career, he had made himself a virtuoso. Many phrases he played seemed derived from practice books. He could now play two notes, or harmonics, and was able to alter his tone to fit the content of a solo. Rhythm and humor were still basic ingredients of his playing, and he continued to employ the quotes, the melodic interpolations, from "corny" or "naive" sources. His once-expressed desire to play completely unaccompanied "works as part of a solo"; long, brilliant, unaccompanied cadenzas often contained the most stimulating portions of his playing.

The powerful build and bold face that had once earned him the nickname "Newk," for a resemblance to pitcher Don Newcomb, still made him a dominant figure on the stand. He would start with his back to the audience, turn around to face them, and often play entire solos leaning, legs crossed, against the unused piano.

Soon, it seemed that every newspaper and magazine in the country wanted a Rollins story. "Conformity is working in my favor," he commented. Patrons constantly engaged him in conversation. As one of Rollins' associates remarked, "Sonny is everybody's friend, because he isn't afraid." And Rollins himself said, "Conditions in clubs are no better than when I left. If there was a dressing room, I wouldn't be available to these people."

"They seem to feel you belong to them," I remarked.

"In a sense," he answered, "I suppose we do."

While fans contented themselves with remarking on the fact that Rollins wears earplugs when he plays, a habit he began to exclude outside noises while he was practicing, musicians had rather more astute comments to make. Drummer Art Blakey, working opposite Rollins at the Gallery, said, "I've never seen a man that determined. He's still experimenting; he doesn't know what he wants to do yet. But he'll do it, or die trying."

Blakey could not have known how accurate he was. The novelist Vladimir Nabokov, speaking of his own work, once said, "Desperate Russian critics, trying hard to find an influence and to pigeonhole my own novels, have once or twice linked me up with Gogol, but when they looked again I had untied the knots and the box was empty." Rollins, similarly, had resisted all attempts at classification: bop, hard bop, "new thing." The first real statement of his music came a few months after the Gallery engagement, when he played a concert at New York's Museum of Modern Art. By then, he had already begun what has become one of his favorite hobbies, firing drummers. He has had at least half a dozen since his return.

He is, fortunately, in an excellent financial position to experiment. Upon leaving retirement, he signed with Monte Kay, one of the busiest personal managers in the jazz business. And he had signed a recording contract with RCA Victor, the reported terms of which called for five LPs over a two-year period, for a fee of $90,000. To date, none of the albums Victor has released approach the work Rollins is capable of in person. "That's the way it's supposed to be," he agrees. "The recording studio is a very cold situation."

For a while, Rollins accepted only engagements in and around New York, preferring to ease himself back into professional life. When I next saw him, in the summer of 1962, he was playing in a small club on Chicago's South Side, McKie's Disc Jockey Lounge. He was back in the jazz life full force. The club, which caters almost exclusively to a Negro clientele, had taken ads in none of the major Chicago papers; no one knew Rollins was in town. When he arrived, he had learned that his sidemen were also expected to accompany Gene Ammons, who had been booked into the club opposite Rollins as a single. He was restless away from home, and had changed drummers again.

After one more New York engagement, guitarist Jim Hall was gone, too. "I have nothing but respect for Sonny," Hall said later. "He was one of my first idols. Working with him is like watching Picasso paint, or Thomas Wolfe write. It was good for me; it made me practice to keep up with him." Many observers found significance in the fact that the new members of the band were trumpeter Don Cherry and drummer Billy Higgins, both of whom had formerly worked with Ornette Coleman. And just as Rollins had drawn upon Hall's knowledge of Brazilian music to record a *bossa nova* or two, he produced an LP set with Cherry and Higgins that reflected many of the aspects of the "new thing." With his followers thus thoroughly confused by yet another change in style, Rollins left for a European tour.

When he returned, the dental difficulties that had plagued him forced him to stop work again for four months, after which he reappeared again in the spring of 1963 minus Cherry, plus two new sidemen: bassist Henry Grimes and another Coleman drummer, Charles Moffett. Then, he began using "new thing" pianist Paul Bley.

He sat in a Long Island club between sets, applauding the intermission pianist, and talking about everything but music. He was reading a book called *Autobiography of a Yoga*, from which he had learned new exercises, and which he heartily recommended. He was to be a member of President Kennedy's Physical Fitness Committee, an honor he regarded as far more important than the *Down Beat* Critics' Poll he had recently won, and he had posed with his bar bells for a muscle-building magazine. He had a new home in Brooklyn near Pratt Institute and was once again accepting students. "They're very important to me. They're non-professionals, but I hope you *will* hear of them."

He was happy to be back in music, because "nothing is as good as the feeling you get from playing." He would, he said, leave again, if there were a necessity for it, and seemed surprised that the question would even be asked. And he made this surprising declaration: "I haven't yet started to play the things I worked on while I was away, I haven't felt ready yet. Maybe soon, I will." (He fulfilled some of that prophecy at the Five Spot in 1964, playing in a new, *vox humana* style, moving around the tables and in and out of phone booths in hat and coat, like a strolling street musician.)

It was time for him to go to work. One knew he would be playing brilliantly, with the old-time show-business flair and humor that stamps all his music, but one could not be sure if the music would be at all similar to what he had played the night before, or what he would play the next night. As he says, "You have to have something else to go to."

Selected Discography

Work Time, PRESTIGE 7246.
Sonny Rollins Plus 4, PRESTIGE 7038.
Saxaphone Colossus, PRESTIGE 7079.
Way Out West, CONTEMPORARY 3530.
Shadow Waltz, JAZZLAND 86.
The Bridge, RCA VICTOR LPM 2527.

Note: Several other LPs contain one or two tracks of unusual interest. Still other superior Rollins solos are found on LPs recorded under the leadership of Miles Davis, Thelonious Monk, and Max Roach.

THE MODERN JAZZ QUARTET

IN MANY WAYS, the development of the Modern Jazz Quartet from its origins to its present preeminent position parallels that of the music which gives the organization its name. Its original members comprised Dizzy Gillespie's 1947 rhythm section, and the Quartet has played *concerti grossi* with the Stuttgart Symphony—a long road to have traveled. That the MJQ has traveled it with such success and apparent ease is largely due to the singleness of purpose of its musical director, John Lewis. It is also an example of an astute use of public relations unparalleled in jazz.

Jazz musicians and commentators have always fought for respectability, determined to prove that the music itself has validity apart from the social situations and myths which have surrounded it. To some, the whorehouses of Storyville are a colorful embarrassment; each new instance of narcotics addiction among jazzmen is treated as if it were unique; every stride toward social acceptance made by the music or by the musicians receives press plaudits often entirely incommensurate with the step taken.

The MJQ is a boon to those who wish well for the music. Impeccably attired, with the bearing, manner, and appearance of gentlemen in the employ of Schweppes beverages, its members play some of the most eminently respectable music ever to be called jazz. Their records are in the homes of suburbanites who might own nothing else more daring than the songbooks of Ella Fitzgerald. They have played places no jazzmen have ever played before, possibly some that no others will ever play.

But there are skeptics. Most of these are passionate adherents of the musical tradition which gave the players in the MJQ their start. They love the music of Parker and Gillespie, and tend to think that any player of that music, whether a top-drawer musician or not, is better than any player of another kind of music. They are proselytizers for such men as Kenny Drew, Kenny Dorham, and Hank Mobley, and tend to view the MJQ's vibraharpist, Milt Jackson, as a man somehow held captive in the sinister thrall of John Lewis, stoutly maintaining that "MJQ" should stand for "Milt Jackson Quartet," as indeed it once did. The main virtue of this viewpoint is that it points up the differences between Jackson and pianist-composer-musical director Lewis, differences that amount to a miniature history of the two main directions jazz has taken since the death of Parker. That prime exponents of these two directions are the major soloists of the same quartet has made the MJQ one of the most fascinating, valuable, successful, and frustrating units of the fifties.

As Lewis told Francis Thorne in *The Jazz Review*, "The formation of the group has little to do with what it is today. At the beginning, it was a recording group that Milt wanted to use for some records for Dizzy Gillespie's Dee Gee label. The original drummer was Kenny Clarke and the bass player was Ray Brown. From that time, we knew how nice the music felt, and how nice it was to play together. Of course it should have been easy; we had played together for two years with Dizzy's band, which didn't have too many arrangements. The trumpet players' music was particularly difficult in that band, and they needed a lot of rest. The rhythm section played quite a lot as relief, and it also gave Milt a chance to play, as he didn't have much chance to do with the band, except for a few solos. We were all working for others when we started, and there was a serious problem about more recording work, because Milt was the leader and could not then afford to pay the others, but we hit on the idea of making the group co-operative so that no one was the leader. This condition still exists, and though it is not perfect, it has worked quite well for a long time."

The recordings Lewis refers to have been reissued by

Savoy. Different bassists and drummers were used on the two dates for Dee Gee, but the four pieces Jackson recalls as the first to be recorded—*Milt Meets Sid, D & E, Yesterdays,* and *Between the Devil and the Deep Blue Sea*—were played by Jackson, Lewis, Brown, and Clarke. The Savoy LP contains a simple repertoire—blues, standards and originals based on popular chord progressions—and reveals an excellent small group powered by Jackson, with fine blues solos, the occasional hint of contrapuntal accompaniment by Lewis, and no hint of the experimental. The unit at the time was called The Milt Jackson Quartet.

There were also Blue Note records under Jackson's name, some with the addition of alto saxophonist Lou Donaldson, but their first work as the Modern Jazz Quartet was in 1953, for Prestige. Bob Weinstock of that company, who is one of those enamoured of "hard bop," had signed Milt Jackson, whose work he greatly admires, to a contract. He recalls using Lewis only because Jackson requested it. According to Ira Gitler, who supervised those first sessions, the original contract was made out for the New Jazz Quartet. Weinstock has a subsidiary label called New Jazz, and hoped to achieve company identification. But the unit, which now included bassist Percy Heath and drummer Kenny Clarke, held out for Modern Jazz Quartet, also in the face of club owners who wanted Jackson's name out front.

That first Prestige record included a far greater incidence of arranged sections than was usual for such groups. Lewis' originals on the set included a Bachlike fugue, *Vendôme,* based on half of *All The Things You Are,* a tune which is also included on the program; *The Queen's Fancy,* for which Lewis invoked the name of Elizabethan composer Giles Farnaby; and Lewis's *La Ronde,* a piece which, when Gillespie had played it, had gone under a rather less prepossessing name: *Two Bass Hit.*

The album stirred considerable interest among musicians, some of whom were already desperately hoping for a small group to challenge the success of Dave Brubeck. But the record which finally established the MJQ was their second. Recorded in December 1954 and January 1955, it contained one of the few indisputable classic compositions of contemporary jazz, John Lewis' *Django*. Dedicated to the late gypsy guitarist Django Reinhardt, it is in two parts: a sad, haunting melody, and a faster, improvised section based on slightly different chord changes. It was the first of several Lewis compositions which justify a remark of Gunther Schuller, who has been a sort of unofficial advisor to the Quartet since its inception: "In a very simple, unspectacular way, he combines the romantic and the classical in a judicious blending. His great melodic gift is very much in evidence. John has that rare ability to create a melody which is thoroughly conventional, immediately hummable, sounds as if one had heard it somewhere before, and yet is in fact absolutely original. Above all, his music has that unassailable quality of rightness for which there is no substitute."

In February 1955, Kenny Clarke left the group to live in Paris. As Milt Jackson says, "John had a very definite idea of the way drums should sound in the group. Kenny already had his thing all worked out—he was one of the first to start dropping those bombs, you know—and it would have meant him changing all around. It wasn't just 'sticks here and the ride cymbal there,' it wasn't that simple." Lewis began coaching young Connie Kay, who had been working with Lester Young, and who was willing to adapt himself to Lewis' ideas. Since Kay joined, the group has remained intact.

In the light of this, it is interesting to compare their next recording, *Concorde,* with the two previous sets. The LP announces the style the MJQ has continued ever since. The fugue which gives the album its title is much less a pastiche than its predecessors; the Gershwin ballad medley and *Ralph's New Blues* contain a great deal of simultaneous improvisation and counterpoint. It is almost as if Lewis' final ascendancy in the group coincided with Clarke's departure. "It had been my group originally," Jackson says, "and I'll admit I felt bad for a while. But John was putting so much time and work into it, more than I would have done. He worked so hard. It was a better idea to be co-operative, and John has been mostly responsible for the way we have gone since."

A Prestige record made at about the same time called *Soul Pioneers,* with Jackson, Heath, Kay, and Horace Silver in place of Lewis, is, in Jackson's estimation, an accurate representation of what the quartet would have been like under his own direction. Silver is dedicated to the kind of free-blowing music Jackson likes, and the record therefore lacks the elements of form and contrast that Lewis would have brought to it.

It was to be expected that Weinstock, who prefers the kind of album Jackson and Silver produced, would not see eye to eye with Lewis musically. Moreover, the MJQ had signed with Monte Kay, a manager who had several artists recording for Atlantic. Soon, the MJQ signed as well.

The switch to Atlantic was one of the final steps in a plan which Lewis had long had in mind. His concept of jazz has to do with more than the music itself. "I am an American Negro," he has said. "I'm proud of it, and I want to enhance the dignity of that position." And he is also a member of a profession whose greatest composer-pianist, a man to whom Lewis is sometimes compared, was once told by a policeman, "If you'd been a white man, Duke, you'd been a great musician." And so Lewis, who is conscious of his world and the promotion techniques pertinent to it, set about creating an image for the Modern Jazz Quartet.

"It wasn't a gimmick," Milt Jackson says in retrospect, "it was a plan, and it was mostly John's. Do you want to know what *really* happened with the Modern Jazz Quartet? We sat down together, the four of us, and talked all this over at the beginning. What we would wear, the way we would bow, where we wanted to play. It was a co-operative group, and each of us had a job to do. John was musical director, he was responsible for that. If the music sounded good or bad on a particular night, that was his responsibility. Percy was responsible for our wardrobe. Connie was responsible for transportation, hotel accommodations, things like that. Originally, I was responsible for public relations, announcements from the bandstand and such, but John started doing that, too, and about all I do now is show up and play.

"We didn't start out to prove anything, it just worked out that way. The French titles we give pieces, the classical forms we use, interested people who weren't interested in jazz. And we work well together—some of the things we do— you know, John and I have been playing together over fifteen years. We play places no other group could play. A place like the London House in Chicago, or the Embers in New York, people don't come there for music, they come for food, and they're talking and drinking. I've seen it happen some nights, we play so quietly that people stop to try to hear what we're doing, and pretty soon the whole room is silent. And we play festivals and concerts. No other group in the world has such a wide choice of places to play.

"In the music, we've been widening the restrictions with our repertoire. And it keeps changing. A piece like *Fontessa* is now the last part of *The Comedy*. That's how we keep ourselves interested. We've been together over ten years now, that's longer than anybody. We have such a large repertoire that we could play three concerts on three different nights and not repeat once.

"And we've proved that we can be respectable, dignified, and gentlemen. A lot of people think jazz musicians are dope addicts, drunks, and sex fiends, and you're branded with that. But we've proved it isn't so. The way the plan worked out, it proved all these things simultaneously."

Lewis has had to work hard on all levels to achieve his goals, musically as well as otherwise. As Miles Davis has said, "John taught all of them; Milt couldn't read at all, and

Percy hardly." Lewis himself, on the other hand, was an unusually well-schooled jazz man. In this, as in many other ways, he is markedly different from the other members of the Quartet.

Born in La Grange, Illinois, on May 3, 1920, he soon moved with his family to Albuquerque, New Mexico. Both popular and classical music were present in his home, a large, pleasant hotel owned by his grandfather, who had come out in a covered wagon. Attending the University of New Mexico, he was an anthropology major before deciding to switch to music. After graduation, he went into the army. "I met Kenny Clarke in the service," Lewis has said, "and Kenny got me to do an arrangement for Dizzy when we got out. Dizzy liked it, and then after a while, when Monk left, I took over the piano. Dizzy's band was such a good idea musically, but it was botched up by appearing in the wrong places. . . . And there I sat at the piano and could see the whole thing happening, and I knew what was wrong, and I couldn't do a thing about it."

After Gillespie, Lewis worked with Illinois Jacquet, but found two much more rewarding associations when he worked for Lester Young and, largely on records, for Charlie Parker. For the latter, he recorded an indelible solo on the classic *Parker's Mood*. While with Parker he also became associated with Miles Davis, then Parker's trumpeter. Lewis was later pianist and a driving force in the Davis nine-piece "cool" band.

But at the same time, Lewis was continuing studies at the Manhattan School of Music, from which he holds two degrees, and singing with the Schola Cantorum. That he sees no incompatibility in such activities (his record-buying, for instance, is likely to include Handel and Schoenberg), is a fact which is likely to have a pervasive impact on jazz—indeed, it has already.

This influence first began to be felt in the summer of 1956, when the MJQ found itself at Music Inn, a resort near Lenox,

Massachusetts, close to Tanglewood. From time to time
Philip and Stephanie Barber, who owned Music Inn, had
presented jazz and folk concerts and discussions. In 1956,
they broadened the program considerably and invited the
MJQ to be what they called the "jazz group in residence."
Those who came to the discussions—such men as Dizzy
Gillespie, Jimmy Giuffre, Max Roach, Rex Stewart, Charles
Mingus, and Wilbur de Paris were present—found them
extremely valuable.

As John S. Wilson remarked on the notes for the Giuffre-
MJQ album which was one of the by-products of this
summer session, "John Lewis, who had been on hand
throughout all the discussions, was disturbed that this ex-
change of such a wide range of jazz knowledge should be
so ephemeral. He urged the Barbers to give it some form of
continuing existence so that both established jazzmen and
youngsters just getting started could benefit from it. The
result has been the establishment of the Music Inn School
of Jazz, an annual three-week workshop course under Lewis'
direction which incorporates the roundtable discussions by
musicians and Marshall Stearns' panels along with practical
experience in writing for large and small groups, playing
with both types of groups, and lessons in the jazz techniques
of various instruments. The first session of the school was
held in August 1957, with a small, carefully selected body of
students."

Lewis was not only involved in the School of Jazz, he
was also, with Gunther Schuller, the founder of the Modern
Jazz Society (later the Jazz and Classical Music Society),
which resulted in a concert, and a Verve Album of Lewis'
compositions, scored for large orchestra by Schuller and
himself, which may be counted one of the initial attempts
at "Third Stream" music.

In the main, the further achievements of Lewis and the
Quartet have been extensions of what had already been
accomplished by 1956. And the basis and evolution of that

accomplishment may best be seen in three quotations from John Lewis. Early in the Quartet's career, in a succinct description of the Quartet's method and desires, Lewis told Nat Hentoff that "the audience for our work can be widened if we strengthen our work with structure. If there is more of a reason for what's going on, there'll be more over-all sense, and, therefore, more interest in the listener. I do not think, however, that the sections in this structured jazz—both the improvised and written sections—should take on too much complexity. The total effect must be within the mind's ability to appreciate through the ear. Also, the music will have to swing. But remember that all music must do this, must have a meaningful rhythmic sense. Swinging is not new in the history of music, nor is improvisation. What makes jazz unique is that it is *collective* improvisation that swings. And the possibilities within jazz are very large. Take rhythm. Any kind of improvisation, unless you're playing for yourself, is going to be more or less contrapuntal. But in jazz, except for the best Dixieland people and a few others, there is often a rhythmic dullness beneath the improvisation. Yet the bass, drums, and piano should and can do more than simply supply chords and a basic pulsation." A few years later, Lewis was telling Hentoff, "The most important thing we're doing, the bulk of what we play is improvisation. The rest is to give us a framework. And even those frames get moved or bent to fit what we're trying to project. A frame may last a while, and if it wears out it has to be changed too. Anything wears out in time, and changes. All of what we do is relative, and can be different at different minutes in different sets in different nights." Soon, Lewis could say to Francis Thorne, "Some of the music we've played, *Vendôme* for instance, was very unnatural when we started playing. On the record it is not natural at all. Now it has become natural, but it has taken a long time. *Concorde* was better in that it had a more inherent rhythmic feeling of jazz, and even *Concorde* took time to find its correct rhythmic feeling, but now it's very good, sometimes . . . I never have a conscious searching for form; I believe that my composing is just a natural music-making. Perhaps years ago I started a composition with a form in mind and then tried to write the music, but it is a long time since I have done this."

"It is his achievement," the English critic Max Harrison wrote of Lewis, "that he has succeeded where all others have failed in grafting a number of classical devices onto the technique of jazz without doing violence to the spirit of the music."

The link between Lewis' and Harrison's statements is a remark made by Gunther Schuller early in the Quartet's career, which now seems, in retrospect, to have been the most prescient of all: "The fact that jazz is acquiring more form does not necessarily mean that jazz will lose any of its emotional power or freedom of individual speech. As jazz grows in form, it will develop a freedom in the use of form that is inherent in all the great masterpieces of classical music. Form does not mean rigidity by rote. And the best and most successful example of how form *is* becoming more meaningfully extended in jazz is the work of the Modern Jazz Quartet."

What Lewis acknowledged after the fact, Schuller seems to have understood at the time: the devices, forms and techniques which were, in the beginning, tacked on in a rather gratuitous manner, have, through years of familiarity, become natural to the members of the Quartet. At first, pieces such as *Vendôme* must have been unnatural to everyone except Lewis, and perhaps even to him. What was once stiff and academic, and later decked out like a Christmas tree so ornamented that the tree itself is invisible, has finally become organic and functional. The evidence of this is the superb 1960 recording *European Concert,* an in-person performance of fifteen pieces, twelve of which had been recorded previously by one or another manifestation of the group, some more than once. The versions on *European Con-*

cert are almost invariably the best. Part of the reason is undoubtedly that jazz players usually record music while it is new to them, and only later become familiar with the piece, so that a version heard later in a nightclub is often a better performance than the recorded one. But, by comparing the *European Concert* recitals of such MJQ staples as *Django, Pyramid* and *Vendôme* with earlier recordings, one can hear the changes that have taken place.

The MJQ has long been known as one of the few jazz groups which truly improvises, and never allows routines to become set. But the recording is a testament to more than that. It is a testament to the work of Lewis in training the other members in methods originally uncomfortable to them, and in finally making those methods the basic, understood vocabulary of the group, so that the powerful jazz sense of the individual players could function out of that vocabulary.

In connection with this, it is interesting to look at another remark of Harrison's: ". . . so far only Morton, Ellington, and now John Lewis have consistently been able to regard a performance as a unit of musical architecture, to see part in relation to whole and to develop an intimate relationship between improvised solos, predetermined ensembles, and a general structure. Lewis might paraphrase Strayhorn's remark about Ellington and say, 'I play the piano but my real instrument is the Quartet.'

"There is a parallel between the way Duke has molded his bands to suit many diverse compositions, using the great soloists as vehicles for his own ideas yet not trespassing on the individuality of their own expression, and Lewis developing his compositional gifts through the more limited medium of the MJQ without confining Jackson's freedom in solos or compromising the basic jazz qualities of the group."

It is necessary to make a modification and say that Lewis is an excellent composer *for the Quartet*, and they are in turn excellent players for him. This is proven by his various nonjazz albums such as *European Windows, The Golden Striker,* ballet *Original Sin,* or even the film score *A Milanese Story,* where his compositions often sound bland and empty —a high grade of background music, but not the work of a great composer, jazz or otherwise. Within the context of the quartet, however, these same compositions sound splendidly exciting and often quite moving. One finally wonders how much of this is due to the subtle recomposition, by use of rhythmic displacement and grace notes, of Milt Jackson. This is not to deny the obvious fact that Lewis knew he was writing for Jackson, to deny Lewis' achievement in the myriad combinations of sound and texture which he is able to get from his seemingly limited instrumentation, to dismiss the contributions of Heath and Kay, or even to fail to recognize that much of Jackson's present prodigious musicianship is due to contact with Lewis. But Jackson is regarded in several areas as being the musical salvation of the MJQ, and it is less certain that the MJQ has done as much for him.

Although Jackson has only rarely been identified with those who treat soul as one of our more readily marketable commodities, he is widely recognized as possessing that intangible in abundance. He has said, "In my case, I believe that what I heard and felt in the music of my church—I went until I was full-grown—was the most powerful influence of my musical career. The music I heard there was open, relaxed, impromptu—soul music." Prior to the MJQ, he was known as a "blowing" musician (much criticism of the MJQ still boils down to the entreaty, "Let Milt blow"), playing with such men as Dizzy Gillespie, both in his big band and in the short-lived combo he had with Charlie Parker, also with Tadd Dameron and Howard McGhee, and contributing heavily to the superb Thelonious Monk Blue Note records, Jackson being one of the few musicians to successfully complement Monk. Asked about two recordings he has made of *Willow, Weep For Me,* one with Monk and the other with the MJQ, Jackson states that "there's no comparison," and, lest he be misunderstood, adds that playing with Monk was "one of the great experiences of my life." Unfortunately, the group he and Monk once had worked only about three weeks.

Jackson, who is one of two or three major innovators on his instrument, first obtained a xylophone while attending high school in Detroit, where he was born on January 1, 1923, and says, in contrast to almost any other vibraharpist, of Lionel Hampton, "I had no eyes to play Hamp's way. I just got hung on the instrument."

Jackson's style, which is romantic although based on his own pitiless folk tradition, is often composed of seeming filigree work that has immediate charm, employing a heavy vibrato, reminding one, especially in the matter of playing what might be called an unessential instrument in a completely personal way, of the late Django Reinhardt. The difference between them is simply that Jackson's folk tradition, unlike Reinhardt's, is the source of jazz.

Jackson's style, which emphasizes sweep and content, is almost diametrically opposed to the ascetic playing of John Lewis, which emphasizes control and form. Unlike Jackson, who is all emotion, Lewis seems almost to be performing an act of criticism as he plays, unconcerned with personal expression or the delineation of fleeting emotion, but interested rather in expressing, in a quite objective way, an esthetic doctrine. The esthetics of his music are always evident, but the emotion which informs those esthetics seldom is, except in his often superb blues solos. The result is an impeccability which causes his adherents to mention Mozart and Bartók's "Mikrokosmos," and his detractors to wish he would allow himself and the group more freedom. The two finally achieved a synthesis of approach, providing brilliant foils for one another, with Lewis symbolizing tension and Jackson release. It is a powerfully effective contrast, which was becoming highly developed in such albums as the Quartet version of the *Odds Against Tomorrow* film music and the *Pyramid* set and came to full fruition in the *European Concert*.

But the better the Quartet played, the more Lewis' interests seemed to lead elsewhere. He writes more and more film music, is involved with Schuller in the large co-operative Orchestra U.S.A., and produces non-MJQ albums for Atlantic. Unlike his fellow members in the group, he enjoys spending his leisure time in Europe. All this led to an arrangement arrived at in the summer of 1962, under which the Quartet would disband for six months every year, while each member pursued whatever activity he wished.

When Jackson speaks about the Quartet, it is with a mixture of fierce pride, slightly sorrowful rationalization, and occasional flashes of anger. Occasionally, when he says something that strikes him as particularly apt, he follows it with the same smile of joyous, slightly puzzled discovery that sometimes lights up the bandstand. Much as he loves his music, he can be quite matter-of-fact about it, as witness the fact that he recorded *The Ballad Artistry of Milt Jackson,* a "with-strings" set, while watching a boxing match on a portable television set he had brought into the studio. "There's nothing strange about that," he says. "I guess it seems strange to some people, though. There was nothing to get bugged about, the music wasn't all that difficult." And then he adds, in irrefutable justification, "Floyd Patterson was fighting, as I recall."

Jackson has been called "instinctive," and his taste runs to musicians who also fit that description. His own ideal group would feature guitar and flute. Besides vibraharp ("It's larger than a vibraphone," he explains) he can play guitar, piano, bass, and drums, and one of his minor ambitions is to record a multi-dubbed LP on all the instruments.

One of the things he says about the MJQ, a remark seemingly designed to convince both the interrogator and himself, is, "I can always go someplace afterward and jam." He continues, "It's no secret that I'm not crazy about everything we do," referring to two of the most controversial topics of jazz conversation in recent years, the Third Stream and Ornette Coleman. John Lewis, because of his interest in what Jackson calls "widening the restrictions," has been a staunch supporter of both.

The Third Stream—a phrase so bitterly discussed that one pianist characterized as a Third Stream musician called it "a term invented to get work for Gunther Schuller"—can be said to have had its origins, as far as the Quartet is concerned, in Lewis' and Schuller's Jazz and Classical Music Society, but is actually the latest in a long line of attempts to effect a fusion of jazz and classical music. Jackson, who has played much of the music, remarks of Schuller, "I don't want to run him down, because he's an excellent composer, but he's not writing jazz—he's not from the jazz environment."

The MJQ has recorded two Third Stream LPs, one of which pairs the group with the Beaux Arts String Quartet, and the other with the Stuttgart Symphony. Lewis' contribution to the string quartet session was *Sketch*, which contrasted the MJQ with Haydn-like string figures in a work that accomplished highly limited goals. Schuller's composition for the same instrumentation, *Conversations*, is probably the most successful attempt so far in the idiom. Schuller's *Concertino for Jazz Quartet and Orchestra*, recorded by the Quartet with the Stuttgart Symphony, is less successful. Schuller remarks that "it would be best to forget all labels and categories, to approach these pieces simply as *a music written today*," but that is difficult to do in the face of Lewis' contribution to the album, the same classic-pastiche arrangement of *God Rest Ye Merry Gentlemen* he had presented three years previously on *European Windows*. It seems unlikely that a contemporary fusion will ever be achieved by a man who remains resolutely in genteel eighteenth-century Europe, particularly when Jackson's instinctive grasp of the pieces seems more complete than Lewis' intellectual one.

For his part, Jackson, who is widely known to favor the simplest, most direct jazz, does not feel that a fusion has been achieved. He favors *Around the Blues*, which André Hodeir wrote for him, and he sums up his feeling toward the advances these works strive for by saying, "In the middle, there's always twenty-four bars of blues."

That the jazz audience probably sides with Jackson is best supported by an incident at an MJQ concert recalled by Don DeMichael in *Down Beat:* "The concert's finale was given over to a several-part composition written by Lewis, who announced and explained each part. Before the third section, as he was explaining his attractive, but complex, piece of work, a man in the first row shouted, *'Bags' Groove!'* Lewis recoiled as if a bucket of ice water had been thrown in his face. He replied with dignity, 'We'll play *that* later. And now, in this third section . . .' When the man had shouted, Jackson threw his head back and laughed a silent laugh."

The other area of differing opinion, Ornette Coleman, is far from a laughing matter to Jackson. It is, however, guaranteed to start a conversation with him, for he seems to feel that Coleman negates everything he believes about music. "Let's face it, nobody's going to do more than Bird did on the saxophone, or Dizzy on trumpet—nobody's going to play faster or higher—so they decided they had to have a departure." Asked why colleagues Lewis and Heath are equally adamant *for* Coleman, his reply is brief: "They discovered him." And of playing with Coleman himself, "I didn't get the message."

The solemnity of the MJQ, then, would seem to be Lewis' contribution. He takes few chances with himself and his music. There are clauses in his contracts specifying particular pianos and sound systems, and he will wipe each key carefully with cold cream, and keep hand-warmers and lotion about. He kept one concert audience waiting until the specified piano, which was not present when he arrived, was brought in. "John would get so mad at the piano," Jack-

son has said of the days when Lewis had to play on whatever was around, "he'd play his head off."

Lewis' quest for dignity has led him to such worthwhile
projects as becoming Music Director of the Monterey Jazz
Festival, the only festival of which the musicians themselves
approve. It has led to the Lenox School, forced to close in
1961 for the lack of funds and students. He is director of
probably the most universally acclaimed jazz group in the
world, which plays only the best clubs—when it plays clubs
—appears in concerts, and at contemporary music festivals in
Europe, and has performed with orchestra for a ballet at
the New York City Center ("There was nothing for me to
do," Jackson says).

One of Lewis' main contributions to the success of the
Quartet is best noted in a statement he made to Nat Hentoff:
"People who play should think more about *where* they're
playing. When you're playing in one kind of place, you have
to do things that fit that place. Now, if you're in clubs, and
feel better off in concerts, you should work in that direction
as much as you can. . . . The quartet, for example, does
much better in places where people can listen attentively."

This is one more example of Lewis' shaping of the image
of the MJQ, an image which may ultimately be as important
as its music, and it is disconcerting to note that the totality
of Lewis' work in that area hits many people in ways they
might prefer not to think about. "I don't go with this bringing 'dignity' to jazz," said Miles Davis, who has himself
brought to it the dignity of a unique individual. "The way
they bring 'dignity' to jazz in their formal clothes and the
way they bow is like Ray Robinson bringing dignity to boxing by fighting in a tuxedo." The aloof formality of the
MJQ has indirectly called into question problems of race and
of the nature of jazz itself. Is it pretentious to title a piece of
music *Baden-Baden*, or is it only pretentious because that
piece was formerly called *Moving Nicely?* In the album notes
for his film score to *No Sun in Venice*, Lewis says of his

Cortege, "This is *my* Venice and that isn't the same perhaps as what Raoul Levy is trying to show in the movie. I know Venice's history, the music it has produced, I love its *commedia dell'arte* and in my *Fontessa* gave it musical expression. In seeing a colorful funeral procession on the Grand Canal, however, I can't help but think of funerals in New Orleans, which are happy as well as sad, and that double image in my mind is undoubtedly reflected in my music." But when Francis Thorne asked him, "When you wrote *Cortege* for *No Sun in Venice* were you definitely planning a funeral march?" Lewis replied, "In this case it was not so much a matter of form but the fact that people asked for a piece that was similar to *Django.* Actually, that was the main reason the producers of the film wanted music from me in the first place; it was *Django* that gave them the idea to use me for the background score." Of course, it is possible to do all these things at once—write a Venice–New Orleans funeral march that is like *Django.* The MJQ has made an enormous reputation by doing—and doing better— many of the same things for which Dave Brubeck has been so thoroughly trounced by the critics. Both units have incorporated classical techniques, including counterpoint and fugue; both employ true improvisation to a degree unknown in most other small bands. Both Lewis and Brubeck adhere strongly to the old rhetorical dictum, "Tell 'em what you're gonna do, do it, and tell 'em what you did." Both units have as their featured soloists men with great, flowing gifts for melody who have the approval which many deny the leaders of those units, soloists who are often at variance with the aims of the group. (In one of his multiple jokes, Paul Desmond, tired of hearing the recurrent stories that he would leave Brubeck, referred to himself as "The divine Milt.") The MJQ undoubtedly has the better rhythm section, and on one of Desmond's recordings as a leader, he chose Heath and Kay to play with him.

But the differences may be more important than the similarities. Why Lewis' self-effacing urbanity is better received than Brubeck's hominess might make a fascinating psychological study which would reveal a great deal about the jazz audience and the extra-musical reasons for the jazz cult. Lewis is a fine blues pianist but is rebuffed in such attempts as his *Original Sin* ballet score; Brubeck can turn out pieces in the style of any composer one cares to mention, but points with pride when Harlem stride-man Willie "The Lion" Smith praises his blues playing. Brubeck hungers for the critical acclaim which Lewis has received almost automatically; Lewis may never appear with Leonard Bernstein and the New York Philharmonic. "One man's mate," James Thurber wrote, "is another man's prison."

If the MJQ has fashioned a prison for itself, it is one which allows for a great deal of freedom. "We decide everything together," Jackson says. "When we go to Europe, we don't go for two weeks, we go for two months. And then, if we decide we don't want to work, we don't." The Quartet will probably go on, despite the differing opinions and personal conflicts of its members, so long as both Lewis and Jackson are free to indulge their personal preferences outside it. And the best and simplest reason is given by Milt Jackson: "We could all get our own groups, but we do better as the Quartet."

Selected Discography

The Quartet, SAVOY 12046.
Django, PRESTIGE 7057.
One Never Knows, ATLANTIC 1284.
Patterns (Music from *Odds Against Tomorrow*), UNITED ARTISTS 4072.
Pyramid, ATLANTIC 1325.
European Concert, ATLANTIC 2–603.

CHARLES MINGUS

"SAY THAT I'm uncooperative, and that I don't want to be in the book. Besides, I'm not a jazz musician, anyway." And then Charles Mingus began to talk.

Much of Mingus' attitude toward the world is contained in that statement. A highly complex man, he is an astonishing mixture of directness, outrageous exaggeration, self-contradiction, hostility, and rare affection. He was attempting, by the latter part of the remark, to disassociate himself from the bland conformity he finds around him. As he puts it, "If Nina Simone is a jazz musician, then I'm not." My bet is on Mingus. Besides being one of the most forceful, personal, and most unusual composers and leaders in jazz, he is one of the greatest virtuosi on the double bass in the world.

None of these talents has done Mingus very much good. Musicians far less capable work more often, and it is safe to say that the majority of them, in a business not noted for the peace of mind of its participants, are more content. It may be that Mingus benefits everyone but himself.

There are stories, real and apocryphal, about Mingus, but Mingus himself has the longest, most involved Mingus story of all. It is a book, called *Beneath the Underdog*, which he has been writing for quite some time. An enormous, handwritten manuscript, it is of Thomas Wolfe proportions already, and when we spoke, had not yet reached the point of its semi-autobiographical protagonist's arrival in New York.

A good deal of Mingus' unwillingness to disseminate information is directly traceable to the book. "I'm telling you too much now," he says after any anecdote, "I should save that for the book." He has another, more pragmatic reason: "I think jazz musicians should write their own books, so they'll get the money. I never got a job from anything that was written about me. I'm on the cover of one jazz magazine right now. Do you think the agents care about that? The publicity has never done me any good."

Nor has it pleased him. An extended tirade he delivered in a nightclub one night was taken down on tape, and appeared in a book called *The Jazz Word*. Mingus complains that the most telling parts have been edited out.

The same attitude is likely to extend to his music. He played the background score for the motion picture, *Shadows*. Director John Cassavetes, Mingus feels, edited the results in such a way that they are not representative of what he wanted to do. But rather than explaining how, Mingus may simply say, "That's not me playing bass."

Even in a situation in which he apparently has control, such as a notorious 1962 Town Hall concert and recording date, Mingus seems to be trying to see to it that things do not go as he plans.

But all of this, Mingus feels, is beside the point. What is important, he says, is his music, and if you want to understand him, you should listen to that music. His music is indeed so personal that it tells quite a bit about him. So, of course, does his life.

Charles Mingus was born April 22, 1922, in Nogales, Arizona. Before he was a year old, the family moved to Watts, California, just outside Los Angeles. He started school there, but had trouble, partially because he was still a little too young.

When he was about six years old Mingus was given a Christmas present—a trombone and lessons. The teacher, it seems, was a poor one, but Mingus was convinced for a time that the problem was his, that he could not play. About four years later, he met Britt Woodman, later to become an Ellington trombonist. Woodman talked the ex-trombonist's parents into buying a cello. Again, Mingus found a poor teacher. Perhaps it was this bad training that made him unable to hold down a cello chair in the high school orchestra.

Mingus was becoming accustomed, by this time, to a bewildering series of musical failures. He had also heard the two kinds of music which were to influence him most deeply: the music of the Holiness Church, and—at a concert to which Woodman took him—the music of Duke Ellington. Today, many of his pieces reflect a simultaneous assimilation of and struggle with the influence of the older man's music.

Mingus joined a jazz band in high school, and another member of the band, Buddy Collette, suggested that bass was more suitable than cello to the needs of the orchestra. Mingus switched, and Collette took him to bassist Red Callender for help. For five years after that, he studied with a New York Philharmonic bassist, H. Rheinschagen. It is this study that made him the amazing player he is. He has told Nat Hentoff that "for a while I concentrated on speed and technique almost as ends in themselves. I aimed at scaring all the other bass players . . . Then one night (when I was eighteen or nineteen) all this changed . . . It was suddenly *me;* it wasn't the bass any more. Now I'm not conscious of the instrument as an instrument when I play."

Probably, Mingus is more responsible than anyone since the late Ellington bassist Jimmy Blanton for the liberation and expanding role of his instrument in jazz. Originally, the string bass was strictly a rhythm instrument; a substitution for the tuba when the New Orleans marching bands came in off the streets (many of the early jazz bassists played both instruments). Blanton had showed that the instrument was capable of subtler melody, both plucked and bowed, and gave the impetus to such virtuosi of the late forties and fifties as Oscar Pettiford and Ray Brown. Bop, however, made the drums more of an accent voice, and the burden of keeping a steady beat fell more heavily on the bass. Most bassists were so steeped in their roles as timekeepers that during their solos, they would simply continue to keep time, but with a more interesting choice of notes. Since Mingus, many bassists have seemed to consider their instrument as a sort of large guitar, and in his wake, the late fifties and early sixties have unearthed perhaps the largest number of young virtuosi to appear at the same time on any one jazz instrument: Wilbur Ware, the late Scott LaFaro, Charlie Haden, Art Davis, Ron Carter, Gary Peacock, Jimmy Garrison, Chuck Israels, Steve Swallow, and others.

Mingus' own career has been remarkable. For a time, in an attempt to be an Ellington counterpart, he was known in California as Baron Mingus. He appeared in two motion pictures, *Higher and Higher* and *The Road to Zanzibar*. (One wonders what kind of role the race-conscious Mingus must have played in them.)

His musical experience was extraordinarily varied. From 1941–43, he was with Louis Armstrong. From Armstrong to Kid Ory, then to Alvino Ray, and from 1946–48, he was with Lionel Hampton. During the stay with Hampton, he was featured on a recording of his own composition, *Mingus Fingers*. Today, he points to a particular section of the new version of *Fingers* and says, with the air of a man to whom justice has come after long waiting, "That's the chorus Hamp couldn't play." In 1950 and 1951, he toured with a fascinating trio led by Red Norvo, which included guitarist Tal Farlow. After leaving that group, he settled in New York and, discouraged, went to work for the post office.

"It was Bird," Mingus has said, "who had called me out of the post office in December 1951, when I had almost decided to stay there. And Bird encouraged me about my writing. He never mentioned whether he thought my bass playing was good or bad, but he always thought I was a good writer."

Mingus, who regards Parker in a manner approaching reverence, heeded his word, and took a job as bassist with the trio of pianist Billy Taylor. While this paid the bills, Mingus became involved in the first of several experiments.

In 1952, he started his own record company, Debut, in

partnership with Max Roach. Mingus' former wife, Celia, was business head of the operation, and the money came, sporadically, from a friend of Roach's. Despite several excellent releases—most notably the recording of a May 1953 concert given in Toronto, Canada, by a Mingus-organized quintet consisting of Charlie Parker, Dizzy Gillespie, Bud Powell, Mingus, and Roach—the company went out of business due to poor management, internecine squabbling, and ego clashes. (The catalog has since been acquired by Fantasy Records.)

One of the purposes of Debut Records was to record a series of Jazz Workshop concerts which Mingus gave in Brooklyn in the summer of 1953. This later became the Composers' Workshop, an organization which included radical experimenters Teddy Charles, John LaPorta, and Teo Macero, and the jazz journalist Bill Coss. The music played at these concerts was almost completely written out, a method with which Mingus felt a growing dissatisfaction. As he later wrote, "I found out two important things from this series of concerts. First, that a jazz composition as I hear it in my mind's ear—although set down in so many notes on score paper and precisely notated—cannot be played by a group of either jazz or classical musicians. Secondly, jazz, by its very definition, cannot be held down to written parts to be played with a feeling that goes only with blowing free. A classical musician might read all the notes correctly but play them without the correct feeling or interpretation, and a jazz musician, although he might read all the notes and play them with jazz feeling, inevitably introduces his own *individual* expression rather than what the composer intended. It is amazing how many ways a four-bar phrase of four beats can be interpreted."

For a while after these concerts, Mingus played in various groups with Parker, Powell, Stan Getz, and Art Tatum, and then disappeared from music for a considerable stretch of time, to reappear around 1956 with a new, and more power-

ful, concept. Disenchanted, with the technical preoccupa-
tions of certain white musicians, he recalled to Hentoff an
incident which occurred when the trumpeter Roy Eldridge
had been a guest with his high school band. Eldridge, preferring not to play a passage which had been written for him,
told Mingus, "You see this horn. I play what I feel on it.
That's jazz. You'd better find out about the music of your
people. Some day you're going to thank me for talking to
you like this."

Accordingly, Mingus wrote in 1956, "My whole conception with my present Jazz Workshop group deals with nothing written. I 'write' compositions—but only on mental score
paper—then I lay out the composition part by part to the
musicians. I play them the 'framework' on piano so that they
are all familiar with my interpretation and feeling and with
the scale and chord progressions to be used. Each man's own
particular style is taken into consideration, both in ensemble
and in solos. For instance, they are given different rows of
notes to use against each chord but they choose their own
notes and play them in their own style, from scales as well
as chords, except where a particular mood is indicated. In
this way, I find it possible to keep my own compositional
flavor in the pieces and yet to allow the musicians more individual freedom in the creation of their group lines and solos."

Basically, Mingus writes cooperatively with his players in
the Ellington manner, but Ellington, of necessity, has to have
many more sections actually written out, simply because
there are so many more men in his band. It is notable that in
the cases of both men, the unit is instantly recognizable, no
matter who is in the band, and so are the soloists. Of his
first recorded compositions, Mingus says, "They sound a lot
like Ellington, but what I was trying to say with them was,
'See, I can write, too.'"

After many changes of personnel, Mingus' new Jazz Workshop eventually recorded an album called *Pithecanthropus*

Erectus. Besides Mingus, the group consisted of Jackie McLean, alto; J. R. Monterose, tenor sax; Mal Waldron, piano; and Willie Jones, drums. One of the tracks, *A Foggy Day,* displays one aspect of Mingus for which many have taken him to task. It is an attempt to convey his impressions of San Francisco, and uses actual sounds (auto and ships' horns), rather than attempting to represent them musically. Of this complaint, he has said, characteristically, "Critics wanted to pigeonhole and stylize me, saying 'Mingus uses whistles and effects,' when I used them on only one piece out of thirty or forty different recorded compositions."

It is the album's title track, though, which caused the up- roar and again brought Mingus to public notice. Critic Mar- tin Williams, on first hearing it, remarked, "I didn't know you could say that with jazz." And five years later, a French group awarded it a *Grand Prix.* "Maybe they're just now catching up to where I was then," Mingus said.

The composition is characteristic of much of Mingus' sub- sequent music. It show traces of Ellington; it is never far from the blues; it has all the virtues and excesses of extreme emotionalism; it contains some false climaxes; and, above all, it is a shatteringly powerful experience for the listener. It is also specifically programmatic, as few jazz composers beside Mingus have attempted to be.

Mal Waldon, the pianist on the album, is a valuable source of information on what it is like to work for Mingus. "He makes you find yourself," Waldron says, "to play your own style. At that time, I played a good deal like Horace Silver, and whenever I did, Mingus would be on me with 'That sounds like Horace.'"

Such remarks from Mingus have caused many musicians to leave his groups, for he does not wait until after the set or until the next day's rehearsal to make them. Any complaint he has against a member of his band is voiced at the moment of the transgression; often loudly enough for an audience to hear. To an over-busy drummer, Mingus will say, "Hey man, it's *my* solo." If a pianist plays a chord which Mingus does not feel to be the right one, he will obligingly reach over (he is always stationed next to the piano), and play the proper one. He has no compunction against stopping in the middle of a number and starting over again from the beginning, giving some club patrons the impression that they are paying to watch a rehearsal. One night, in the middle of *Mood Indigo,* Mingus stopped the performance to remark, "I'll have to apologize for our pianist. He's a young man, and doesn't know all the old songs."

Waldron is perhaps less offended than most by these and similar hazards of being in Mingus' employ. "Probably it doesn't bother me," he says, "because I was in the Composers' Workshop. That was the idea of that group, to study and to learn, and so when I joined the group, I knew that's how it would be. Naturally, something like that can be harmful to a guy's ego, but when Mingus says something like that, he's always right. And it does a lot more good to be told about something when you do it than later. I don't believe Mingus thinks of himself as a teacher, though, because he's too in-volved with Mingus. If you play in his band, you play his way. Mingus is the personality. But at the same time, play-ing with him brings you out, and forces you to play yourself. And when that time comes, when you've reached that point, you have to leave."

Some have suggested that Mingus feels a sense of personal betrayal at a player's defection. "He does," Waldron says, "and he has good reason to. People think Miles Davis is the great talent scout. But Paul Chambers was already winning polls before he went with Miles. And all the musicians knew what a great drummer Philly Joe Jones was. He was there. He was complete. There was no work to be done. When Mingus finds these guys, sometimes they haven't worked anywhere. And they way he teaches them the book, he sings or plays their part to them. I was always after him to write it down. That way, if someone left, a good man could read it right down, and we could work the next night. But Mingus didn't think that was the way to learn. So that way, if anyone leaves, Mingus is back where he started. He has to begin all over again, from scratch. For a while, he has to play all standards, and he has this great number of tunes of his, that he'd rather play. And while the new guys are rehearsing, the other members of the band who had stayed—sometimes I was the only one—would have to play the same thing, over and over again, until the new guy got it."

At the same time that his music began to be known, Mingus acquired his vast reputation as a battler. He reacts directly, sometimes before thought, and since he is a large, powerful man who can inflict great physical damage, he has come to be feared. About the incident which launched the stories, Mingus told Ira Gitler, "I only had three fights since I've been in New York. One was when I took my band on the road for the first time. One of the guys in the band was late for the job. He was a junky and when I got mad at him he pulled a knife on me. I only hit him because he had the knife. I didn't want to hit him because I loved the cat. He's my friend today. He knows I was right. But that's when my reputation spread."

Waldron, who was there when it happened, says, "Everybody expected it long before it happened, even the guy he hit. The guy was asking for it, and then one night he got it."

Mingus was perhaps not entirely blameless in the affair, because both Waldron and Jackie McLean report that while they, on the assumption that Mingus had no money, were subsisting on Cheez Whiz and crackers, Mingus, who *did* have money, was eating steak.

Mingus' next major bout took place not long afterward, at Music Inn at Lenox, Mass. Nat Hentoff, who was present, recalls the incident: "He can be very wrong. He sometimes reacts to an actual or invisible hurt with instantaneous, un-reasoning, out-of-proportion emotional directness. And yet sometimes he does all he can to avoid a situation he knows will detonate his rages. I've seen him leave the room when a drunken Southerner began to make all too explicit racial allusions. Mingus didn't want to embarrass his hosts, and he was in the midst of another of his frequent resolutions not to explode, whatever the provocation. The drunk followed him, backed him into a corner, and finally, with shattering quick-ness, Mingus knocked him out. He was shiveringly upset, angry at himself more than at the man. 'I wouldn't have hit him at all,' he said, 'but I was afraid he was going to hit me.' "

It is probably significant that today, in a prominent posi-tion on Mingus' bookshelf, is a volume entitled *The Power of Nonviolence*, which looks as though it has been read sev-eral times.

He was also, of course, continuing to make music. Several albums were released. The most impressive of them, called *The Clown*, was even better received than *Pithecanthropus Erectus*, primarily because of the overpowering *Haitian Fight Song*, and *Blue Cee*, which Mingus refers to as "the first blues I've made on record." While the band underwent further personnel changes, Mingus became involved in vari-ous disparate projects. For a time, he had been connected with the ill-fated jazz-and-poetry movement, for which his unique programmatic sense ideally suited him. He had written the *Shadows* score, an extended work called *Revela-tions* for the Brandeis Music Festival, and played some ex-cellently received concerts, one of which is preserved on records under the title, *Wonderland*.

His most important opportunity, though, came in 1959, with the release of an album called *Mingus Ah Um* (a Columbia Records executive's attempt at Latinate declen-sion of Mingus' name). Mingus' old Composers' Workshop associate, Teo Macero, was now a Columbia A & R director, and produced an album which enabled Mingus to show a larger audience than he had ever had that he was one of the leaders of the "soul" movement.

By the time *Mingus Ah Um* was released, "soul" music, which took much of its inspiration from the Negro church, had become an unstimulating backwater devoid of all freshness. Too many of the young musicians attempting this style satisfied themselves with a mere aping of its devices. Much of what they did could have been learned from Horace Silver, without once going to the church music that is the source of the style.

Mingus had not only gone to the source, but had grasped its essence, and added elements peculiarly his own. Rather than approaching church material as a set of currently popular conventions which might be turned to advantage, he saw a living tradition on which to impose, and through which to express, his own vision. The result, a piece called *Better Git It In Your Soul*, complete with handclapping and Mingus shouting "Yes, Lord, I know," was stunning proof that nothing is cliché in the hands of a great musician.

There are eight other Mingus compositions on *Mingus Ah Um*, some of which may have more eventual pertinence to Mingus' compositional development than *Soul*. Among them are *Pussy Cat Dues*, which is a lovely tribute to Ellington; *Open Letter to Duke*, which is not; *Boogie Stop Shuffle*, an object lesson in how to generate the kind of excitement for which movie and TV jazz scorers are constantly, and unsuccessfully, striving; and *Jelly Roll*, a delightful, affectionate burlesque done with real understanding, which stems from Mingus' purchase of a book of Morton tunes.

Several typically Mingus incidents stemmed from the album's release. New York's most influential jazz disc jockey, Symphony Sid, creates hits by finding one track from an LP and playing it three or four times a night. He did this with *Soul*, and it *was* a hit. Atlantic, for whom Mingus had previously been recording, offered an album of previously unreleased material called *Blues and Roots*. A darkly oppressive record, it contained pieces—*Wednesday Night Prayer Meeting* and *My Jelly Roll Soul*—that sounded like earlier, less successful versions of what had appeared on Columbia. "Do you know how long that was on the shelf?" Mingus asked Gitler. "Two or three years. Atlantic put it out because my Columbia had come out. They had that before I ever had the Columbia done."

Mingus launched a campaign whose ultimate effect was to undermine his opportunity. At one point he claimed that *Mingus Ah Um* had sold ninety thousand copies (an astronomical amount for a jazz LP), a figure with which Columbia officials did not concur. And he attacked Julian "Cannonball" Adderley, whose quintet had popularized the "soul" movement, mostly through Bobby Timmons' gospel-derived *This Here*. Mingus told Gitler, "Cannonball don't know nothing—may I say this right now—and he's a rock 'n'roll musician, No. 1," and now claims that the Adderley brothers have stolen tunes from him. "They have something called *Work Song*. I have *Work Song* on my *Mingus at the Bohemia* (now re-released on Fantasy as *Chazz!*)."

But if one presses Mingus for specifics, he becomes evasive. "He exaggerates to make his point," Mal Waldron says. "Actually, he did do a lot of those things before anyone else. When I was with him, all the guys were playing very 'hip' blues, with all kinds of extra chords and passing tones. Mingus got rid of all that, and made it basic. He made us play like the old, original blues, with only two or three chords, and got a basic feeling. And he brought in some gospel music, too, the first time that was done. And suspensions. The way Miles and Coltrane play, getting to a particular part of a number and staying on the same chord for several bars before going on. Mingus was the first one to do that."

Mingus refused to take the most obvious course in attaining the recognition he so obviously wants. "Everybody wants me to play *Better Git It In Your Soul* and *Wednesday Night Prayer Meeting*," he says, "but I'm past that. They were written years before they were recorded, and I'm doing something else now."

Pianist Billy Taylor, Mingus' old employer, says, "He really had something there, if he had stayed with it. But he wouldn't do it. If he had had someone he respected, who had the business sense he doesn't have, and who knew jazz—even if he didn't know jazz, just someone he could respect—a Martha Glaser or a John Levy, he could have been a star. When he talks about the Adderleys, I think he's referring to *Wednesday Night Prayer Meeting*. But all gospel songs sound similar. If you have five different men playing a B-flat blues, there are going to be many similarities."

Mingus did, however, record again for Columbia, and the album included two gospel-type pieces which, as it happens, had been written previously on commission. There were several other things, too, for Mingus says, "a composer writing twenty pieces should write twenty pieces that are different." At the time, I tried to sum up my impressions of the album (called *Mingus Dynasty*), and Mingus, for *The American Record Guide:* "This does not pretend to be a review; it is an appreciation. God Bless Charlie Mingus. He can see the humor in Negro Church music in a piece like *Slop;* he can play the bass like no one in the world; he can be sprawling and excessive in his conception; he can be as tender as he is in *Diane;* he can take himself as solemnly he does on these liner notes while making an offhand reference to Gauguin that might make you ponder several things for several hours; he can write and execute a piece as unusual and important as *Far Wells, Mill Valley;* he can be as lovingly respectful to the man who has probably shaped his musical life more than anyone, while adding something important of his own that was not there before, as he is on his version of *Mood Indigo;* he can be more poignant and original with the theme of Frankie and Johnny as a ballet than Jerome Moross was (*Put Me in That Dungeon*); he can prattle for hours like an adolescent about the freedom and responsibility of the artist; he can create an endlessly fascinating jazz album like this one; and then he can turn around and pose for the front cover."

The cover, in line with the title, shows Mingus attired in mandarin robes and hat, and it is surprising, after some of the things he has said, that he would have been party to such exploitation; he is, as he puts it, "a protest cat."

One of most telling and constructive manifestations of that protest occurred on the July Fourth weekend, 1960, during the Newport Jazz Festival. Since its inception, Newport had become more and more an overtly commercial enterprise, catering to mass taste rather than presenting jazz as it had set out to do—booking such nonjazz performers as Pat Suzuki and the Kingston Trio, in an attempt to swell the "nonprofits", and turning the island, by 1960, into a haven for the beer-drinking college crowd who eventually ran amok, making Newport an area of limited war, with tear-gas-armed police and barbed-wire compounds thrown up on the beaches.

Mingus, in the company of Max Roach and several others, seceded from the festival, and set up one of their own at Cliff Walk Manor, elsewhere on the island. The musicians involved did all the organizational and production work themselves, and were running concerts in direct opposition to the NJF. It is generally agreed that the music at Cliff Walk was superior to that of the scheduled festival. (Some of the highlights were recreated for a Candid LP called *Newport Rebels.*)

What began at Newport continued in the fall as the Jazz Artists' Guild, giving a random series of concerts at the small York Theatre in Manhattan. Roach and singer Abbey Lincoln were also leading members, and the plan was that, in an attempt to protect themselves from the business machinery of jazz, which they deeply mistrust, the Guild members would book and manage themselves. But apparently they did not have the necessary business acumen, and the venture failed.

Mingus feels that much of his trouble is due to these business forces, and constantly claims that gangsters are in control of all jazz outlets. "You know gangsters run jazz," he shouted at Martin Williams at a United Nations Jazz Club symposium. "Why don't you say something?"

"If there are gangsters," says Billy Taylor, who was also at the symposium, "they aren't interested in Mingus. If they were, he wouldn't be out of work, he'd be dead in an alley someplace."

For these and musical reasons, it has always been Mingus' ideal to be "in residence" at a particular club. Rather than traveling constantly, he would remain in one place for several months, building up an audience and working with one group at perfecting his music. That was his situation for a while at Greenwich Village's Half Note. After that he went to another Village club, The Showplace, and even talked of holding a school for musicians and theatre people there in the afternoons. When he left, in October, 1960, he had been there for nearly a year, refining his ideas and changing his personnel. When the group disbanded, it included drummer Dannie Richmond, who has remained with Mingus longer than anyone; trumpeter Ted Curson; the late Eric Dolphy, a brilliant young multi-instrumentalist; and Mingus. Just after Dolphy and Curson decided to leave, Nat Hentoff, determined not to let the group go unrecorded, made an album with them for Candid, *Charles Mingus Presents Charles Mingus*. It is, in many respects, the most remarkable set Mingus has ever made.

In several places, particularly in Dolphy's work, the set was said to reflect the considerable impact of saxophonist Ornette Coleman. *Folk Forms No. 1* is based on a motif comparable to Coleman's *Ramblin'*. *Original Faubus Fables*, in which Mingus verbally gives his opinion of the governor, seems to be more propaganda than art. *All The Things You Could Be By Now If Sigmund Freud's Wife Was Your Mother* is a variant on the outline of *All The Things You Are*. There is generally one piece on a Mingus album that stands out, and on this, it is *What Love*, loosely derived from the structure of *What Is This Thing Called Love?* After the opening theme, Curson has a solo, accompanied by Mingus in a cello-like fashion, which is at times startlingly like Jewish liturgical music. It seems to be in several rhythms, and at times, in no rhythm. Mingus solos next, in an amazingly musical virtuoso display, completely unaccompanied. Dolphy solos on bass clarinet, again with several rhythmic shifts. Following that, Dolphy and Mingus "converse" in what may be the most successful recorded attempt to duplicate the human voice with instruments.

Before the release of this album, Mingus took a group to Copa City, in Queens, once again with the idea of being "in residence." But he had to leave there, too. Bill Coss recalls, "Mingus went in on an arrangement whereby he would remain indefinitely, building up a clientele for the room. The lady who owned Copa City was perfectly willing to go along with him, but the room wasn't doing the business it needed to do. If she had kept Mingus, she would eventually have gone out of business. It's a rare club that can remain in business without changing attractions, but Mingus doesn't take that into consideration. All he knows is he feels betrayed."

It was during his Copa City tenure that Mingus first announced he was no longer a jazz musician. What he played he now termed "rotary perception," explaining that what is generally known as jazz has, to a much greater extent than suits him, disregarded the all-important element of improvisation. Those who heard him at Copa City maintain that what Mingus was playing could only be called jazz, and excellent jazz at that, but he seemed to feel the necessity for the different label.

It is interesting that everyone approached on the subject of Mingus feels that he is the only one who understands him. An exception was Dolphy, who, feeling that only the music is important, said, "He writes wonderful music and is a ball to play with," and let it go at that. Two jazz writers, Bill Coss and Nat Hentoff, seem to find symbolic value in Mingus' personality and spend much of their time trying to unravel his paradoxes. Coss, amazed that he is still Mingus' sometime friend after all these years, shows the strain of constantly trying to figure out in advance which of several ways Mingus may react to the same stimulus. Hentoff, on being told of a particularly puzzling incident, says, "Sometimes he laughs at himself when he does things like that."

Perhaps the most cogent evaluation comes from Billy Taylor. "Very few people," Taylor says, "have ever really made the attempt to understand this terribly complex human being. I knew him in a different way than most musicians. They've worked for him, and he worked for me. I first used him when I got a job at Storyville, in Boston, in 1951. I'd heard him with Hampton, and hadn't been that impressed. Then I heard him with Red Norvo, and he sounded like an extension of Tal Farlow's guitar. He had fantastic technique, but I didn't know if it was what was needed in my group. But Jo Jones kept telling me, "Use Mingus," and I've always had an enormous respect for his opinion, so I did. Charlie was with me about eight months. We never had any trouble. We used to have some long talks, and he'd tell me what he wanted to do, and I'd tell him what I wanted. We had some musical disagreements and differences of opinion, of course, but never had any trouble. The only time I ever saw him lose his temper was one night when a drunk kept leaning over Mingus to try to talk to me while I was playing. Charlie pushed him away.

"We see each other every once in a while, and I talk to him. I think he listens to me. I remember once when he was in the hospital, I went to see him, and sent some other people to see him. I'm not saying that was such a big thing, it's only what anyone would do for a friend. But a lot of other people, people who are supposed to be a lot tighter with him than I am, never showed up.

"Of course he's resentful, of course he's bitter. He wants fame, and recognition for what he's done, and he sees other people, not as talented as he is, getting credit for his accomplishments. But you can't think about things like that, or you'd never do anything. He's like a lot of big men. He's very emotional, and very direct, and sometimes he goes off half-cocked, without thinking things through. And because he's a big man, he can do a lot of damage. I've told him that if he did that in his music, he wouldn't have accomplished very much. His music is so well thought out and organized, but he doesn't act that way in his personal life. He's very sensitive to rejection, and sometimes he feels it when it isn't there."

In his home, Mingus graciously explains why, because of his book, he cannot, in all conscience, give interviews. "But if you've got a mind," he says, as he tells you he cannot help, "you're getting a lot right now."

A highly sensitive barometer of current events, he scans the newspaper accounts of the civil rights struggle in Mississippi, Alabama and elsewhere: "Why do you want to waste your time writing about jazz musicians when there's a war going on? But I'm not a jazz musician anyway, so I shouldn't be in the book."

He reads accounts of his friend and ex-partner Max

Roach, who broke up a Miles Davis benefit concert for the African Research Foundation by appearing on the stage from the audience with propagandistic placards: "I told Max," he says, "that if he wanted to become famous, he'd have to do something crazy."

And then, because he wants very much to be helpful, although his conscience tells him he should not be, he produces documentary evidence. "All the biographical stuff is on liner notes," he says, "but you might get something from this." ("This" is a carbon copy of a lengthy letter he wrote to a friend, explaining how he has been cheated by agents, why bookers and clubowners will not accept him, why Symphony Sid will no longer play his records, why the Syndicate has him staked out for special attention. The letter is an eloquent, impassioned statement of his side of the story.) He plays an unreleased record, so that I may hear it before I write. He gives me the telephone number of a person who can supply additional information.

His wife, who is white, pauses in her work to look at their baby Caroline, saying, "Maybe she'll be a genius, too."

And then Mingus says once again that the lack of assistance is not personal, smiles, shakes hands, says, "Good luck to you," and goes back to *Beneath the Underdog.*

Mingus has made a film in England, *All Night Long,* a story of jazz musicians based on *Othello.* Unfortunately, the theatrical, violently suspicious Mingus did not play the lead, but he did film a piano-bass blues duet with Dave Brubeck which both men were surprised and pleased to learn was one of their most enjoyable musical experiences.

On his return, he had assimilated enough of English customs to appear everywhere in a black bowler, black-rimmed glasses, black topcoat and carrying a black briefcase. In such periods of insistence on the outward trappings of dignity, he refers to himself as Charles; at other times he is Charlie. One evening, attired in his London clothes, he walked into the *Metronome* offices to attend a wake for that magazine. As his contribution to the party, he brought with him several bottles of liquor in a paper sack. Seeing his former trumpeter, Ted Curson, on the other side of the room, Mingus shouted happily, "Jazz is dead, baby, ain't you glad?"

When Mingus again began performing in public, he had solved his perpetual problems with pianists by becoming one himself. The thankless task of playing bass for pianist Mingus was at first performed by the late Doug Watkins. The direct, uncluttered Mingus piano style was proof of a line of descent from Ellington to Monk to Cecil Taylor: at times, Mingus sounded astonishingly like each of them. He also sang the blues, with little technical skill but powerful conviction. Aside from Mingus, the most notable member of the group was Roland Kirk, a remarkable musician who plays tenor, siren, a couple of flutes, two odd saxophone off-shoots called the manzello and the strich, and almost any other odd instrument that comes to hand, sometimes three at a time. Kirk bursts with self-expression like Mingus, and he made a perfect complement to him. The permanent record of this collaboration is the album, *Oh Yeah.*

At the same time, Mingus had been agitating for the release of an album called *Tijuana Moods,* which had been lying unreleased in RCA Victor's vaults since 1957. Mingus called it "the best record I ever made," and while its release in 1962 did not necessarily prove his point, the album is certainly one of his better efforts, and his agitation had constructive results.

The results of his agitations are not always constructive. Mingus sometimes tries to convey what cannot be expressed by singing, playing bass or piano, or shouting, with his fists or through the mails. He has written an acid series of letters to *Down Beat,* offering, for instance, to punch in the mouth the reviewer who took exception to his blues singing. This destructive side of his nature took over in the summer and fall of 1962, resulting in one debacle after another.

When the Five Spot Café closed that summer, Mingus played the closing night. It was fitting, he said, because he had been the first "name" artist to play in the club. (He had been one of the early ones but not the first.) Afterward, he told reporters, he was going to Ibiza, an island off the coast of Spain, to get away from the New York rat race. He might stay two years; he might never come back. The general press, less familiar with Mingus than the trade papers, dutifully printed the story.

He never went. He remained, he said, because he had received a large advance on his novel from McGraw-Hill. The novel, of course, might have been written in Ibiza, but he also had to record an album on November 15, in a combination concert-record date at New York's Town Hall.

The concert was a shambles. The thirty musicians had not been well prepared; numbers started, stopped, and started again. From the stage, Mingus blamed everyone but himself, and advised the audience to ask for its money back. Later, everyone else blamed Mingus. Somehow, United Artists records managed to salvage enough music for an LP, released in mid-1963.

Not long afterward, he punched his trombonist of long standing, Jimmy Knepper, and knocked out two of his teeth. Knepper was suing, and Mingus turned up at the Village Vanguard, leading a strongly Ellington-influenced orchestra. At the same time there was a remarkable trio LP with Ellington on piano, Mingus and Max Roach. Later, he was in semi-residence at the Five-Spot's new location.

But with all his trouble, with all the accusations and self-justifications, his music still stood. It was impossible to tell what Mingus might be playing next; in his own way, he had gone through nearly everyone else's style of jazz, a few of his own, and was still as unsatisfied as when he had begun. "When I went to a Gauguin retrospective," he once wrote, "I saw a great painter: no painting looked like the other, each was done by a new genius, unimpressed by himself and his previous creation." He might have been speaking of himself.

Whatever else he is, Mingus is one of the great jazz talents. If he has been that talent's worst enemy, perhaps that is the price he pays for having it. He is a fascinating, complex, even tortured human being, and if his personality sometimes is more noticed than the music which results from it, one can only echo the sad, ironic words of Billy Taylor: "He sees to that."

The last time I saw Mingus was in a Greenwich Village bar. The pianist Cecil Taylor was standing at the bar, and Mingus, who was walking across the room, stopped and looked at him. "Haven't I seen you around someplace?" asked Mingus, knowing perfectly well to whom he was talking. Taylor, at least as wary as Mingus, said, "I think so."

Mingus stared at Taylor for long moment, then impulsively threw his arms around him. "I love you, baby," he said.

Selected Discography

Pithecanthropus Erectus, ATLANTIC 1237.
The Clown, ATLANTIC 1260.
Mingus Ah Um, COLUMBIA CL 1370.
Mingus Dynasty, COLUMBIA CL 1440.
Charles Mingus Presents Charles Mingus, CANDID 8005.
Oh Yeah, ATLANTIC 1377.

PAUL DESMOND

"There is also a Scandinavian version of the ever-famous story
which Sir Walter Scott told to Washington Irving, which Monk
Lewis told to Shelley and which, in one form or another, we find
embodied in the folklore of every land—now, Tommy, pay
attention—the story of the traveler who saw within a ruined
abbey, a processon of cats, lowering into a grave a little coffin
with a crown upon it. Filled with horror, he hastened from the
spot; but when he had reached his destination, he could not
forbear relating to a friend the wonder he had seen. Scarcely
had the tale been told when his friend's cat, who lay curled up
tranquilly by the fire, sprang to its feet, cried out, 'Then I am
the King of the Cats!' and disappeared in a flash up the chimney."

"THE KING OF THE CATS"—STEPHEN VINCENT BENÉT

ONE MARCH AFTERNOON in 1955, alto saxophonist Paul Desmond and some friends were sitting in a restaurant in
Chicago when someone saw a headline in the paper: BOP
KING FOUND DEAD IN BARONESS' APARTMENT. The story told
of Charlie Parker's death. Desmond didn't spring to his
feet and cry out "Then I am the King of the Cats!"—it is
doubtful that he springs or cries out under any circumstances. But even that long ago he was probably resigned
to the fact that he was never going to be the King of the
Cats.

"Unfashionable" is a word that crops up frequently in
Desmond's conversation. "I was unfashionable," he says, "before anyone knew who I was." Today, everyone has known
who he is for quite a while. He is the other solo voice of the
Dave Brubeck Quartet, which is the most maligned, and possibly the most affluent, small group in jazz. As such, he is in
an almost unique position. He has been a sideman in the
same group for over ten years, although he could undoubtedly lead his own combo whenever he wished. He is greatly

admired by several musicians, critics, and fans who have far less use for his employer's playing. And he is acutely aware of his situation.

Unlike most jazz musicians, Desmond is an intellectual. As much of his energy as he devotes to his music is consumed in living the gracious, if somewhat lonely, life. The theater, foreign films, ballet, good books, and good food count for much with him, and his friends are likely to be well-known in areas of show business other than his own. A diffidently epigrammatic conversationalist whose acquaintances pass his casual remarks back and forth as if they were suppressed literature, he has all the qualifications for the perfect extra man at a dinner party, and only two essential differences: he doesn't bother with details like pressed pants and shined shoes, and he is an exceptionally gifted musician.

It is a gift that has long been overlooked or taken for granted for several reasons. One of them, Desmond feels, is that "I'm not hostile enough to be currently acceptable." And indeed, in a period characterized by musical anger, his essentially melodic, lyrical talent was as unlikely to find favor as the delicate tone which complements it so well. (Eddie Condon, who is not fashionable either at the moment, said, "He sounds like a female alcoholic," and Miles Davis, who is probably the most fashionable of jazz musicians, has said, "I just don't like the sound of an alto played that way," even though Davis' fans might be shocked at the similarity in the way he and Desmond play the blues.) Also, the Dave Brubeck Quartet has so long been summarily dismissed by most people involved with jazz that very few of them any longer give themselves the opportunity to hear Desmond play. And he is white ("the real underground," in his phrase), which, in his profession, doesn't necessarily help. As successful as he is, he pays dues, which are no less costly for being of a different nature than those of his colleagues.

Desmond was born Paul Emil Breitenfeld on November

25, 1924, in San Francisco. His father was a musician, accompanying vaudeville acts and silent movies. Because of an illness of his mother's, Paul went to live with relatives in New Rochelle, New York. Moderately interested in music, he took the mandatory courses, but nothing more. It was not until 1936, when he was going to high school back in San Francisco, that he began to study with any seriousness. The instrument he chose was the clarinet. "I was a real clarinetnik," he says. "I could play entire Artie Shaw choruses." His teacher was a pit-band associate of his father's, and Desmond found himself being steered toward that kind of music ("I could have been Al Gallodoro"). Except for that and an elementary course in music theory, he never had any formal training, and attributes such knowledge as he has to "looking over the shoulders of piano players."

The shoulder he has looked over for most of his professional life belongs to Dave Brubeck, whom he met in 1943 through a mutual friend, Dave Van Kreidt. Tenor saxophonist Van Kreidt and Desmond had both been in the reed section of an army band stationed in San Francisco ("It was a great way to spend the war"), and one night Van Kreidt's friend Brubeck, also in the army, played a session with them. Desmond, whose conversation is made up of equal parts of Holden Caulfield, Mort Sahl, and James Joyce, is pleased to relate his initial confrontation with Brubeck as follows: "I went up to him and said, 'Man, like Wigsville! You really grooved me with those nutty changes.'" If that were actually what was said, it would be a partial explanation for the fact that the two men didn't meet again for four years.

Later Brubeck was working in a San Francisco club for Darryl Cutler, a tenor saxophonist. Desmond recalled their second meeting for Marian McPartland in *Down Beat:* "I went down and sat in, and the musical rapport was very evident and kind of scary. A lot of things we've done since, we did then, *immediately*—a lot of the counterpoint things, and it really impressed me. If you think Dave plays far out now, you should have heard him then. He made Cecil Taylor sound like Lester Lanin." Shortly afterward, Desmond got a job for a Paul Desmond Trio, and since such a group was nonexistent, he hired away Cutler's bass player, Norman Bates, and his pianist. The difficulties involved were sufficient to make Desmond recoil—as he remarked to Mrs. Mc-Partland, "That's when I decided I really didn't want to be a leader." But he also said, "A lot of the things we did later with the quartet began there . . . that's where the empathy between Dave and me began, and it's survived a remarkable amount of pulling and pushing in the eleven or so years since."

The first strain on that empathy occurred soon afterward, when Desmond was offered a summer resort job and disbanded his trio, leaving Brubeck out of work and in no strong position to re-apply to Cutler. They were reunited in 1949 for the Dave Brubeck Octet. Half the membership of that group—Brubeck, but not Desmond, included—had studied with the composer Darius Milhaud (Desmond has referred to this contingent as the Four Frenchmen), and the music attempted a fusion of jazz and classical techniques. The Octet was able to get only two days' work that year, and so disbanded. One more job playing a wedding accounted for all of Desmond's musical income for a while, and so, when he was offered a job with pianist Jack Fina, who had become so popular playing "concertos" with Freddy Martin's hotel band that he formed his own, Desmond took it. He hoped to get to New York with Fina and then leave, but found to his dismay that most of the musicians he talked to in New York wanted *his* job.

Brubeck, in the meantime, had been leading a trio in Honolulu, and had formed, with the Weiss Brothers, San Francisco plastics manufacturers, Fantasy Records. Largely through the help of disc jockey Jimmy Lyons, Brubeck got himself an engagement at an important San Francisco night-club, The Blackhawk. The group included Desmond.

Desmond says of the fortunes of the group, "It was timing, and luck, and a lot of very careful planning." It is easy to forget, now that Brubeck has become so famous that he can be safely ignored, the very considerable achievements of his quartet. He was, for example, the first leader to discover the financial and sociologically symbolic opportunities of the college circuit. It was probably necessary that someone like Brubeck, who is in many ways the antithesis of the stereotyped jazzman, be the one to establish this as a pattern. It was also Brubeck who first realized the musical and commercial potential of recording these concerts, a practice the quartet has since largely abandoned. "If we record a concert now," Desmond says, "Columbia is out there with two sound trucks, and a vice-president, and stereo. But when we first started recording, the record business was different, and the sound from one little home tape recorder was acceptable." A series of three recordings, made either in concerts or at clubs, provided the first major breakthrough for the quartet, and still, to some, represents the musical highpoint of their achievement.

They were *Jazz at Storyville*, *Jazz at Oberlin*, and *Jazz at College of the Pacific*. On them, the format the group usually uses was employed: an opening solo by Desmond, followed by a Brubeck solo, then Desmond either took the tune out or engaged with Brubeck in the improvised counterpoint which has become one of their trademarks. Then, as now, the main point of interest was in the contrast which the two men provide for one another. Brubeck's approach is essen-tially rhythmic and harmonic; rarely does his solo depend on melody for its impact. Desmond, on the other hand, is one of the supreme creators of original improvised melody. He can create an exquisite melodic line without seeming to try, carrying a long, logical melody of sometimes chilled perfection past the point where other musicians would falter. He is all delicacy and subtlety, endlessly fascinating and intricate. He depends a great deal on facility and a rare sense of how one song is related to another (he loves to quote musically, to interpolate recognizable fragments of other melodies, and he does it with great humor). From the time of his first recordings, he could play anything on his horn that anyone else could, and many things that no one else would even attempt (Brubeck has said that Desmond used to have another octave in range until he explained to someone how he did it and, in figuring out the technique, lost the ability). When one stops to consider that what he plays comes from a relatively unschooled musician it is rather surprising. Not surprising, though, is the answer Desmond gives to questions about his facility: "It's all a fraud."

By 1954, when Brubeck got a Columbia recording contract and his picture on the cover of *Time*, many people were beginning to cry "Fraud!" about the quartet. The situation has since become such that Desmond says, "Most jazz fans wouldn't be caught dead listening to us any more. But we've picked up a whole new audience. Just people."

Ever since the end of 1954, Brubeck and Desmond have been fighting, in various ways, an unending battle against the perils of success. They continue to make albums which continue to sell, and have been involved in various promotional schemes and searches for new material, the latter concerned mainly with the use of unusual rhythms. But though critical interest picked up for a time when Brubeck hired drummer Joe Morello, the jazz writer and the jazz fan are apparently gone forever, a fact that Brubeck, who feels that some of his former close friends are now in the vanguard of the enemy, is particularly bitter about.

Desmond himself has reacted differently at different times to Brubeck's music, but he is most likely to laugh and say, "Ambivalent City. I think he's great on ballads. Maybe I feel that way because I'm a secret German romantic myself. A lot of people have never heard Dave under the right circumstances. If you catch one set at Basin Street East or Newport, you won't really hear what he does." He pauses for a moment, trying to think of a recorded example, shrugs, and goes on. "He's done some wonderful things with polytonality and has a fantastic harmonic sense. You know, he's not as well schooled on the piano as people think. Things he plays, Chopin and Rachmaninoff, he may never have actually played. His mother is a piano teacher, and he probably heard her play them, but he never played them himself.

"We have occasional disagreements, but basically it's been just about an ideal relationship. There's certainly nobody else with whom I would have stuck around all this long. Aside from everything else, Dave can really be fantastic as an accompanist, which is getting to be something of a dying art. He plays behind you in a very self-effacing, intuitive way—sometimes you can even pick the wrongest note imaginable on a certain chord and he'll revoice the chord around it so it sounds beautiful. Not too many guys play this way— usually they just run through the same changes, chorus after chorus, like a hand-organ. Or, worse yet, they wait for you to leave a hole and play some tricky little thing that sounds great for them but hangs up your line of thought. As I said, it's a dying art. And that quality of Dave's alone is really enough to make up for the occasional arguments we get into about tunes, tempos, or whatnot."

Brubeck, on the other hand, has called Desmond "the best saxophone player in the world," and told Marian McPartland, "I've heard him play more than anyone else has, and even after all these years, he still surprises me. There are so many imitators of Charlie Parker, and to me Paul is one of the few true individuals on his instrument. . . . Paul's big contribution is going to be that he didn't copy Charlie Parker."

Over the years, Desmond has evolved into the musical magician, the juggler *par excellence*. The most curious aspect of his playing is a seeming detachment, a disinvolvement that enables him to play as well as he does with his mind, apparently, on something else. This quality translates itself in the minds of some of Desmond's critics into hesitancy and lack of assurance (in the case of a jazz writer of whom he is particularly fond, Desmond solves what might become a personal problem by reading his reviews as little as possible). Rather than hesitancy, the quality seems almost the same one Truman Capote described in the book *Writers at Work:* "My own theory is that the writer should have considered his wit and dried his tears long, long before setting out to invoke similar reactions in a reader. In other words, I believe the greatest intensity in art in all its shapes is achieved with a deliberate, hard and cool head." This approach sometimes works to Desmond's disadvantage. His average solo is a highly ordered, logical melodic flow, and the man playing it sounds and looks as though he might be reading the stock reports at the same time. Before audiences accustomed to having passion signaled for them with physical action, Desmond's best work sometimes goes by unnoticed.

Fans, though, are somewhat less disenchanted than the critics. Starting in 1955, Desmond began to win the *Down Beat* and *Metronome* readers' polls with monotonous regularity (Parker, the King of the Cats, was, according to the rules of these polls, no longer eligible because of his death that year). He also won the *Playboy* poll when it began in 1957, and continued to win them all until 1960, when the heavy odor of funk replaced Desmond with one of the most notable of the soul-brothers, Julian "Cannonball" Adderley. In 1962, however, he again won the *Down Beat* Readers' Poll.

Desmond seems little disturbed by his fluctuating popularity and has one brief, but extremely revealing, remark to make about his total situation: "There are many parallels with the Modern Jazz Quartet."

Aside from such obvious similarities as the use of some classical devices and simultaneous improvisation, the main parallel between the two units is in the personal situations and attitudes of the major soloists.

Desmond has a lucrative percentage deal with Brubeck, and a guaranteed minimum annual wage. And he is disinclined to form his own group because "You could wind up on the road with two junkies and a guy who can't play." But, like Milt Jackson, he makes his own records, although Brubeck was less than happy about it ("I wanted people to know that when you hear Desmond you hear Brubeck, and when you hear Brubeck you hear Desmond," the pianist says), and he has done so, with what seems to him a crushing lack of success.

"Nobody ever found out about them," he says. They usually follow a musical pattern similar to Gerry Mulligan's, as Desmond is quick to point out. "I like to work without piano," he says, "and Dave feels there's less confusion if I don't work with another piano player." He has recorded twice with Mulligan, as one of the countless artists who "met" the baritonist on Verve, and on Desmond's own RCA Victor album. "He met everybody," Desmond says, "but I only met him."

His most musically successful small-group effort under his own name, *Paul Desmond and Friends*, appeared on the Warner Brothers label. He is more satisfied with the music than is usual for him. The rhythm section, interestingly enough, was made up of Percy Heath and Connie Kay from the MJQ, and the other soloist is Jim Hall, whom Desmond calls "the Pablo Casals of the guitar." Hall is as lyrical a musician as Desmond, and an element of contrast, so evident with Brubeck, is missing. And Desmond, even though he is unusually sensitive to what his fellow musicians are playing, relies, as a result of having played for over ten years with one group, on techniques that have their greatest effect with that group, and have become favorites with him. The difference is most noticeable when Desmond, the master of re-entering after another man's solo, does so in his familiar way: it is as if he were replying to a statement which has not been made.

On *You Go To My Head* Desmond evidently decided that he had to be more than a contrasting element, and that, in this case, the passion and involvement would have to come from him. Midway in this solo, the best on the record, the hesitancy is gone, and there is a dominant, assured voice, which shows that Desmond might be capable of leading an excellent jazz group—if he chose to.

Whether or not he ever will is an open question. Brubeck has become increasingly more involved with composition, and wishes to perform less frequently. The problem, Desmond feels, is one of having men with whom he can get along personally as well as musically, and it is because he has that sort of rapport with Brubeck that he has remained so long and is so reluctant to leave. "Eventually," he says, "it will probably have to happen, if only because of the way Dave's career goes."

"He stays," Brubeck says, "because he can't find as much creative freedom anywhere else. If he ever does, he *should* leave." Desmond has any kind of freedom in the quartet, creative or otherwise, that he is willing to take; when he does not get what he wants, it is invariably because he has chosen to walk away rather than fight. Joe Benjamin, who was the group's bassist for a time, recalls a pertinent incident: "When he wants to, Paul can play so much more than he does. One night, we were playing an average set, and Joe Morello and I really got something going together. When it came time for Paul's solo, I started to dig in harder. Paul felt it—he looked over at me—and then he started to *play*.

For chorus after chorus. I think Dave was a little troubled, he didn't expect it. But that doesn't happen very often. I wish it did, though, because Paul's one of the loveliest guys in the world."

Desmond himself says, "It might sound arrogant, but I'm never satisfied with my playing, partly because of some technical things I've never mastered. I don't feel I've played up to my potential capacity." Another reason might be the personal and musical tensions that exist in the Dave Brubeck Quartet. Since Brubeck hired Morello in 1956, the group has undergone a significant change, one that greatly pleases Brubeck. "The character of the group changed when Joe Morello became our drummer," he says. "Before that, I'd never had a rhythm section that allowed me to do what I wanted. Morello is the best drummer in the world for rhythms." Originally, Brubeck had been the star of his own group, but by 1956, most astute listeners were in Desmond's camp. Then, with the arrival of Morello, Brubeck began the rhythmic experiments with the out-of-the-way time signatures and meters he is so fond of. Morello is a flashy, crowd-pleasing drummer, and he began to dominate the situation, particularly before the musically naïve audiences Brubeck often plays to, to the extent that many might think they were watching the Joe Morello Quartet. Desmond's personal diffidence in such matters sometimes manifests itself as musical diffidence; much of the harsh excitement that was present on the old recordings is gone. He stands apart from his associates at a concert, both literally and figuratively: they seem part of a friendly gathering from which he has excluded himself. Crowds cheer Morello's stickwork and Brubeck's rhythmic pounding; some of Desmond's most intricate lines get only token appreciation. If he does not always do his best work, there is ample reason.

A typical incident occurred one day in New Jersey, when the quartet played late afternoon and evening concerts at a summer theater. Morello and Wright were nearly always talking together; Brubeck was taking care of several different details; Desmond was alone. At the end of his final solo of the first concert, he capped his mouthpiece and was out the door before the piece was finished. When Brubeck, having patiently signed autographs afterward, walked into the town's best restaurant, Desmond had nearly finished eating. During the second concert, while Morello was in the midst of a ten-minute drum solo on Desmond's piece *Take Five*, then high on the popularity charts, the composer was seated backstage, reading a paperback collection of Dostoevsky short stories. "It was supposed to be a drum solo," he remarked wearily, "but it wasn't supposed to be a hit record."

These might sound like the actions of a man who is doing exactly what he is paid to do and no more, but after the concert, Brubeck advanced another theory. "Paul was fighting to say something all night," he said, "but in that one place, when Joe started that conga rhythm, he let it stop him. Every once in a while, though, when he gets stopped, he gets mad, and sort of says, 'I'm Paul Desmond, and the hell with you.' That's when he plays best. He's achieved so much, even if he'd never done anything but not play like Parker, but he's capable of so much more. He could be a composer, he could be a lyricist, he could be a writer, but he doesn't seem to have the ambition." Part of Morello's value, Brubeck feels, is that he may someday goad Desmond into realizing his potential.

Desmond did begin to show signs of more activity on his own. When A&R man George Avakian joined RCA Victor, he signed Desmond to a contract calling for two albums a year—three if he should leave Brubeck. The first release, with attendant publicity unlike any the saxophonist has received before, was *Desmond Blue*—a quartet featuring Jim Hall played over a string section conducted and arranged by Bob Prince. The set also contains a lovely Desmond composition,

Late Lament. After so many years, both Desmond and Milt Jackson, with Riverside, signed recording contracts with companies other than the ones to which the Brubeck quartet and the MJQ are committed.

Desmond professes unconcern with the final results of his albums, saying, "There is a hard core of three hundred and twenty-four people who will buy any album I put out, and maybe they'll like it," but unconcern is his standard pose. He is resigned to being unfashionable, and seems not to care. At the same time, he has given up other things that once interested him deeply. He is an excellent amateur photographer; at one time Desmond and his camera were inseparable, and he used to amuse himself at jazz festivals by taking pictures of the people who were taking pictures of *him.* But he has given that up. "It happens," he says. "You see a guy, and he always has a camera around his neck, and then one day he just shows up without the camera." At one time, he wanted to be a writer—that was his major when he attended San Francisco State College—but that, too, has apparently gone by the boards. "You can't say I gave that up, because I never started it." His standard reason for not pursuing a literary career, which his conversation and letters indicate might have been a considerable one, is: "I could only write at the beach, and I kept getting sand in my typewriter." His only professed ambition is to make a record on which he would play successive choruses like Johnny Hodges, Charlie Parker, Cannonball Adderley, and Ornette Coleman.

So perhaps Desmond will continue to be the "illustrious sideman," as he puts it sardonically, living the urbane bachelor's life that suits him so well, keeping a distance between himself and whatever he might actually feel about his musical and personal situations, and making the music that comes so easily to him. "I will become the Mantovani of 55th Street," he says. "I will make a series of lush string albums and retire into fashionable obscurity." Taking a cue from

Charlie Mingus' phrase "rotary perception," he calls his music "Kiwanis Perception." But perhaps he only says that because, as he wrote in the notes for his first Fantasy album, "the uncrafty approach doesn't always get it these days."

Selected Discography

Dave Brubeck: Jazz at Storyville, FANTASY 3240.
Dave Brubeck: Jazz at Oberlin, FANTASY 3245.
Dave Brubeck: Jazz at College of Pacific, FANTASY 3223.
Paul Desmond and Friends, WARNER BROTHERS 1356.
Desmond Blue, RCA VICTOR LPM-2438.

RAY CHARLES

Nesuhi Ertegun, the Atlantic Records executive who supervised some of Ray Charles' most successful recordings, has said that "he who is a jazz instrumentalist, if he has any voice at all, is *ipso facto* a jazz singer." That comment notwithstanding, it is hard to escape the suspicion that no one knows what jazz singing is. No one has come any closer to a definition than a list of names—Bessie Smith, of course, and Billie Holiday, and Louis Armstrong (if he isn't singing jazz, then what is he doing up there?). And, despite her own protestations, Mahalia Jackson. There are others who are, apparently, jazz singers at some times and not at others —Sarah Vaughan, Billy Eckstine, Dinah Washington, and Ella Fitzgerald—and this seems to be more a matter of material and accompaniment than of the singing itself. Then there is Frank Sinatra, who has even been called a "semi-jazz" singer. If we follow a standard vocabulary, that might place Sinatra in the same general category as the derivative Australian Jazz Quintet or the *Rhapsody in Blue,* which doesn't seem to be right.

While attempting no definition, it might be good to set down a few basics which are so simple as to be often overlooked. There has always been disagreement over the balance between the creative and the interpretive in jazz instrumental music. But the singer, by the nature of what he does, is forced to be more interpreter and less creator than any other musician. He is singing words; he is interpreting another person's story.

Take, for example, a very good melody with a fairly banal lyric:

> Was I gay, till today?
> Now she's gone and we're through,
> Am I blue?

That is stated simply enough, and is a common enough situation, except for the word "today." If one reacts to the lyric when sung by an average singer, it is on the lowest level of appreciation—recognition of a common experience. But in the hands of a Ray Charles, the lyric takes on all the painful immediacy implied by the word "today," and one is wounded for the singer and himself.

Since most popular song lyrics are on that level, it becomes the task of a singer to bring a poignant personal involvement to an otherwise banal situation, and not too many are up to it. It is, originally, a problem in interpretation—it is the lyricist's story, but the singer must make it his own, and by doing so, make it the story of the audience.

There are many names for the quality possessed by the singers who can do this. Some of them—Billie Holiday and Ray Charles—are jazz singers; others—Judy Garland and Mabel Mercer—are not. But they all share in common an individual identity; a soul, if you wish; a personality, certainly; the ability to rise above material; or even an artistry that allows an emotion to pass from the depths of the singer's heart to the depths of his listeners'. Singers such as Charles and Miss Mercer, who have that as their prime vocal ability, prove that it is worth everything else in the book. All else—technique, vocal quality, swing, and the jazz feel—is incidental. And this quality cannot be learned or faked.

Perhaps this is only to say that the singers mentioned are sufficiently talented to refract banal emotions (for Ray Charles and Miss Holiday, through an ever-present reservoir of pain), and make those emotions come out bigger and more meaningful. In such cases, you get what the song means to the singer, not what it meant to the man who wrote it. As Ray Charles has said, "I sing the songs for what they mean to me."

Apparently, the songs mean the same thing to a significant number of Charles' contemporaries. He is simultaneously considered to be the best of the rock-and-roll singers, the best of the jazz singers (he has won the *Down Beat* International Critics' Poll in that category more than once), and one of the best pop singers, perhaps second only to Sinatra (his single records and albums consistently top the popularity charts). The high regard in which his singing is held has tended to obscure rather considerable accomplishments as a blues pianist, bandleader, composer, and arranger.

How Charles has achieved his present position is one of the most fascinating stories of recent show-business history. The operative word is "soul," a euphemism for the music of the Negro church, which was, by the late fifties, the most pervasive influence in contemporary American popular music. Besides being the basic informing influence in rhythm and blues (and hence rock-and-roll), the music of the Sanctified Churches also made its presence felt in the country and western field. Since these two strains account for all of our general popular style that the theater does not, we find hit tunes strongly tinged with this music have been recorded by people as far from the tradition as Eydie Gormé. At the same time, jazz has rediscovered an *overt* use of Negro church material, an uncompromising blues singer like "Lightnin'" Hopkins becomes a national figure, and we see the rise to enormous popularity of Ray Charles, a performer who might otherwise have remained firmly categorized as a rhythm and blues artist, and whose own music, lowered to a tasteless common denominator, has dominated the Twist.

Charles' popularity is explained by his long-time friend, arranger Quincy Jones, far more succinctly: "He gets everything inside of him out." And it is true that Charles displays open, unselfconscious emotionalism, probably more so than any major jazz singer. But as many people are repelled by that kind of naked emotion as are attracted to it. I have seen people suddenly become nervous, restless as Charles' raw shouts of pain filled a room, literally embarrassed by a kind of emotional honesty which they themselves are probably never able to summon up.

Such is not the case, however, when Ray Charles works the Apollo, in Harlem. One of his shows there is likely to take on all the aspects of a combination revival meeting and breakfast dance, with shouts, choral response, and dancing in the aisles. The most astonishing thing about Ray Charles is that, on his own terms, he was able to capture a much wider audience than the Apollo regulars; some feel that the most saddening thing is that he altered those terms as soon as he had captured that audience.

Charles, though, has lost few of his old fans, and picks up new ones by the carload in whatever new musical area he attempts. This, in spite of the fact that, apart from his music, Ray Charles does not have what is commonly thought of as "star quality." Blind and highly nervous, he can be a disconcerting performer to watch. His valet brings him out onto the stage (when possible, he is already seated at the piano at curtain rise), and he walks with a side-to-side jerky movement suggestive of a nightclub comic imitating a robot. While he plays, his knees execute a quick scissoring movement. He is likely to scratch himself. If one looks, as many do, for an added emotional charge from being in The Presence, one is likely to be disappointed. Some of his fans actually prefer not to see him in person, and confine their pleasure to the recordings.

Constantly, one hears of or is present at incidents which reflect that Charles is doing nothing to abet one of the finest natural talents of our time. One example was his 1961 three-day engagement at Small's Paradise in Harlem. Since Charles has no New York Police Department so-called cabaret card, he is unable to work in New York night clubs, although any of them would be delighted to have him. However, a cabaret card is not necessary for a booking of up to three days, and for three days Small's became a Mecca for Charles fans who had never heard him in such circumstances. He was also, for the first time, employing a nineteen-piece band playing Quincy Jones arrangements. Crowds overflowed onto the street, and such jazz luminaries as Jimmy Rushing and Erroll Garner had trouble getting in, even though they had reservations. "There was no presentation at all," Jones says. "The lighting was bad, the mikes were set up so that you couldn't hear him sing in front of the band, it was a mess. If he knew as much about presentation as Nat Cole or guys who don't have one quarter of his talent, he'd be the greatest thing in the business."

There was also a concert Charles gave at the Brooklyn Academy of Music. Scheduled to begin at eight-thirty, it started about forty-five minutes late. When the curtain finally rose, the Ray Charles band was there, with one of the saxophonists in the piano chair. The band played several instrumentals while its members looked nervously off-stage, as if wondering whether or not their leader would appear. He did, finally, and led the band in two more instrumentals, as if he were unaware that any music had preceded his arrival. Then he began to sing, masterfully, and the effect was hypnotic. He sang some of the rawest blues that had ever been heard in the Academy, he sang his hit record of the moment, *Georgia On My Mind,* and he wound up the first part with his crowd-pleaser, *What'd I Say.* He was a superb musician and a gracious master of ceremonies, and completely captivated the audience.

After the interval, the band played more instrumentals, and Charles again returned. In contrast to his former manner, he seemed truculent and depressed. He announced his first number, *Hallelujah I Love Her So,* by saying, "You've heard this next piece sung by such great *showmen* as Harry Belafonte and Sammy Davis, Jr.; now we'd like to give you the original version." At the conclusion, he said, "I hope you don't mind if I repeat myself," and proceeded to sing *Georgia* again. That segued without stop into the evening's second performance of *What'd I Say,* after which he got up and walked offstage. The audience, which had been in Charles' pocket for the first half, made not even a token attempt to get him to return. They seemed to sense it would do no good. And the entire concert had lasted less than an hour and a half.

In one form or another, this incident has often been repeated when Charles has played. He had been four hours late for a concert; he had not shown up at all. And this from the man who says, "I want to be a good entertainer."

But by that he obviously does not mean punctual arrivals, nor attractive band uniforms, nor psychologically apt lighting. Duke Ellington once answered, when questioned by an overly analytical critic: "Look," pointing to his band, "what you see there is just sixteen men earning their living." Ray Charles, too, is just earning his living, and a handsome living it is, in spite of occasional impositions on the goodwill of his audiences. And though some of his fans and critics feel that he has compromised, he does not feel he has.

No one ever had less opportunity for success. Reports on his early years vary. As Ahmet Ertegun, who supervised many of Charles' first sessions, says, "He has three or four homes. Baltimore claims him, Seattle claims him, Georgia claims him and Florida claims him." According to Leonard Feather's *Encyclopedia of Jazz,* Charles was born in Albany, Georgia, on September 23, 1932. At the age of six, living in Greenville, Florida, he went blind. He is uncertain about the actual cause. "Whatever I had," he has said, "couldn't be cured. It didn't make a hell of an impression on me. I don't remember much about it because I don't want to remember much. It's not the kind of thing you keep turning over in your mind."

He was enrolled in a state school for the blind at St. Augustine, Florida, where he first began to study piano by Braille.

By the time he was seventeen, both his parents were dead.

and Ray was a thoroughly accedited professional, playing with everything from rhythm-and-blues groups to hillbilly bands. Of the latter experience, he says, "I wouldn't say it was the music I like most to play, but there were some very good musicians in those bands." He played both piano and alto, and in 1948, wound up in Seattle, Washington, with a trio.

It was in Seattle that he met Quincy Jones, whose comment on Charles, in the light of Charles's past circumstances, is startling: "Ray never had to pay any dues. He was always working, I never knew him when he was without a job. He was sixteen and I was fifteen, but he always seemed five or six years older, even then. Whenever he was at a session, it went well. He'd be sitting at the piano, playing those hip blues and boppish things, even then."

The group Charles had at the time was called the Maxim Trio. Of that period, he has said, "I used to sing like Charles Brown and King Cole because they were making money. I wanted to make money, too. So I tried to copy them." And earlier, in Florida, he was in another group that "could play everything Louis Jordan played and sound just like him. He was doing well, and we thought if we imitated him, we'd make money." He has refuted the press-agent-inspired rumors that he was a member of the famous Five Blind Boys gospel group. "If you love something, it's bound to run off on you. But I never sang in any church choir or anything. My first singing was in a rhythm and blues kind of thing. No, I didn't have too much time for choirs and things; I was too busy trying to make two dollars 'round about then."

The next few years were spent trying to make two dollars, and he was fairly successful locally. He worked with such bands as Lowell Fulsom and Bumps Blackwell, and made a record for a small California label, Swingtime, called *Baby Let Me Hold Your Hand*. In the limited field of rhythm-and-blues it was a hit, and one of those who heard it was Ahmet Ertegun.

"I don't buy very many records," Ertegun says, "but when I heard that one, I flipped. We bought his contract from Swingtime, for two or three thousand dollars, I think, and it was no trouble at all. Ray was getting to be known, but just in the rhythm-and-blues field, and Swingtime was a very small company. That was in 1952.

"Naturally, what we wanted was a hit. Ray wanted one, too—every artist does. It's very hard getting work in the rhythm-and-blues field. At that time, he played piano for a while in Joe Morris' band. It was a rhythm-and-blues band, but it was a great one.

"Ray and I started to make records. I've never met a musician with such strong and stubborn ideas about what he wants. He wanted to record with his own band and his own arrangements. But I also had very strong ideas about what constitutes a good blues record, and I'll admit that in the beginning, I imposed my ideas on him. He was willing to do anything I suggested, because he wanted a hit. I had good blues arrangers, like Jesse Stone, and we gave Ray songs to do like Charles Brown had done, and Amos Milburn. Ray was very fond of Charles Brown, and so was I.

"I used to play records for him," Ertegun continues. "One day we sat in the studio all day playing Jimmy Yancey records. And I wrote some of those tunes. Things like *Heartbreaker* and *Messaround*. I played Cow Cow Davenport records for him, and *Messaround* is just the bass to *Cow Cow Blues*. We got some very good blues records that way, like *Losing Hand*.

"But Ray still kept saying that he wanted to record *his* way. He told me about songs his uncle used to sing. I asked him if he remembered any of those songs. He said yes, so we tried it. That session had *A Fool For You* and *Hallelujah I Love Her So*, and from then on, Ray was made. But maybe I'm overdramatizing."

If one compares those early records, it becomes apparent that Ertegun was not overdramatizing at all. For what

Charles had worked out, on those early records, whether consciously or not, was a fusion of styles that would make him one of the most popular entertainers in the world. Nesuhi Ertegun, Ahmet's brother and partner, cautions, however, that "Ray was not the first to do this, combine gospel and blues. He is the best of a long tradition, but there were people singing this way twenty years ago. But Ray was able to bring so much of his own to it."

Blues singer Big Bill Broonzy once made an accurate, though disapproving, estimate of Charles' method: "He's got the blues he's cryin' sanctified. He's mixin' the blues with the spirituals. I know that's wrong. . . . He should be singin' in a church." Although he never sang in church, Charles attended, as does everyone in a southern town. "Everyone in a small town went to church," he said in *Ebony*, "and I mean you had to go, too. Sunday school in the morning, then regular services, home for dinner and back for BYPU. Then there were evening services, and you'd get home about ten at night." Dominant conventions in Charles' music are those of the gospel song, and his performances are replete with choral effects, call-and-response patterns, piano triplet figures and the 6/8 time that gospel singers made swing long before the advent of the "new" jazz waltz.

Broonzy criticized him for it. But an artist should be free to employ any vocabulary or set of conventions available to him in order to make his statement, and perhaps the personality of the artist is made most clear when it operates through such a set of conventions.

When Charles speaks about his work, as he did in *Ebony*, he speaks as an "entertainer": "The things I write and sing about concern the general Joe and his general problems. There are about four basic things: love, somebody running his mouth too much, having fun, and jobs are hard to get. You know, the general Joe's problems are the problems of everyone. He fools around, falls in love, would give the woman his right arm, then she leaves him but he loves her just the same. Or, a guy works hard, brings the old lady all his money, and she's out all day while he's gone, double-timing him. There are things like people talking, trying to break us up . . . songs that make sense—that mean something. Seeing people or not seeing them, life is still life. The same match that burns you burns me. When I put myself in the place of the guy, the general Joe I'm singing about, I want to feel that his problem is real. So I sing with all the feeling I can put into it, so that I can feel it myself. I sing the songs for what they mean to me."

The great early Charles records were based on blues and gospel forms. The lyrics were concise, full of sharp psychological truth, and, for the most part, conspicuously lacking in the self-pity that is the stock-in-trade of most popular songs. Perhaps the most deeply moving are the sad, chantlike, gospel-derived songs of unrequited love: *A Fool For You, What Would I Do Without You?, It's Allright,* and *Drown In My Own Tears.* There are examples of popular material being transmuted into infectious gospels: *My Bonnie, Yes, Indeed!,* and the small satiric masterpiece, *Swanee River Rock.* One also finds the uptempo, rocking, happy gospel-derived songs like *Talkin' 'Bout You, Hallelujah I Love Her So, I Got a Woman, This Little Girl Of Mine,* and a few splendid contemporizations of such material as *I Want A Little Girl.* Such performances, initially released as single records on Atlantic, constitute the nucleus of Charles' achievement.

"Those sessions," Ahmet Ertegun says, "were recorded everywhere—Florida, Atlanta—we had to record Ray on the fly; he was always working, and seldom in New York. I remember once we recorded in New Orleans. He has a fantastic memory; he knew where all the best Negro hotels were. He was running so fast down the street I could hardly keep up with him." Nesuhi Ertegun feels that there was a decided advantage in this method of recording. "On his own arrangements, he had a chance to work them out on the road. It was almost like Ellington. He'd play a number for two or three months, changing things, and when he felt he had it at just that point, he'd record. This is in contrast to most singers, who see a piece of music for the first time in the studio."

Since much of Charles' impact depends on direct communication with his audience, we are fortunate that Atlantic has also recorded two in-person appearances, *Ray Charles at Newport* and *Ray Charles in Person*.

In the presence of an audience, the vocals take on a different cast than in the studio. On the Newport album, *I Got A Woman* has the addition of a mournful, chantlike introduction in startling contrast to the body of the piece and a seemingly endless tag that includes everything from wordless shouting to an "entertainer's" gimmick like "I got a woman right here in Newport." The Newport set also contains Ray Charles' masterpiece, the in-person performance of *A Fool For You*. A slow, agonizing recital of pain, with a powerful cumulative effect achieved by Charles' seemingly uncalculated repetition of the word "Yeah" over an apt, organlike arrangement, it ends with a hair-raising cry of anguish that is the emotional equal of anything that has ever been recorded. It is not a performance to hear when one is morose.

The *In Person* set was recorded May 28, 1959, in Atlanta, Georgia, when Charles appeared at Herndon Stadium there as part of a rhythm-and-blues package show. It is the most natural setting in which he has been recorded, and proves that Charles is what he intends to be, a popular entertainer. He teases the audience with sex; encourages them to participate in call-and-response; plays *Frenesi* for them as a cha-cha; offers the kind of rhythm that encourages the gallery to clap hands, stamp feet, shout, and dance in the aisles; makes gracious announcements; bandies words with the Raylettes, his vocal group of young girls; takes the next-to-closing spot with an overt tear-jerker; and finishes out with a stomping finale in which he finally enters as soloist, whooping and shrieking, with every stop out, for a shattering finale that makes one afraid of what he might be able to do to the emotions of the wrong audience. But at the same time, to the segment of his audience that is attuned to the essence of his personality, he offers an emotional experience of a depth that negates some of the obvious methods by which that experience is achieved.

Atlantic also began to release instrumental sets. Even though Charles is capable of accurate self-appraisal ("Four pianists influenced me most when I was a kid learning how to play the piano: Art Tatum, Bud Powell, King Cole, and Oscar Peterson"), he was reluctant, according to Ahmet Ertegun, to make straight jazz instrumental recordings, although they have, in the main, been quite successful. The first, *The Great Ray Charles*, revealed that he is a fine blues pianist with an excellent small band. This band, the favorite of Art Blakey, among others, plays in the same general "soul" category as Blakey or Horace Silver, but leans more to overt use of gospel forms. His touching piano solo, *Sweet Sixteen Bars*, is simply an instrumental version of *A Fool For You*. As Charles told Gary Kramer, "All music is related. Gospel music background is important to a jazz musician for it draws out feeling. What you speak of as *soul* in jazz is *soul* in gospel music. The important thing in jazz is to feel your music, but *really* feel it and believe it—the way a gospel singer like Mahalia Jackson obviously feels and believes the music she is singing, with her whole body and soul. And if you feel and believe in your music, that conviction carries over to the public. You can create a very strong emotional bond between yourself and your listener that way." These again are the words of an entertainer. Apparently everyone thinks Charles is an artist but Charles himself.

By this time, he had a considerable reputation among the cognoscenti, and Peggy Lee was paying him the ultimate compliment of singing his songs and telling audiences, "If you think I sound like Ray Charles, that's because I'm trying to." And Nesuhi Ertegun reports that "Jazz musicians were the first to hear about him. Five and six years ago, people like Miles and Dizzy would always ask about him, did he have a new record coming out, and where was he playing. I don't know if they bought those records, but they knew every note by heart, and could play all the riffs." But at that time, if one called a jazz disc jockey like Symphony Sid to request a Charles record, the answer would be, "We don't play rock-and-roll." What freed Charles from such pigeon-holing was the release of his Atlantic recording, *The Genius of Ray Charles.*

"Everybody knew right away," Ahmet Ertegun says. "Sometimes you can listen to a record years later and say, 'that didn't sound so bad,' but two hours after the session, the musicians were still sitting in the studio listening to the playbacks over and over. And they weren't just average musicians, they were the best. The album will last forever."

Even this is not a record executive's exaggeration. The musicians on one of the two sessions in the album included top men from the Ellington and Basie bands—such men as Clark Terry, Joe Newman, Frank Wess, Freddie Greene, Quentin Jackson, Al Gray, plus other jazzmen like Zoot Sims and Charlie Persip. The other session, arranged by Ralph Burns, featured strings and a vocal chorus.

The three triumphs of the set are on the side with strings. *Don't Let the Sun Catch You Cryin'* is an old Louis Jordan specialty. *Am I Blue* is almost unbearably poignant, reminiscent of other examples of deep sensibility transcending limited vocal equipment such as Walter Huston's *September Song* or Adolph Green's *A Quiet Girl.* And on the final track, *Come Rain Or Come Shine* (supposedly one of Charles' favorites), he justifies Harold Arlen's incessant flirtation with the blues by turning the song into a magnificent blues performance. "Ray is really as much responsible for those arrangements as Ralph Burns," says Nesuhi Ertegun. "You can be sure that anything he does is ninety per cent his own idea. The three of us sat down for hours, and Ray would practically dictate. 'In the third bar, I'd like the low strings to play this figure,' he'd say. It was really a collaboration. He's a fantastic, complete musician."

Whether or not the strings were apt, whether or not the Erteguns had to convince Charles to make such a record, it was a certainty that a jazz singer of great depth and importance had finally arrived. Even Symphony Sid made a shift of position and began calling Charles "Mr. Soul."

And then, the inevitable machinery began to roll. There is a law operating in the record business that goes, roughly, like this: A performer starts out on an "independent" label. He achieves success, and leaves his old company for a "major" label. The idea men who work for his new company—using some such phrase as, "Now then, my thinking on this . . ."—decide that whatever the performer does that induced them to sign him is the sort of thing he must stop if he is to achieve popularity. They are paid to know what the public wants, and the performer only knows what he feels a need to perform. So a new style, in which the performer quite likely feels uncomfortable, is adopted, and the only question that remains is whether the new fans thus acquired will outnumber the old ones who will turn away in disappointment.

Just how and why Charles left Atlantic in the summer of 1960 is not fully known. His road manager, Jeff Brown, has power of attorney, because of Ray's inability to read contracts, and some have said that the move was made without Ray's knowledge, but that seems doubtful. One Atlantic official said, "We always had the best kind of relationship with Ray, and let him do whatever he wanted. When time came to sign again, we thought it would be a matter of course, because we would have met any of his demands. We were very surprised when we got a phone call from an ABC executive telling us Ray had signed."

As Charles once told an interviewer, "This success thing is very simple: if all artists would do just the things that are really right for them, they would stay up there a lot longer."

Whether or not the things Ray has done since he signed a lucrative contract with ABC-Paramount have been musically right for him is a matter of opinion. One man who was involved in several of Charles' records says, "Don't they understand he doesn't *need* an A & R man? It's just a matter of understanding Ray, of understanding his soul." And Nesuhi Ertegun says, "I'm very sorry that Ray's not writing now, or at least he doesn't seem to be. He's as great a composer as anybody. And for me, the great Ray Charles records are the ones where he sings his own tunes. *Hallelujah, A Fool For You*—that's my favorite—and the rest. Singing standards is only one small part of what he does."

And whatever needs to be said about the ABC releases, about the gimmick programming (an album of place name songs; two miraculously successful country-and-western sets; one with girls' names in the titles; a collection of duets with Betty Carter; an album on which he plays organ) or about the inapposite arrangements, there can seldom be a quarrel with Ray Charles himself. If he has compromised in matters of material and arrangement, there has been no compromise in what he himself contributes to a performance.

Jazz musicians speak of a quality called "the cry," a quality that echoes the blues no matter what is being played. The cry of blues permeates every Charles performance. By contrast, he sometimes scores most effectively on the most unlikely songs; his hoarse, harsh voice comes cutting through like a razor through cotton batting.

There are two ways to approach a performance. Either the performer conforms to the obvious implications of his material, or else he reshapes the material to fit his own personal style. Since Charles is generally doing the latter while the band is doing the former, he stands out, in most places, like a diamond on a dungheap. He often uses his voice as a horn. He takes chances, perhaps because he is a showman; sudden whoops and falsetto passages. And as Frank Sinatra will alter lyrics slightly to allow for his own hipsterisms, Charles constantly interpolates the standard phrases of the blues shouter or gospel singer, no matter what the context: "I say moon over Miami"; "I'm talking 'bout, deed I do." Some tunes cannot be salvaged by any means; others become outrageous put-ons. The one noticeable change is in his ballad style, since it was first revealed on the *Genius* album. He has refined it, until he sometimes sounds like a male counterpart of Billie Holiday, but some practices which once seemed the result of honest emotion now seem the effects of a master showman.

One thing, though, has not changed: he still plays piano on recordings, no matter what the instrumental setup. "Listen," Quincy Jones told Nat Hentoff apropos the *Genius* set, "to how his piano holds the band together. In his own rather subtle way, he's just as moving a force as the orchestra. When he plays, he sets the tempo and establishes the groove right away. Without him on piano, the results wouldn't have been as good." The piano he plays is still the funky, down-home variety. He is always seated at it whether it is a concert grand or the small electric one he travels with to avoid the out-of tune pianos on the road. (Its unusual sound can be heard on *Ray Charles in Person.*) While his visual "act" might be better if he stood down front, he remains basically a musician-singer, the spiritual brother of everyone who plays the piano and sings the blues in all the small local clubs around the country, and he sits close to, even within, his orchestra.

He has little patience with those who think he has compromised. "I want to get one thing straight," he says. "Nobody tells me what to record. They might suggest, and say, 'Ray, what do you think of this?' but the final decision is mine. Musicians," he adds, pointedly, "don't buy many records." When told that he has successfully avoided all attempts to categorize him, he replies, "I consider that a compliment. I don't want to be branded. I don't want the rhythm-and-blues brand, or the pop brand, or any other. That's why I try all these different things."

Financially, at least, his judgment has been superb. Charles is undoubtedly at the top of the entertainment world. He owns a Cessna plane and a Cadillac; he has a ranch house with swimming pool in Los Angeles, where he lives with his wife Della, a former gospel singer, and two small sons, Ray, Jr. and David James. He is understandably reticent about speaking of his private life. As he said in *Ebony*, "I hope you don't misunderstand me, but my family life is one thing I don't talk about. I figure an entertainer may be public, but at least his family life should be private. Just say that I'm an extremely happily married man and proud of it."

Successful as he is, he cannot escape the great leveller of the entertainment world, the backstage dressing room. The one he uses at the Apollo Theatre, where an interviewer may, after complex negotiations, spend twenty minutes with him, is as drab as any other. A tape recorder was in one corner. A large part of his record collection, which consists mostly of gospel and hillbilly records, has been transferred onto tapes for the machine. His valet and a few other members of the Charles inner circle lounged in chairs, looking like stock players in a Negro gangster film.

Ray Charles sat at a card table in the center of the room, a tall, handsome man in sportshirt and slacks, eyes hidden behind dark glasses, playing dominoes by feel. "The things in magazines are true, if they wrote what I told them," he said. "So why don't you ask your own questions?"

As he talked, he moved, jerky and restless, around the

room, and now and then someone would move a chair out of his way. Once he sat down and leaned back, resting on the chair's two rear legs, and for a moment everyone in the room tensed, fearing that he would fall.

"I told you about that chair, Ray," someone said.

"Oh yeah, I forgot," he laughed, and righted himself.

The phone in the dressing room rang, and someone picked it up. "It's Mrs. Charles."

Answering, he sounded like a Ray Charles song. "Hello, Mama, do you still love your man?" And after the conversation, putting the phone unerringly back on the hook, he resumed, "Now, where were we? I have a bad memory. I'm not proud of it. I have to write everything down."

It has been said that he is suspicious and hostile toward whites, but none of that attitude is revealed in an interview, unless the frank, open attitude is a mask. He has a keen, inquiring mind, a wide grasp of current affairs, and a quick booming laugh. He is deprecatory and almost religious about his talent: "I've been blessed."

About his having a big band, "I've always wanted to do it. I know a lot of good men have tried it and failed, but I'm stubborn."

Then he talked about his inability to work in New York. "I guess you've heard, I've had some trouble with the police." (In Philadelphia once, narcotics charges were dismissed when he told the judge he believed he was getting anti-flu shots.) "All they have to do is *say* you've done something."

Knowing that some of the top New York clubs are waiting to hire him whenever he can work for them, one wondered why he had not tried to fight the vicious cabaret card practice. "He doesn't need the card, he can work anywhere else," Ahmet Ertegun says. And Charles says, "Some guys were talking to me about fighting it, and I thought maybe I would, but I decided against it. I heard that Sinatra was going to work the Copa without a card. What's he going to do if they arrest him, sue them? They're just doing their job. One week after he goes in there, he'll be just another cat who got arrested."

And about his several careers, "I know not everybody likes everything I do. Some like one thing, and some another. But I try to please everybody, while doing what I want. I'm an entertainer."

Then it was time for him to go back onstage. He stood up, walked with me to the door, and extended his hand in a firm grip. "I'm sorry I don't have more time," he said, "but I surely hope I was able to help you." And then he returned to the business of being Ray Charles.

On November 14, 1961, the Associated Press wire service carried a story from Indianapolis: "Ray Charles, one of the country's top jazz recording singers and pianists, was arrested on a narcotics charge in his downtown hotel room today. Detective Sgts. William Owen and Robert Keithby reported heroin and marijuana were seized, along with a hypodermic needle, eyedropper, and other equipment. Charles was taken to police headquarters for questioning. Sgt. Owen said Charles, who gave his age as 31, said he had been a drug addict since the age of 16. He called Charles needle-pricked arm 'one of the worst I've ever seen.' The blind Negro singer said he and his troupe of 20 appeared in Anderson, Ind., last night and have a date in Evansville, Ind. tonight."

Charles was indicted on two counts of possession; a third charge, that of common user, had been dropped. One wondered how the Indianapolis police had found him so unerringly when he had spent only one night in their city. In February 1962, in a surprising move, the Indiana judge, learning that the police had gained admission to Charles' hotel room by announcing themselves as Western Union messengers, dismissed the case on the basis of the manner in which the evidence was acquired.

About Charles' missed dates, lack of attention to detail,

search for big money, and his apparent waste of an enormous natural talent—one close friend says, "You just can't talk to him about that. He doesn't give a damn."

But others do, among them Nat Hentoff, who wrote a stinging article on the subject. Some of the quotes he gathered make a jagged mosaic of Charles' personal situation. From George Pitts in the *Pittsburgh Courier:* "Many in the trade are asking why don't those around him, such as the Shaw Agency, which handles his bookings, or his many aides, such as road manager, personal manager, etc., try to help him. Or is it a case of too many people depending on the loot that Charles' voice brings in to help support themselves?" From Quincy Jones, "The best thing that could happen to Ray is to get rid of everybody around him on the road." In explanation, the Reverend Henry Griffin: "This guy is a blind man. He can't get it by himself and he can't stick it into his arm by himself." And most poignantly, from Charles himself: "The daily grind gets to be too much. A fellow who lives in the dark has to do something." . . .

"ABC–PARAMOUNT RECORDS, INC.," read the invitation, "cordially request the honor of your presence at a Cocktail Party and Record Preview in honor of MR. RAY CHARLES to introduce his new long-playing album, 'MODERN SOUNDS IN COUNTRY & WESTERN MUSIC' on Tuesday, February Twenty-seventh, 1962 at PARK AVENUE SUITE (CENTER) HOTEL WALDORF–ASTORIA Five o'clock to Seven-thirty." The guests at such functions are seldom those the host would like to see attend. The powerful figures in the music business who receive the invitations do not always take the time, and so pass the printed talismans on to assistants and friends who may be seekers after curiosity, free food and drink, or a new playmate. This particular cocktail party sported the regulation number of hangers-on and sinister Broadway types as well as genuine well-wishers and those who could, through their command of communications media, do the enterprise good. The new album played constantly from a phonograph in the corner.

"How did the Ertegun brothers ever let him get away?" asked one disappointed listener.

"That was a whole different world."

"Are you in the music business?" someone asked a beautiful Negro girl.

"My boss is in public relations," she said, "but I am here to honor Ray Charles."

Charles, wearing a tuxedo, arrived a little before six, was introduced to disc jockeys and PR men, and spent the rest of his time sitting at a table sipping champagne while people fought for his ear. Shortly before the party broke up, the president of ABC-Paramount made a speech announcing that Charles would now have his own company in association with ABC, Tangerine, which would produce records and discover new talent. Charles, in answer to the applause, stood up and made a short, halting speech about how pleased and gratified he was that so many people still listened and came to see him.

Afterwards, as he stood in a beautiful gray tweed coat with a velvet collar, surrounded by cronies, waiting for the elevator, one remembered the words of one of Charles' closest friends: "His expenses right now are five hundred dollars a day, and he'll be dead in three years."

Selected Discography

Ray Charles Story, ATLANTIC 2-900.
Ray Charles at Newport, ATLANTIC 1289.
The Genius of Ray Charles, ATLANTIC 1312.

JOHN COLTRANE

"HE PLAYED quite a few solos back then that hippie-in-the-street began to hum," Julian Adderley said, recalling John Coltrane's tenure in the Miles Davis group. "I challenge them to hum some of his solos now."

No statement more accurately reflects the problem that critics and fans have with John Coltrane's music; it comes close to isolating the problem that Coltrane himself has with it. A writer in the December, 1960 issue of the men's magazine, *Nugget,* remarked that "One of the best things that ever happened to John Coltrane was the discovery of Ornette Coleman by the jazz avant garde . . . Coltrane . . . has been able to continue his search for his own musical personality without the onus of having everything he does, missteps and all, hailed as evidence of genius." It would have been nice had it been true. By comparison, the Ornette Coleman controversy was an argument carried on by physicists on the blackboard of the Princeton Institute for Advanced Study; discussions about Coltrane can take on some of the truculent, hysterical aspects of political arguments in neighborhood bars.

Often, the participants in arguments about Coltrane have about the same amount of accurate information as barroom philosophers. Coltrane is as undecided about his music as those who discuss it. Since 1959, he has run through several musical ideas so rapidly that a given Coltrane record may be obsolete before its release; it will almost surely be outdated before reviews of it are published. He therefore identifies with very little of what he reads about himself.

The tenor saxophonist first came to prominence in the middle fifties, reflecting compulsion, anxiety, anger, and fear, what pianist Cecil Taylor calls "the realities of the day." For all its seeming chaos, the music had deep and direct emotional meaning for many listeners, and some insiders began to mark Coltrane as "the man." But it did not become Coltrane's year until 1961, when he won three divisions in *Down Beat's* International Critics' Poll, best tenor saxophonist of the year, and, in the "New Star" division, "Miscellaneous Instrument" (for soprano saxophone) and "New Combo." It behooves a musician to take such "honors" with a grain or two of realism. For as often as not, some of the same writers who make a current victory possible are those who once maintained that their favorite did not know how to play his instrument. The experience of Sonny Rollins, for one, indicates that it can be detrimental to read one's own press notices. It would have been disastrous for Coltrane too, had he taken his to heart, for his early notices were frequently negative, and he has been under fire several times since. That he continues to progress in the inexorable glare of a scrutiny that invests his most casual acts with significance is evidence of unusual conviction. Coltrane is probably the first major soloist of the contemporary era whose development largely took place under such scrutiny, and it should be of some value to examine that development.

Very little is known about Coltrane's personal life; on the face of it, there is not much to tell. As his wife Juanita, who is an avid partisan of her husband and his playing, puts it, "He doesn't think about anything else but his music." He was born John William Coltrane on September 23, 1926, in Hamlet, North Carolina. His father was a tailor who loved music, and played several instruments around the house. John himself played a variety of reed instruments: the E♭ alto horn, the clarinet, and then the tenor saxophone in high school. A few years after his father died, Coltrane's family moved to Philadelphia, and he continued his studies there at the Granoff Studios and the Ornstein School of

Music. By 1945, he was playing professionally in that city with a cocktail combo. Then in 1945–46 he was in the Navy, and despite what writers were later to say of his playing, he had evidently mastered the rudiments of his instruments enough to satisfy the more conservative elements of our society, for he toured with a Navy band in Hawaii during those years.

He once outlined his early professional experience for August Blume in *The Jazz Review:* "My first job was with a band from Indianapolis, led by Joe Webb. This was in 1947. Big Maybelle, the blues singer, was with this band. Then King Kolax, then Eddie Vinson, and Dizzy's big band. Earl Bostic, Gay Cross from Cleveland. He used to be with Louis Jordan. He sang and played in Jordan's style. Then I was with Daisey May and The Hep Cats, and then with Johnny Hodges in 1953 for six or seven months. Richie Powell was on piano, Lawrence Brown on trombone, Emmett Berry on trumpet, Jimmy Johnson on drums and I can't seem to remember the bass player's name . . . I enjoyed that job, we had some true music. I didn't appreciate guys like Bostic at the time because Bird had swayed me so much. After I'd gotten from under his spell I began to appreciate them more. After Hodges I spent a couple of weeks with Jimmy Smith. Wow, I'd wake up in the middle of the night and hear that organ. Those chords screaming at me. Back in 1949 I worked one job with Bud Powell. It was a dance gig at the Audubon in New York. Sonny Rollins and Art Blakey were with him. Those guys you can call really great."

In tone and style, that extract is reminiscent of nothing quite so much as the recitations of past battles which club fighters give reporters. Understandably so, for any talented young Negro hoping to achieve some stature is likely to be telling a reporter either of drummers he has played with or welterweights he has fought.

Coltrane's early experience, which for the most part could

be dismissed superficially as local rhythm-and-blues work, all points in one direction. If one looks in the windows of record stores in Harlem, Chicago's South Side, or any other of the large Negro areas of the country, he will see such music on display—tenors, organs, vocalists, and a few comedy or "party" records. This music has been given different names, but as soon as one admits that the Negro and the white have largely different cultures, then it becomes apparent that it is simply Negro popular music; the equivalent, in a sense, of Lawrence Welk, Les Brown or Doris Day.

Local Negro bands around the country play for social situations. In the small clubs and roadhouses, the patrons are drinking, dancing, talking, and laughing, often paying little or no attention to the musicians. The music becomes, in the most exact sense, background, and the performing musician must first of all cater to the taste of his public and try within that framework, if possible, to satisfy whatever private esthetic standards he holds.

It is perhaps this sort of training, still evident even in Coltrane's most advanced work, which accounts for two extremely revealing remarks he has made. I once questioned him about an album he had recorded, one side of which was a trio with only bass and drum accompaniment. When I first heard these performances, I wondered why he had chosen to record that way. Did he feel more freedom, or was there constriction? Sonny Rollins had made considerable impact by recording and playing personal appearances without piano; was Coltrane challenging Rollins? His answer was brief and to the point: "The piano player didn't show up." Another time, he was speaking of the writers who were nearly unanimous in their dislike of his first widely-heard efforts, seeming to feel that he did not know how to play. "I was hurt by it," he says, "but I was surprised. I don't know why they talked about me the way they did. I wasn't original then; I wasn't playing anything new or different."

In the light of what Coltane has done since, the statement

is true. But it is puzzling when one thinks of the turbulent saxophonist heard on the Miles Davis Quintet record which first brought him to public notice. The conductor Ernest Ansermet once remarked on "what a moving thing it is to meet" Sidney Bechet, the first great jazz virtuoso of the soprano saxophone, ". . . who is very glad one likes what he does, but can say nothing of his art except that he follows his 'own way' . . ." At one time, the same could have been said of Coltrane, and it might account for the self-deprecation. But one is also reminded of some remarks apropos guitarist Charlie Christian which novelist Ralph Ellison printed in *Saturday Review:* "More often than not (and this is especially true of its Negro exponents) jazz's heroes remain local figures known only to small-town dance halls, and whose reputations are limited to the radius of a few hundred miles. . . . Some of the most brilliant of jazzmen made no records; their names appeared in print only in announcements of some local dance or remote 'battles of music' against equally uncelebrated bands. Being devoted to an art which traditionally thrives on improvisation, these unrecorded artists very often have their most original ideas enter the public domain almost as rapidly as they are conceived, to be quickly absorbed into the thought and technique of their fellows . . . Thus, because jazz finds its very life in an endless improvisation upon traditional materials, the jazzman must lose his identity even as he finds it—how often do we see even the most famous of jazz artists being devoured alive by their imitators, and, shamelessly, in the public spotlight?"

Those remarks belong on Coltrane's wall, next to the *Down Beat* plaques which hang there, for he has been living them for years. It seems quite likely, for one thing, that Coltrane was simply playing out of a background which was known to him but not to the writers who found him so unusual. Ira Gitler, the first critic to recognize that Coltrane was not an imitator of Sonny Rollins, feels that the saxophonist is indebted to Dexter Gordon and Sonny Stitt for much of his style, but Coltrane himself has acknowledged Lester Young, Johnny Hodges, and Charlie Parker, and has said—significantly, in the light of Ellison's remarks—"I have listened to about all the good tenor men, beginning with Lester, and believe me, I've picked up something from them all, including several who have never recorded."

But Ellison was talking about Charlie Christian, and the situations in which Christian and Coltrane came to prominence are different. Roughly twenty years separate the influence of the two men, a fact whose importance can best be judged by noting that even though Christian's music is universally acknowledged to be a source of modern jazz, there is no complete LP by him currently in print.

Even though Christian died young, it is unlikely that there would have been so few recorded examples of his playing had he worked in the fifties. As one recording executive puts it, "A man can get on an album if he's had two lessons; if he's had three, he can be a leader." It is highly unlikely that any musician of real talent will remain unknown today, as companies beat the bushes in a desperate search for new people to record. One could say that several young musicians have not received the exposure warranted by their talent, but most of them have had their music committed to disc at least once. Today's young jazzman believes that if he is to be successful, he ought to come to New York. During the fifties, there were mass exoduses to New York from both Detroit and Philadelphia. The danger now is more likely to be that the young musician will be over-recorded, perhaps before he is ready to be recorded at all. It seemed, for a time, that this was happening to Coltrane.

When he came to New York with the Miles Davis Quintet in 1955, Coltrane encountered difficulty, at first, in trying to get a recording contract. At that time, Davis has recalled, "people used to tell me to fire him. They said he wasn't playing anything." Coltrane presented himself to the officials at Blue Note, who were unwilling to sign him to a contract, but agreed to make one album, which, ironically enough, contains some of his best and most famous early work. In April 1957, he recorded one piece with Thelonious Monk which impressed Riverside's A & R man, Orrin Keepnews, so much that he offered Coltrane a contract on the spot. But Coltrane had signed with Prestige two weeks previously. And he has never lacked for work since. The problem with which he then became confronted was one I attempted to discuss in a piece written in 1958:

When John Coltrane is left to shift for himself, those facets of his style that make him a candidate for greatness and those that may well keep him from achieving it are both thrown into sudden relief. On the back liner of his new Blue Note album, Robert Levin speaks of Coltrane's "spearing, sharp and resonant" sound that creates an "ominous atmosphere," and of his "veering, inconsistent lines." Those phrases, I think, characterize Coltrane about as well as it could be done, and highlight the qualities of original thinking that have made him the first major new saxophone innovator since Sonny Rollins, who in turn was the first since Bird. But change is not always progress, and to a large degree Coltrane contains within himself the elements that make his kind of jazz the most exciting being played, and the elements that often seem to be leading it (and him) down a blind alley.

Excitement is there, certainly, of an incomparable nature, and surprise. Most often, at the beginning of a solo, Coltrane enters from the unexpected place, creating a shock effect in the first phrase that leaves the listener limp for two or three choruses. Listen to him on *Blues By Five* on the Miles Davis *Cookin'* album (Prestige 7094). He is also possessed of an unmatched energy by which, in two choruses, he can lift an average, flaccid bop record out of its rut and into the realm of major jazz. Hear his solo on *Light Blue,* in the album *Interplay for Two Trumpets and Two Tenors.*

Two new Coltrane records have just been released which illustrate the right and wrong ways to present his music. The title piece on *Blue Train* is an exceptional blues, loaded with menace, perhaps the best Coltrane has ever recorded. Few current bop releases have the musical value of that one solo, which sounds in many ways like back-country guitar. Unfortunately, on the rest of the record, his material seems casually put together, and the other musicians are of no great assistance. The soloists, in particular, have little on-the-job familiarity with each other's work. *John Coltrane with the Red Garland Trio* (now called *Traneing In*) is another matter. Here he is surrounded exclusively with sympathetic musicians—men who have played and recorded as a unit and with Coltrane over long periods of time. All four men—Coltrane, Chambers, Garland, and Taylor—have Miles Davis as a common mentor. The result is a cohesive, thoughtful album which represents Coltrane's most consistent recorded work to date. Only one track, *Soft Lights,* is at all disappointing. His second appearance on the blues *Traneing In* might well be the most advanced statement of his ideas. On the two ballads, he displays a delightful sound and approach, reminiscent of the small local bands which gave him his start. It is, literally, a dancing approach, a wonderful ballad style which record-date musicians never have the chance to learn.

His attributes are to be admired and respected, and if Coltrane played always what he only plays at times, he would be great. But he has all the lack of discipline of jazz itself. He has his standard runs and phrases, as does everyone, and often must play them for quite a while before they take him to the point in his solo that is art. Although he has worked extensively with Miles Davis and Thelonious Monk, he has not yet mastered the sense of compression that is at the center of their music. When Monk, for instance, takes a solo, it is often a very short one, getting as much exceptional music out of one chorus that Coltrane gets in three. If that is the way Coltrane plays, that is how he plays, and we should be glad we have him, whatever his limitations . . . But why has Coltrane been a part of one unorganized blowing session after another?

Of his role as everybody's recording sideman, Coltrane says, "I wouldn't do it now." At the time, he needed the money. The result is that he appeared on a few records on which his is the only music likely to last. (Johnny Griffin's *A Blowing Session,* for example, which has a fascinating solo on *All The Things You Are;* and *Tenor Conclave,* which has a *How Deep Is The Ocean* that is the best early recorded instance of Coltrane's unique ballad style.) He also played on many others on which he merely juggles his own stock of pet phrases from one tune to the next, justifying his own assessment of himself as not "playing anything new or different." There are two Gene Ammons records on which he even reverts to his original instrument, the alto.

Aside from his regular work with Davis, his best musical opportunity at that time was the chance he got to record an album of Tadd Dameron compositions with the composer on piano.

He profited from contact with musicians who, like Dameron, were more adroit than himself, and his main source of knowledge in those days was his work with Miles Davis. An uncertain musician when he joined the quintet, Coltrane has been reluctant to talk about exactly what he learned from Davis, but it was obviously a great deal. The record of the original Davis group called *'Round About Midnight* first

brought Coltrane to the attention of that segment of the
jazz public which had been ignoring him. Davis has always
been the star of his own group, but as Cecil Taylor said on
first hearing the Davis set, "Coltrane's what you hear on
that record." He had gotten his style under control, and for
the first time, it seemed sure that he would fulfill his promise
as a soloist.

The major turning point in Coltrane's career seems to
have come in the summer of 1957, when he left Davis, who
was temporarily dissatisfied with his group, to join Thelonious
Monk. "Working with Monk," he wrote in *Down Beat*,
"brought me close to a musical architect of the highest order.
I felt I learned from him in every way—through the senses,
theoretically, technically. I would talk to Monk about musical problems, and he would sit at the piano and show me the
answers just by playing them. I could watch him play and
find out the things I wanted to know. Also, I could see a lot
of things that I didn't know about at all.

"Monk was one of the first to show me how to make two
or three notes at a time on tenor . . It's done by false fingering and adjusting your lip. If everything goes right, you can
get triads. Monk just looked at my horn and 'felt' the me-
chanics of what had to be done to get this effect."

The Monk group apparently had its origins in that single
track, *Monk's Mood,* which Monk recorded with Coltrane and
bassist Wilbur Ware in April 1957. That summer, Monk
added another Davis sideman, drummer Philly Joe Jones,
and formed a quartet which he took into New York's Five
Spot Café. Coltrane recalls that rehearsals consisted largely
of his going to Monk's house and waking the pianist up. Monk
would play a piece, and wait while Coltrane tried to learn it
on the saxophone, preferring not to produce sheet music
unless aural methods failed. "I always had to be alert with
Monk," Coltrane has said, "because if you didn't keep aware
all the time of what was going on, you'd suddenly feel as if

you'd stepped into an empty elevator shaft." The unit which resulted, one of the greatest in modern jazz, was unfortunately never recorded, although Riverside released three tracks with Jones' replacement, the late Shadow Wilson. Coltrane, however, has some tapes made at the club, and "I really treasure them."

In the fall of 1957, Coltrane, a greatly improved musician, returned to Miles Davis, who was now beginning the modal experiments which were, in their use of fewer and fewer chords, to affect Coltrane greatly. The saxophonist had also changed. He had previously fallen prey to self-destructive practices that lurk in the jazz world but had, by now, suddenly and definitively stopped. An interview with Ira Gitler reflected his new attitude: "Live cleanly . . . do right . . . You can improve as a player by improving as a person. It's a duty we owe to ourselves."

Not surprisingly, it was at this time that Coltrane began to be an influence on other players. He had also become a careful student of his own work, analyzing it to a point that once caused him to remark, "I'm worried that sometimes what I'm doing sounds just like academic exercises, and I'm trying more and more to make it sound prettier."

In *Down Beat,* he was able to dissect his style in a way that he had never done before: "About this time," he wrote, referring to his second stint with Davis, "I was trying for a sweeping sound. I started experimenting because I was striving for more individual development. I even tried long, rapid lines that Ira Gitler termed 'sheets of sounds' at the time. But actually, I was beginning to apply the three-on-one chord approach, and at that time the tendency was to play the entire scale of each chord. Therefore, they were usually played fast and sometimes sounded like glisses.

"I found there were a certain number of chord progressions to play in a given time, and sometimes what I played didn't work out in eighth notes, sixteenth notes, or triplets. I had to put the notes in uneven groups like fives and sevens in order to get them all in.

"I thought in groups of notes, not of one note at a time. I tried to place these groups on the accents and emphasize the strong beats—maybe on 2 here and on 4 over at the end. I would set up the line and drop groups of notes—a long line with accents dropped as I moved along. Sometimes what I was doing clashed harmonically with the piano—especially if the pianist wasn't familiar with what I was doing—so a lot of time I just strolled with bass and drums.

"I haven't completely abandoned this approach, but it wasn't broad enough. I'm trying to play these progressions in a more flexible manner now."

In those days, Coltrane was in marked contrast to the other two horns in the Davis sextet, sometimes taking interminable solos that seemed little more than scales. One speculated on how much of some men's personalities are released only in music: the quiet, pleasant Coltrane played fierce slashing lines in direct opposition to the gentle, delicate phrases of the often blunt, arrogant Miles. "Cannonball" Adderley, the group's other saxophonist, recalls of those solos, "Once in a while, Miles might say, 'Why you play so long, man?' and John would say, 'It took that long to get it all in.'" Coltrane himself told Gitler of the "sheets of sound" that "Now it is not a thing of beauty, and the only way it would be justified is if it becomes that. If I can't work it through, I will drop it."

It is unfortunate that a phrase like "restless search" has become a cliché used to describe anyone who plays a solo differently from one time to the next, for it accurately describes the thing in which Coltrane has long been involved. At this time, when his whole life had become music, he turned his back on his own considerable achievement and attempted new advances in his style.

By now, he was recording regularly as a leader for Prestige.

As he became better known, Coltrane placed himself on the recording auction block (which had then begun to hear wild excesses in the bidding for major jazz performers) and left Prestige to record for Atlantic. His first Atlantic record, *Giant Steps,* showed a more assured Coltrane than ever before, on an album made up entirely of his own compositions.

In the summer of 1959, the growing critical and public dispute over whether Coltrane or Sonny Rollins was the most influential modern tenorman was settled, at least temporarily, by Rollins' retirement. Coltrane, once maligned, was now indisputably on top. Early in 1960, he made the obvious move: he left Miles Davis to form his own group.

In the group's early stages, it was, according to reports, a chaotic venture. Coltrane, driven by his own needs, was experimenting publicly with his method of playing two or more notes at once on his instrument. It was apparently an extremely exciting experience when it came off, but when it didn't, he would play for a few minutes and walk off the bandstand, disgusted. Recorded examples of the technique are to be found on the Atlantic record, *Coltrane Jazz.*

But he had another idea, one which was eventually to place him so firmly in the public eye that he received a feature story in *Newsweek,* something which rarely happens to a jazzman. "Three of us were driving back from a date in Washington in 1959," he told that magazine's interviewer. "Two of us were in the front seat and the other guy, a sax-player, in the back. He was being very quiet. At Baltimore, we made a rest stop, then got back in the car and 30 miles later realized that the guy in the back wasn't there. We hoped that he had money with him, and drove on. I took his suitcase and horn to my apartment in New York. I opened the case and found a soprano sax. I started fooling around with it and was fascinated. That's how I discovered the instrument."

Eventually, he got a soprano of his own ("it helps me get away—lets me take another look at improvisation. It's like having another hand"). Until Coltrane, the instrument had been irrevocably associated with the New Orleans style of Sidney Bechet (Coltrane's lovely *Blues to Bechet* is a demonstration of the linkage); only Steve Lacy had attempted to adapt the difficult, hard-to-tune instrument to the modern idiom.

His use of the soprano not only brought him greater popularity, it helped make him an influence so powerful that one thinks of another of Ansermet's remarks about Bechet: ". . . perhaps his 'own way' is the highway along which the whole world will swing tomorrow." And Ellison's comment— "how often do we see even the most famous of jazz artists being devoured alive by their imitators, and, shamelessly, in the public spotlight?"—is brought forcibly home every time one hears the younger players—even some of the older ones who have revamped their styles to accommodate the pervasive Coltrane impact. It might be expected that the soprano saxophone should become a more popular instrument; not so expected is the presence of one young man in Greenwich Village who plays Coltrane lines on a kazoo.

The first Coltrane recording to employ soprano was *My Favorite Things*. Some idea of the effect it creates is indicated by the experience of Cecil Taylor, who heard Coltrane play the piece in a club and was unable to convince several young musicians present that it was a Rodgers and Hammerstein song made famous by Mary Martin, rather than the East Indian folk music they took it to be.

Coltrane had, indeed, become deeply involved with the music of India, going so far as to study briefly with the Indian musician Ravi Shankar. Although he is not what he calls "an astute observer of the music," he has found much of what he has learned of it applicable to the sort of jazz he wants to play. Indian music is based on ragas, Indian scales which ascend differently than they descend. There are countless ragas, and each has a particular significance, concerned with religion, time of day, etc. Coltrane had found that *My Favorite Things* could be played almost as a raga. His next soprano recording, *Greensleeves,* also played on principles of the raga, was an even more eerily hypnotic performance. Coltrane had been fascinated by the Indian water drum, essentially a drone instrument which keeps a steady tone going while others improvise around it. To simulate this, he used two bassists ("I like music to be heavy on the bottom"), one of whom was virtually imprisoned while the other remained almost completely free. Coltrane was quite pleased when he later discovered that Ali Akbar Khan, considered the greatest Indian musician, likes to play *Greensleeves.* "I wish I could hear him do it," was his disarming remark. "Then I'd know if I was playing it right.

"Most of what we play in jazz," he continues, "has the feeling of just that one raga. The Indian musicians don't play the melody, they just play their scales. But maybe that's the melody to them. But what they do with it, the little differences, that's the improvisation." For a time, Coltrane pursued this so far that he would call off a chord sequence for his sidemen to play on, rather than an actual tune. They would then improvise on the mood suggested by the chord sequence and the tempo. "Yeah, I did that," he admits somewhat ruefully.

To be able to keep the feeling of the raga, but yet not play just chord changes ("I want to play tunes," he says, "I want to play the feeling of the song"), he began looking through old song books for folk tunes, perhaps turning to folios rather than recordings so that he would not be influenced by another's interpretation. He came up with *Olé,* based on the Spanish folk song *Venga Jaleo.* It is a remarkable synthesis of Indian elements, ideas propounded by Miles Davis in *Sketches of Spain,* and a growing concern with multiples of

3/4 time. Coltrane contributes one of his most furious solos, and Art Davis plays some of the most intricate, superbly musical bass that has ever been heard on a jazz record. In another song book, he found a piece he calls *Spiritual*, which he plays with the irreducible minimum of one chord.

Coltrane's approach may owe as much to Miles Davis as to India. Davis had become preoccupied with "modal" jazz, based on scales rather than chords. As he remarked to Nat Hentoff in 1958, "When you go this way, you can go on forever. You don't have to worry about changes and you can do more with the line. It becomes a challenge to see how melodically inventive you are. When you're based on chords, you know at the end of 32 bars that the chords have run out and there's nothing to do but repeat what you've just done—with variations. I think a movement in jazz is beginning away from the conventional string of chords, and a return to emphasis on melodic rather than harmonic variation. There will be fewer chords but infinite possibilities as to what to do with them." Davis thus predicts the development of both Coltrane and, to a lesser degree, the more extreme, more melodic Ornette Coleman.

Coleman, who is also interested in the music of India, has, conversely, been an influence on Coltrane. It is not surprising that Coltrane's insatiable curiosity and insistence on fewer and fewer chords should have led him to Coleman's music. For Coleman, who has all but done away with traditional harmony, had taken the step which Coltrane's deeply harmonic sensibilities might not allow him to take. As the composer George Russell put it, "Coltrane, it seems to me, is just bursting at the seams to demolish the chord barrier, and because of this, he is enlightening everyone to what can happen on a single chord."

Coltrane and Coleman are good friends, and when they were working a few blocks from one another in New York, each would leave his own club between sets to hear the other man play. Coltrane said of Coleman to French jazz writer François Postif, "I have only played with him once in my life; I went to listen to him at a club and he asked me to join him. We played two pieces—twelve minutes to be exact —but I think that was the most intense moment of my life."

It was quite likely Coltrane's interest in Coleman which led him, in 1961, to invite the late Eric Dolphy to "come on in and work" in his band. Dolphy, who played alto, clarinet, bass clarinet and flute, was as addicted as Coltrane to long solos. Although Coltrane was delighted with the association, there was such a storm of critical protest that Coltrane's advisors eventually convinced him to ask Dolphy to leave. Coltrane had tremendous respect for Dolphy's formal education ("I'm into scales right now," he said one evening, and when asked if Dolphy was doing the same, replied proudly, "Eric's into everything"), and, when his explorations led him into a new area, traces of Dolphy's work began to show up in his own playing. Dolphy, for his part, felt that "I can't say in words what I've learned from John, the way he handles things. He's such a pro."

One remarkable example of Coleman's influence on Coltrane is a fifteen-minute blues accompanied only by bass and drums, called *Chasin' the Trane*. Recorded when Coltrane had only recently become interested in Coleman, it is, as is usual when a new idea strikes him, pure music, exhibiting a concern with notes and sound for their own sake, going painfully through ideas which a more sophisticated musician such as Dolphy might long ago have worked out. Later, significantly enough, Coltrane hired an ex-Coleman bassist, Jimmy Garrison.

A synthesized recorded statement of Coltrane's musical ideas was made after Garrison joined the group. This is not surprising, since each of his musical discoveries has immediately been reflected in changing personnel. Adding, subtracting, changing players, he gathered around him an impressive cadre of young musicians. "I keep looking," he explains, "for different ways to present my music. I don't think it's as presentable as it could be." He once mentioned that "I'd like to add an instrument that can play melody and percussion, maybe a guitar." Thus, Wes Montgomery joined the band, but the guitarist soon noted that the spaces between his solos were longer than the intervals between sets, and left. For a time, the second bassist was Art Davis, a brilliant young musician from Harrisburg, Pennsylvania. When Coltrane became involved with his new ideas about the use of the bass, he got into the habit of driving over to Davis' home and picking him up for a practice session. But Davis will not travel, preferring to remain in New York, where he often works in a non-jazz context. Coltrane uses Davis when he can. "I don't think Trane thinks of anything but music," Davis says. "He'll come back off the road and call me up to say, 'We're opening at the Vanguard tonight.' I say, 'We are?' and then I have to tell him that I'm working somewhere else. He never seems to think to let me know in advance, so I can stay free." Asked one night during a one-bass engagement in New York, why Davis was not with the group, Coltrane replied with some puzzlement, "Art's a very busy guy." For such reasons, he generally bills himself as "John Coltrane and his Group." "I'm playing it safe," he says.

Long permanent fixtures were the heavily chordal pianist McCoy Tyner ("McCoy has a beautiful lyric concept that is essential to complement the rest of us") and Elvin Jones, the most fiery, compulsively brilliant of modern drummers, in many ways the finest now playing. "Even I can't play with him," Coltrane says bemusedly. "He uses so many accents."

With these two and Garrison, Coltrane produced a nearly shattering recording of *Out of This World*. Critic-saxophonist Don Heckman said of it in *Jazz* magazine, "Some of the principles that seem to be basic to (Coltrane's) music are: (1) he rarely cares to explore the development of extended harmonic variations drawn from the chords of a stated melody; (2) color, rhythms, and emotional tensions (often expressed by nontraditional instrumental sounds) replace harmony as cadential signposts; (3) like the improvising musicians of the East, Coltrane prefers that his tonal accompaniment remain static, and that motion be derived from a sympathetic and nearly equal rhythmic percussion—in this case, Elvin Jones. When this happens all at once, the results are very startling indeed. *Out of This World* is surely one of the best things Coltrane has ever done, and its success is as much due to the brilliant drumming of Jones as it is to Coltrane. In combination they have very nearly solved the problem of the essential differences between Eastern and Western improvisatory music. One of the strengths of Indian music is a long, regular metric pulse that stimulates a constant interplay of tension and release between the soloist and the percussionist. By opening up the rhythms of their material (in this case to a rather complex 6/4) Coltrane and Jones are finding a successful solution to the problems of overextension and listening tedium that had nagged much of their earlier work in this vein. The problems for the listener are increased, however, in that he must now meet the music on its own terms."

Not all criticism has been this sympathetic. Coltrane is puzzled by the fact that one critic may praise him for exactly the same qualities another writer uses to damn him. Too often, the opposition to his work has assumed a hysterical cast, his detractors employing words like anarchistic, nihilistic, gobbledegook, confusion, amorphism, nonsense, and the dread epithet, antijazz. More reasoned questioning of his approach dealt with the extreme length of his solos, his use of suspensions ("vamps," he calls them) and the essential emotional sameness of his performances, no matter what the material. As Martin Williams summed up reviewing *Africa Brass* in *Down Beat*, "Coltrane has done on record what he has done so often in person lately, make everything into a handful of chords, frequently only two or three, and run them in every conceivable way, offering what is, in effect, an extended cadenza to a piece that never gets played, a prolonged *montuna* interlude surrounded by no rhumba or *son,* or a very long vamp 'til ready."

With this in mind, it is extremely enlightening to listen to a Miles Davis album, *Someday My Prince Will Come,* recorded during the time that Coltrane was making such controversial music. Coltrane appears on two of the selections ("I sneaked down one afternoon and made it," he says of the record), the title track and a Spanish-influenced piece called *Teo.* In the stricter, long-familiar setting of the Davis group, Coltrane contributes not only the most exciting, impassioned music on the set, but two of the best solos he had played in a long time. What Nat Hentoff called the "cry" in his playing, each note sounding incomplete, only a link between the surrounding ones, was once again present, and he displayed his talent in magnificent relief against another man's contrasting discipline, just as he had been able to do in former years. There were rumors that Davis wanted Coltrane to rejoin him, but even though Davis consistently outdrew Coltrane in the same clubs ("He has a wonderful name," Coltrane says, "he'd hire Sonny, he'd hire me, he'd hire all of us, just to hear us play. He's got a lot of money, and he loves to listen to music"), it seemed unlikely that the merger would ever come to pass.

For "everybody's sideman" is now indisputably a leader himself. He has created a music which is identifiably his, even during the long stretches of any selection when he is not soloing. How he has arrived at this new status is a fascinating question.

To see Coltrane in action is only to increase one's puzzlement about him. A quiet, pleasant, shyly friendly man who dresses simply and speaks softly, he is likely to be found between sets seated on his horncase, reading and eating an apple. At the conclusion of a solo, he wanders off-stage, Miles Davis fashion. He may talk to friends who have come to hear him—Ornette Coleman, for instance, or Davis—or he may sit quietly at the far end of the club, listening to his band. But on the stand, he becomes impassioned and engrossed; it is as if setting the instrument to his lips completed an electrical circuit. As the music takes hold, he leans far back, eyes tight shut as if possessed with instant frenzy. Then, after the solo, he may move to the side of the stage, light one of the long, thin cigars he has begun to affect, and adjust a reed.

He once said of his work with Dizzy Gillespie, "I was playing clichés and trying to learn tunes that were hip, so I could play with the guys who played them." It is hard to equate the Coltrane of today with the hip saxophonist he says he was. In a little over a year, he passed rapidly through several different styles of music, a man with a sudden thirst for knowledge, and each new thing he tries only opens up wider areas to explore. Basically a romantic player—the rage in his playing is only the reverse side of the lyricism—he has accumulated in his search, as most romantics do, an ever-growing list of what he knows he does not want. It may be pertinent that he has retained his original slow ballad style. When playing other music, though, he is in a dangerous position. The first attempt at any new thing inevitably involves awkwardness, and the listener on any given night may find Coltrane struggling through his own musical vocabulary. This has caused many to turn away in exasperation, but the saxophonist is apparently willing to take that chance. All he can offer his audience on such occasions is the excitement of participating in the creative process. It is a thrilling thing to be able to share, but obviously not everyone is willing to share it.

This concern with pure music is easily understood. Jazz began as music-at-home, in which almost anyone could participate. Today, when many jazz musicians can in some respects outplay their symphonic counterparts, it has become a virtuoso's music, a music in which one *begins* as a virtuoso and goes on from there. But technical facility is not Coltrane's only concern. He would like, he says, for his music to have "strong emotional content."

Some of that emotion comes out in his compositions. Now determined to play songs instead of chords, he has found none that completely satisfy him, and has turned to writing his own, more from necessity than a desire to compose. One night at the Jazz Gallery, he premiered a new untitled piece, (now called *Big Nick*), so simple and charming that several members of the audience immediately began whistling it. Coltrane was unable to believe he had been successful. "I'd like to know what the hell they were whistling," he said, puzzled. "I thought it was mine." Some of his pieces do sound familiar. His *Blue Train* is the prototype of much of his work, and some of his blues sound like classic lines from the thirties. "What John has done," says Cecil Taylor, "is take the concept of time he learned from Miles Davis and extend it. You can hear it on *Blues Minor*. It's *Bags' Groove*, sure, but what he's done is tighten it up, take the unnecessary parts out." Coltrane has expressed a desire to write in the twelve-tone system. Asked about the seeming impossibility of improvising serially, he replies, "Damn the rules, it's the feeling that counts. You play all twelve notes in your solo anyway."

Despite the increased emphasis on composition, improvising remains the primary vehicle of Coltrane's emotions. If we are, in Heckman's words, to "meet the music on its own terms," to understand the menace of its almost crushing energy, then some attempt must be made to understand Coltrane himself.

One clue is in his Jamaica, Long Island, home. There are few records in his library, but what he has is almost all folk music from India. For a long time, occupying a considerable part of the livingroom was a large rented harp, which he was learning to play "because it helps me with harmony." His only apparent hobby is a telescope in the back yard, which he looks through on the rare occasions when he has the chance. His group works constantly. "I don't know what you mean by a dedicated musician," his wife says, "but all he does is practice. Many nights he'd fall asleep with the horn still in his mouth." "When you talk to him," adds young trumpeter Freddie Hubbard, "he's always looking off somewhere, like he's thinking of the next note he's going to play."

Scant attention has been paid to furnishing; ceramic wall plaques provide almost the only decor. Coltrane, the most pleasant of men, seems almost naïve; his musical sophistication is not hinted at by his manner. ("A lot of 'literary' people say that," comments Cecil Taylor. "I always feel good about being with John *after* I've talked to him.") "White Americans," James Baldwin has written, "find it as difficult as white people elsewhere to divest themselves of the notion that they are in possesion of some intrinsic value that black people need, or want." In that remark may lie the ultimate significance of the power and danger of the jazz of quiet, naïve John Coltrane, who has taken his musical imagination from India, from Africa, and from the blues.

While displaying an ever more voracious appetite for all things new (Coltrane does not tend to think of himself as a leader, but as a student of music who is in the remarkable position of being paid to do what obsesses him), he has still managed to combine commerce and art. Although his playing is basically the same on both his instruments ("I think you have to have musical conviction, rather than let the instrument dictate to you"), his soprano sax is primarily responsible for a popularity that, in 1961, enabled him to appear at all four of New York's major jazz clubs. He has judiciously combined the elements of his success. Early in an evening, he will feature the soprano on pieces like *My Favorite Things* and *Greensleeves*. Afterwards, he might say to a friend, "The next set will be different. The next set I'll play all my non-hits." The soprano disappears, to be replaced by the tenor and long, furiously impassioned and basic blues.

Off the stand again, he once more becomes the shy, friendly man whose cigar is the only indication that he knows he is a success. His main concern with his constant work on the road is the protracted absence from his wife ("She really knows me, and understands the problems I have as a leader"). Perhaps he takes his preeminence with such equanimity because, having made it the hard way, he has an extremely realistic view of the business he is in. "Every time I talk about jazz," he says, "I think of prizefighters. One year it's your year, like it's mine now, and the next year everybody's forgotten you. You only have a few years, and you have to stay up there as long as you can, and do the best you can, and be graceful about it when it's someone else's turn."

I was interested to know what John Coltrane would do when the young musicians who are learning so much from him overtook him.

"I'd just keep playing," he said. "It's all I know."

Selected Discography

Blue Train, BLUE NOTE 1577.
Traneing In, PRESTIGE 7123.
My Favorite Things, ATLANTIC 1361.
Coltrane "Live" At The Village Vanguard, IMPULSE A-10.
Coltrane, IMPULSE A-21.

Note: Several of the best examples of Coltrane's work are to be found on various albums recorded under Miles Davis' name for Prestige and Columbia.

CECIL TAYLOR

"NEGRO SPEECH," the novelist and essayist James Baldwin has written, "is vivid largely because it is private. It is a kind of emotional shorthand—or sleight-of-hand—by means of which Negroes express, not only their relationship to each other, but their judgment of the white world. And, as the white world takes over this vocabulary—without the faintest notion of what it really means—the vocabulary is forced to change. The same thing is true of Negro music, which has had to become more and more complex in order to express any of the private or collective experience . . ."

Cecil Taylor, the most controversial jazz pianist since Thelonious Monk and certainly the most complex, would probably agree with Baldwin's estimate. "Anybody's music," Taylor says, "is made up of a lot of things that are not musical. Music is an attitude, a group of symbols of a way of life, whether you're conscious of it or not. Any music is an expression of those who created it. So that jazz would naturally have to be an expression of the American Negro, his feelings, within the tradition of his folk songs, the church, those swinging funeral bands. Simply the feeling of the American Negro within that tradition. That's what it is. It's quite simple, really. And, of course, it naturally reflects the social and economic and educational attitudes of the players. And that's why the fools don't think I play jazz."

The "fools" include listeners who maintain, as has been maintained of nearly every important jazz innovator, that Taylor does not know how to play his instrument; owners of jazz rooms who have fired him after one example of "music like that in my club"; critics who have said that his music is little more than a mélange of Bartók, Stravinsky, and Debussy; and perhaps most inimical of all, other critics who have found it necessary to erect complex structures of rationalization and evasion when praising him.

Musicians have been no kinder. Many have walked off the stand when Taylor has appeared at a jam session. He is never asked to be a sideman; he must get his jobs for himself. In 1962, six years after the release of a first recording which *The New Yorker*'s Whitney Balliett said "could have the same revolutionary impact upon modern jazz as the recordings of Charlie Parker," the participants in the *Down Beat* International Critics Poll finally got around to voting Taylor "new star" pianist. The recipient of the award was out of work at the time, as he has been most of his professional life.

All of this leaves Taylor bitter and amused. "Now there's one thing that has to be said about critics," he remarks. "Certainly they did attempt to raise the level of writing about jazz. And my appeal to certain of these people, I can understand it. But it's also like being grateful for small favors. And most of their information was inaccurate. The trouble was they couldn't hear. It was certainly valid for them to say 'I heard such-and-such a composer,' and perhaps so, but what I also heard, and what was also there, were jazz personalities and jazz musicians which they didn't bother to identify because their reference eluded that. Like Horace Silver, like Thelonious Monk, like Duke Ellington, like Milt Jackson, like Miles Davis, all that was there."

Perhaps essential to the confusion surrounding Taylor's music is that, in his phrase, he "accepted Ellington's word," a casual remark of Ellington's to the effect that it would be necessary for the coming generations of jazz musicians to have conservatory training. "You need everything you can get," Ellington has been quoted as saying. "You need the conservatory—with an ear to what's happening in the street." The problem, as Taylor sees it, "is to utilize the energies of the European composers, their technique, so to speak, *consciously* and blend this with the traditional music of the American Negro, and to create a new energy. And was it unique? No. Historically not. This is what has always happened. Ellington did it."

The essential word is "blend." From the time when New Orleans bands played marches and quadrilles, jazz has borrowed from Europe, and the borrowing has persisted up to the present, when some of the younger jazzmen are experimenting with serial techniques, chance, and indeterminism. The criterion is how nearly assimilation is achieved: does a musician simply play a popular tune in the manner of a certain "classical" composer, as the pianist Don Shirley does, or does he, like John Lewis, compose a fugue that is truly a jazz piece? "The object of any musician who has had this background," Taylor says of the conservatory, "is to bring it to jazz—combine it with jazz, and see what happens." Not all of his sources are musical, for, as Taylor says, "you are the recipient of all the cultural things around you that you wish to be—things like dance, theater, literature, the people that you see—so you are a departure."

The music that comes from these theories is an accurate reflection of the highly complex individual who plays it. Difficult and unrelentingly powerful, there is seldom rest or relaxation in it; dissonant and battering, it demands the total attention of the listener. Only a superb technician could execute it. But if listening to Taylor can be strenuous, watching him perform can be exhausting. He once said, "I try to imitate on the piano the leaps in space a dancer makes," and Taylor himself, at the piano, is a darting, spidery dancer. His entire body follows his fingers as they approach the keyboard, as if to attack the notes unaware. He recoils quickly, singing to himself, and leaps elsewhere. The forbidding, nearly opaque dark glasses he usually wears are always in imminent danger of falling off, and in the midst of an especially involved solo, as his musical and personal tension build to an excruciating pitch, he will whip them off in anger, toss them onto the piano, and forget them for the rest of the set. He often wears a sweatshirt under his shirt and tie, to prevent the necessity of changing after every set. It is clear to see why he is the darling of photographers, although he is unavailable to most of them, and why the word "energy" crops up so frequently in his discussion of music. "Playing," he says, "is very difficult. Practicing is preparing for the playing, and the playing is always total, and the result—you lose a lot of weight."

He has lost more jobs than weight because of his music, but musicians—at least the younger ones—no longer leave the stand when Taylor plays. On the contrary, the bar is likely to be lined with musicians, hoping to be asked to sit in.

Jazz makes legends easily, and for the past few years, Taylor has been something of a man of mystery. Some of this is the inevitable result of being known more by reputation than through infrequent personal appearances; more, it must be said, is the result of calculation. He will enter a club without speaking to anyone, listen to a few numbers, and leave suddenly. His telephone number, when he has one, and the location of his apartment, are closely guarded secrets. Still he manages to keep in constant touch with the few people he feels close to. The phone rings late at night, and it is Taylor, calling from a pay booth. "I'm around the corner," he says. He will arrive, as likely as not, three days later.

One reason so little is known about him is his general dislike and distrust of the people who promote and write about jazz. One writer, for instance, congratulated Taylor in print for a lovely recording of Rodgers and Hammerstein's *This Nearly Was Mine,* a piece the writer called "one of the most terrifyingly maudlin pop tunes of our times . . . a frighteningly fragile piece of 'midtown' fluff." Taylor looked at the review in stunned amazement. "Doesn't that fool know," he asked finally, "that I recorded that tune because I *like* it?"

Such hostility is a large part of Taylor's makeup, and many find it reflected in his music. "Hostility's a genuine emotion," he replies. "Why shouldn't jazz have hostility in it? That should be the one thing that would make everybody in the United States dig it. Most people in the United States shield their hostility with smiles. Jazz musicians don't bother." Taylor himself seldom bothers, and is even half in love with the idea of himself as a mysterious figure, but is also a close and generous, if sardonic, friend to those few people he has decided *are* his friends.

His obsession with mystery extends to keeping his birth-date a secret, but it is most commonly accepted that Taylor was born in New York City on March 15, 1933. His mother, who died when he was quite young, was a dancer who could also play piano and violin. His father sang around the house, Negro shouts and field hollers remembered from his youth, things that Taylor says "go back farther than the blues." When he was about six, Taylor decided he wanted piano lessons, and his family was more than happy to oblige. The music heard most often around the Taylor house was Duke Ellington's. Many people think Taylor bears a remarkable resemblance to Ellington's alter ego, Billy Strayhorn, which may be why members of the Ellington band, most notably drummer Sonny Greer, befriended him. (Today, Taylor refers to Ellington as "Uncle Ken"—the full name is Edward Kennedy Ellington—but the relationship, apparently, is a spiritual one.) He was also exposed very early to the music of the Negro church, and as he told Nat Hentoff, "even when we were going to a middle-class one, the one around the corner was sanctified."

Because of Ellington, Taylor—after studies at the New York College of Music—went to Boston to attend the New England Conservatory. At the time, he says, he did not "grasp the nature of improvisation" necessary for a jazz musician. His style of playing, however, began at the Conservatory. "It began on a very small basis, based on scales. At the time it began, it was based on one single scale which soon became many scales, scales made up of different intervalic constructions, then chords, then diads, and then just combinations of tones, and then just intervals spaced differently, not scales at all, just groups of notes." The Conservatory, where Taylor eventually wound up in the popular music division, proved to be an enlightening, if exasperating, experience.

"I heard Stravinsky for the first time," he recalls, *The Rite of Spring.* I heard all the formalized music, the hipped-up music of the twenties. I became aware. But I consolidated all of those things the year *after* I got out of the conservatory, alone by myself. There were certain Bartók scores in which I saw things no teacher told me anything about." One of the things a teacher did tell him was that no one could possibly sing his vocal arrangement of *Why Was I Born*, his choice for a graduation exercise. His interest in the composers he heard at the conservatory, as well as a later involvement with Schoenberg and Webern, has given rise to critical phrases like "classical pastiche" in discussing his work, but Taylor says in rebuttal, "I think it is the right of any would-be artist to try and get material from as many places as possible."

One of the most unfashionable places he went for his material was the music of Dave Brubeck, in the days before Brubeck had toned down his style. "I learned a lot from him. When he's most interesting, he sounds like me." Taylor did listen to Brubeck a lot in those days, and it was later a source of great satisfaction to him when, one night, Brubeck walked across the street from the Lower Basin Street club where he was then working to listen appreciatively to a Cecil Taylor set in a small bar. Perhaps it is economic security which makes Brubeck one of the few pianists who will openly praise Taylor. "As far as borrowing from classical music goes," Brubeck says, "there has never been a jazz musician who didn't. I think Cecil has a very exciting, important concept. I wish him all the luck in the world. Jazz needs twenty more Cecil Taylors, or individuals like him. It needs a hundred."

After the Conservatory, Taylor found that others would not be so generous. It is never easy for the young musician in New York, but it was more difficult for Taylor than most, with his completely different, demanding, often frightening style. "Of course," he remembers, "the reality was, you come back and you work in Harlem. You go there and try to get gigs, you come to grips with Miles Davis, come to grips with the evolution of the language, where contemporary jazz is going, as well as being aware of other musics."

Taylor has shown, when necessary, that he is fully capable of playing any kind of piano called for in a specific situation, but in general, he has preferred not to. And he was, and is, completely unwilling to participate in the shaking-hands-and-smiling routine that is often a necessary prerequisite of employment. Once, a well-meaning friend, who felt that Taylor's intransigence was keeping him from getting work, showed him an article by the extremely successful Gerry Mulligan which dealt with the proper way for musicians to present their music and themselves to club owners. Cecil, shocked that the friend would take Mulligan's word on any subject, walked out.

The one job he remembers with affection from those days was a weekend spent in Pennsylvania with a combo led by Ellington saxophonist Johnny Hodges. He was too overawed to play well and was given notice, but the band included a sufficient number of Ellingtonians to represent the fulfillment of an old ambition.

He sustained himself by carrying out orders from a mid-

town coffee shop near Madison Avenue. One can only speculate with some horror upon the encounters between Taylor,
sandwiches in hand and hidden behind dark glasses, and the
executives in the office buildings.

The year 1956 was the first break in what had been a wall
of indifference. With soprano saxophonist Steve Lacy, bassist
Buell Neidlinger, and drummer Dennis Charles, Taylor recorded an LP, *Jazz Advance,* for the now-defunct Transition
label of Boston. 1956, he says, "gave me enough time
to have gotten over the academic thing, to have gotten
further away from it." Transition also issued a sampler record, containing work not available on their regular releases,
and Taylor's moody, jagged *Sweet and Lovely,* included on
it, is perhaps the finest work he has ever done. (Blue Note
Records, who purchased the Transition catalog, has not reissued either set.)

That fall, Taylor played his first extended New York club
date. His was the first jazz group to play regularly at the
Five Spot Café, where he remained for six weeks. The following summer, he was invited to play at the 1957 Newport
Jazz Festival, at one of the afternoon sessions devoted to
"experimental" music. Although that word has been connected with him on several occasions, he objects to it violently, saying, "Experimental means that you're trying to do
something. I'm *doing* it."

Taylor has been plagued throughout his career by attempts
at labeling. On the Verve LP recorded at Newport, he can
be heard referring to his music as "traditional," and, when
shown an item that called him the only musician now improvising Third Stream music, he said, "I play an extension of
period music—Ellington and Monk. Third Stream is George
Gershwin and Ferde Grofé." When called a conservatory-
trained musician, he snaps, "I like hell am. If my musical
training stopped when I left the conservatory, you wouldn't
be talking to me today."

A highly-regarded first LP, a successful engagement at a New York jazz club, praise from some of the most respected critics, an engagement at Newport that resulted in a second LP—all this sounds like the beginnings of a most auspicious career. But Taylor has seldom worked since. Jobs in Village bars and coffeeshops have been interspersed with periods as a record salesman, dishwasher, and cook.

No one, least of all Taylor himself, ever expected him to have the kind of popular acceptance given an Erroll Garner. (Although he made one attempt to get such acceptance several years ago, during a brief period of night club singing.)

But Taylor didn't count on being ignored. Most people found his music too complex and demanding. This may have been a function of Taylor himself: immensely articulate, he is still able to communicate only to a few people; his music, with all its technique, may still be expressive of too private and fragmented an emotion to gain acceptance or followers. This, despite his growing tendency to listen to his own comment, "music consists of sounds and silences," and avoid his previous habit of playing each song as though it were his last, using everything he knew in every number, leaving nothing out.

There is, though, another possible reason for the lack of acceptance, one to which Taylor has given some thought. "The jazz musician," he says, "is quite apart, because the black bourgeousie is interested in identifying with Sammy Davis and Sidney Poitier. They consider Billie Holiday a drug addict, that's what they know about her. The middle-class scene is the middle-class scene. The Negro middle class, as best I can see, is very busy trying to emulate the white middle class. I'm a part of the tradition of the American artist. That's the only thing to hold onto. It's the most vibrant and alive thing that there is to hold onto." Which means that he is separate even from his own people. When he is not playing or practicing, which he sometimes does for ten or twelve hours a day, one of his main pleasures is walking about New York, looking at the architecture. A highly verbal, astute observer of the theater and dance ("I think I should really write dance criticism"), he attends as often as possible. When economics make this difficult, he reverts to the official pastime of solitary New Yorkers, the double feature, and has been known to attend two in one day.

A Negro, particularly a Negro jazz musician, is not supposed to have Taylor's interests and talents. To play a Don Shirley Chopinesque arrangement is charming; to revere Handel, as John Lewis does, is expressive of dignity. But to play jazz piano, as Taylor does, with strong intimations of Stravinsky, Webern, Charles Ives, and most particularly the Prokofiev of the final movement of the *Seventh Piano Sonata*, is unexpected and somehow unsettling. Out of the wall of indifference and his own insistence on himself as a Negro, Taylor has fashioned a mordant, often destructive wit which has played as much a part as his music in keeping him from getting work. Of Miles Davis: "He's the first millionaire I ever heard play pretty well." Of European influences on Ellington: "He doesn't look European to me." Of Ralph Ellison's *Invisible Man:* "That's a nice novel. After he said the title, however, you didn't need to read the book." Of Dizzy Gillespie's comedy: "I don't put him down for it, I just don't go to hear him." Of white jazz musicians: "All white musicians try to cop the feeling. That's all they're involved in, copping the feeling. What any musician must do, and this is why most white musicians fail in jazz, they never come to grips with themselves and their own musical traditions. They always get involved in competing. What they should do is recognize the function that they have in a jazz group and to function out of it with the whole history of America which is theirs. That's what America is. All these people. And to know what to do with all these things, blend them and make them go on, that's what creating the new music is about."

But rather than believe that such blunt attitudes have helped keep him out of work, Taylor believes it has been strictly a musical matter. "They thought I was denying," he says of his critics, "because that's their thing, to kill fathers, because that's what America is built on, the slaying of tradition. Jazz is the only art form in which the tradition can be seen, and you consciously can gain from it if you wish. Jazz is the only art form in which you can see four different generations working together, and see how they're growing."

Probably the single most crushing blow to Taylor's musical career came in 1959, with the enormous impact on the New York musical scene of the alto saxophonist Ornette Coleman. Taylor says accurately of Coleman that "we play music differently, in every way," and some influential critics who had thought that Taylor would bring about the breakthrough they had been expecting abandoned his cause and made Coleman the center of the most violent jazz controversy in several years.

Since that time, Taylor has gone about his work practically without notice. Associated with such musicians as Charles, Lacy, and the late vibraphonist Earl Griffith in groups with uncompromising names like "The Bleecker Street Devils," he has been pursuing his primary aim, which is to compose a body of music and have a group to play it. Six Taylor LPs have been released on five different labels since Newport, all of them well received in the press. Of them, the Contemporary album *Looking Ahead!* probably contains his best work. (It is a comment on the business aspects of jazz that one of these LPs, originally recorded as the Cecil Taylor Quintet, on which tenor saxophonist John Coltrane appeared under the contractually necessary pseudonym "Blue Train," has since been reissued, now that the saxophonist is a top draw, as a Coltrane album.)

Some of these groups have been interesting, with slight ensemble overtones of Mingus and early Monk, but the strong possibility exists that Taylor, who says "I think of the piano as an orchestra," is, like Art Tatum, a pianist who functions best alone. Like Tatum, he often overwhelms his sidemen; like Monk, his accompaniments, which many consider inapposite, are often more fascinating than the solos they are intended to support.

He has, however, come to be recognized as an important jazz composer, in a direct line from Ellington and Monk. A composer's job is to "organize sounds," he says, utilizing a "compression of energy," and Taylor has an extremely explicit philosophy of jazz composition. "Thelonious Monk and Charlie Parker," he explains, "wrote heads that have all the energy and all the rhythmical and musical qualities of a symphony in twelve measures. They say I follow Europe, but every hipster knows that the Europeans are looking, really, at jazz. The long form is exasperated. Nobody writes long form music any more. It's nineteenth century. The sonata is out, old-fashioned. That's what all Webern is about. So, it means that what they're trying to get to is the kernel, the short musical statement. When they come to the point where everything happens, where the development, the climax is, that's good. Why not just give me that? That's music, that should stand by itself."

Such audience as he has had perhaps allows his insistence on not choosing a "pretty" melody because of his enormous technique and a stage presence that almost makes him a "visual act." This last quality made him an ideal replacement for the regular group of actor-musicians who went on three-week vacation in the summer of 1960 from the cast of Jack Gelber's *The Connection*, the Pirandello-like, supposedly improvised play about narcotics which had such a long run at New York's Living Theatre. His presence came as a shock, to audience and actors alike. "I'll never forget the first night we played," Taylor recalls. "One of the actors said, 'What the hell is going on up here?' Gelber told me that I was changing the meaning of his play. I was destroying the meaning of his play by the music I was playing. Mr. Gelber wished music that was in what he considered, I imagine, the Charlie Parker idiom, the Bud Powell idiom. I, of course, knew that I was going to do music that was for a theater piece, which meant that it would be music that I would create because of the situation presented. For the first time in that play, the actors were not mere props, they were integrated with what was going on. They called it improvised theater, but the only improvising that was going on, we were doing it, most of the time. It was a marvelous experience. It's like life, it was both hell and beautiful." After six weeks, an extension of the original three, it got more and more like hell as Taylor would arrive late as a protest against an untuned piano ("They'd fix a broken seat, wouldn't they?"), and his career as an actor came to an end.

Taylor is an acute, waspish critic, good enough to be a professional, not only of his own sidemen, whom he reprimanded from the stage during the run of the play under the guise of "improvisation," but of all musicians. He has little respect for any but his totems, Ellington and Monk, who might be surprised to hear themselves referred to as "period" musicians ("We're all period musicians"). Although he can be difficult to get along with, the players who have worked with him have all benefitted from the situation ("He puts himself into the music," one associate has said, "with such a beautiful drive and so *fully* that he makes me get that way"), and most of them would be happy for the opportunity to play with him again. Practice sessions with Taylor sometimes closely resemble school.

When Taylor plays in public, the response is still likely to be divided. One night, I stood at the bar of the Five Spot, where he was appearing. After the first number, a crew-cut, tweedy young man to my left said, "They must all be smoking that pot. They couldn't play that way unless they smoked that pot." After the second number, the standee to my right, bearded and dishevelled, said, "That's the most beautiful music I've ever heard in my life. That man must have the answer to everything." At the end of the set, a well-dressed, mild-mannered man came up to Taylor and said, "I think you're the world's greatest living performing artist."

Taylor tries not to think about such remarks. He feels reasonably certain that he will always eat, but refuses to concern himself with the problems of fame. "I, certainly, will never become a success, so I don't have to worry about it. Who wants art here? We want viable, bended plants that can be put in anybody's garden." He believes implicitly in his role as an extension of traditional music—"What I'm fighting against is the group power that says you can't go *here*"—but has little time for the kind of personal advocacy that leads many musicians into agents' offices: "What's the point in it? They pick *you*. They want *you*. They get *you*. They find *you*." When reminded that it took Thelonious Monk, to whom his career bears startling resemblances, fifteen years to become a success, he replies mysteriously, "I don't have that kind of time."

The only indication of a commercial breakthrough he has had came in November 1962, when he took a trio, including alto saxophonist Jimmy Lyons and drummer Sonny Murray, on a tour of Scandinavia, portions of which are preserved on a Fantasy LP. The music, apparently, met the same mixture of adulation and puzzlement that greeted it in the States. On his return, Taylor said only that "they have good pianos over there."

One night after watching ballerina Maria Tallchief, Taylor remarked, "She made me think, for about five minutes, that the only worthwhile thing in the world to be was a dancer." There have been nights when he has made people feel that way about the piano; there have even been nights when he has made people think that the mild-mannered man at the Five Spot might be right. But even if popular success never comes, he is prepared for that. "If you want to be a jazz musician," he says, "there's a price you have to pay. You have to know who you are. *You* have to know, and that has to be enough."

Selected Discography

Jazz Advance, TRANSITION 19.
Looking Ahead!, CONTEMPORARY 3562.
The World of Cecil Taylor, CANDID 8006.

ORNETTE COLEMAN

"A bomb outrage to have an influence on public opinion now must go beyond the intention of vengeance or terrorism. It must be purely destructive. It must be that, and only that, beyond the faintest suspicion of any other object. You anarchists should make it clear that you are perfectly determined to make a clean sweep of the whole social creation. . . . The demonstration must be against learning—science. But not every science will do. The attack must have all the shocking senselessness of gratuitous blasphemy. Since bombs are your means of expression, it would be really telling if one could throw a bomb into pure mathematics. But that is impossible. Go for the first meridian. You don't know the middle classes as well as I do. Their sensibilities are jaded. The first meridian. Nothing better, and nothing easier, I should think."

THE SECRET AGENT—JOSEPH CONRAD

IN THE SUMMER of 1959, the pianist and composer John Lewis gave an interview to an Italian jazz magazine which was subsequently printed in the original English in *The Jazz Review*. Asked about new trends, Lewis replied that "there are two young people I met in California—an alto player named Ornette Coleman and a trumpet played named Don Cherry. I've never heard anything like them before. Ornette is the driving force of the two. They're almost like twins; they play together like I've never heard anybody play together. It's not like any ensemble that I have ever heard, and I can't figure out what it's all about yet. Ornette is, in a sense, an extension of Charlie Parker and the first I've heard. This is the real need that I think has to take place, to extend the basic ideas of Bird until they are not playing an imitation but actually something new. I think that they may have come up with something, not perfect yet, and still in the early stages but nevertheless very fresh and interesting."

Many who read the interview were doubtless intrigued; Lewis is a figure of substance and an often astute judge of musicianship. But the announcement was misleading in its casual understatement. Although Lewis, a career diplomat of impeccable grooming and bland self-effacement, was not likely to be carrying a bomb in his briefcase, the equally mild-mannered Ornette Coleman of whom he spoke was, indeed, carrying a bomb—a *plastique*, as it happened—which would explode accepted notions of jazz rhythm, melody, and harmony.

Coleman's music was seen not as a bomb but a panacea in an October, 1959 *Jazz Review* piece by Martin Williams dealing with The School of Jazz at Lenox, Massachusetts, at which Coleman was a student. John Lewis, the school's director, had arranged for Atlantic, his recording company, to send Coleman to Lenox on a scholarship. Coleman was by then under contract to Atlantic. "I honestly believe," Williams wrote, "(not that I am alone or particularly original in believing it) that what Ornette Coleman is doing on alto will affect the whole character of jazz music profoundly and pervasively, and that the first consideration is that what he plays can be very beautiful. . . . When he stood up to solo on the blues with the big band on the first day of school, I was taken. It was as if he opened up something in one's soul and opened up the way for jazz to grow. His music makes a new sensibility for one's ears and heart and mind, all the while including the most fundamental things in jazz. It seems impossible for Ornette Coleman to talk about music without soon using the word 'love' and when he plays one knows that, undeluded, it is love of man his music is talking about. As is so necessary with an innovator in the beginning he is not afraid of what his muse tells him to play: 'I don't know how it's going to sound before I play it any more than anybody else does.' The step he is taking, like all great steps, seems inevitable only when someone has taken it and Cole-

man is taking it with a sublime stubbornness: if you put a
conventional chord or rhythm under my note, you limit the
number of choices I have for my next note; if you do not,
my melody may move freely with far greater choice of directions. . . . Several of the faculty justly hoped that 'the
critics' would not fill him full of wrong ideas about his duty
to be 'the next thing'—or whatever. Somehow, one has the
feeling hearing him play or talk that he will simply do what
he must do, not taking credit for his talent but simply feeling
a duty to explore and use it, so long as he can work not
deluded about 'recognition,' that he will play the music he
hears, obey his muse, and fulfill his destiny as an artist, perhaps listening to what advice seems just and helpful but
forgetting the rest, and resign himself patiently to the fate
that any innovator must have. If he does that, he will be one
of the very few American artists who has ever followed his
talent without letting himself be somehow exploited by his
'public' or his 'notices.' But, honestly, I really think he will."

Some saw in Coleman a repository of peace, wisdom, and
inner serenity. But Coleman is highly complicated, sometimes naïve, sometimes mystical, sometimes suspicious, and
dedicated to the point of obsession. When he came to New
York he became the public darling for a while (Leonard
Bernstein and Dorothy Kilgallen said yes, Kenneth Tynan
said no), then was out of work and living in a succession of
cold-water flats on the Lower East Side.

In between, Coleman became the center of the most violent controversy to divide the jazz world since the arrival of
Charlie Parker. While there were outspoken voices pro (Williams and Nat Hentoff) and con (John Mehegan and Leonard Feather), most critics and musicians equivocated and
evaded, not wishing to make the error of out-of-hand con-
demnation that many of them had made with Parker, yet
unwilling to approve of music that offended and outraged
them. Only Milt Jackson, of the Modern Jazz Quartet,

seemed willing to state pointblank that he saw no clothes on the emperor. "They're afraid to say it is nothing," Jackson said. "There's no such thing as free form. We're just getting around to knowing what Charlie Parker was playing. They threw him on the public and said this is it. You can't do it." And Miles Davis remarked, "Hell, just listen to what he writes and how he plays. If you're talking psychologically, the man is all screwed up inside."

Coleman himself stayed apart from the battle. "I haven't been hurt," he says, looking back on his journey, "I haven't been made happy, I haven't been anything. To me, I haven't been. I'm interested in playing my music. All these other things have nothing to do with it."

Coleman has gone his own resolute way, often unencumbered by assistance, for most of his life. He was born in Fort Worth, Texas, on March 19, 1930. A cousin, James Jordan, was a saxophonist, and largely due to his influence, Coleman bought himself an alto when he was fourteen. Unable to afford lessons, he got a piano instruction book and proceeded to teach himself. He decided that C on his horn was A in the book, and continued playing in that fashion until the leader of a church band set him straight. Still, he believes that "the only way you learn is when you teach it to yourself." Two years later, he switched to tenor, on which more jobs were available. "At first," he has told Nat Hentoff, "I used to be one of those people like Big Jay McNeeley. I'd lie on the floor and play and do all those other gimmicks." Years later, after his reputation had been established on alto, he returned to tenor for a recording, telling A. B. Spellman, "The tenor is a rhythm instrument, and the best statements Negroes have made of what their soul is have been on tenor saxophone. Now you think about it and you'll see I'm right. The tenor's got that thing, that honk, you can get to people with it. Sometimes you can be playing that tenor and I'm telling you, the people want to jump across the rail.

Especially that D flat blues. You can really reach their souls
with that D flat blues . . ."

When he first played tenor, his message only inspired his
auditors to fire him or beat him up. After playing around
Fort Worth for a few years, he got a job with a carnival
band whose leader fired him and left him stranded in
Natchez, Mississippi. The Natchez police, displeased with
the long hair and beard Coleman affected at the time, ran
him out of town. He went to New Orleans, where he found
work with a rhythm-and-blues band led by Clarence Samuels.
One night, he was invited to meet some men in Baton
Rouge. Their object in meeting him, it developed, was to
provide an object lesson for traveling musicians who were
too attractive to the local girls. Coleman lost some teeth
and his tenor.

When he bought another horn, it was an alto. He returned
to Fort Worth, where he stayed until he joined another
rhythm-and-blues band, led by Pee Wee Crayton. By the
time the band got to Los Angeles, Crayton was paying Coleman not to play, so Coleman left.

He worked as a house boy in Los Angeles, and attended
sessions where the musicians were nearly unanimous in their
hostility. Going back to Fort Worth for two years, he formed
his own band, playing "what the people liked." Coleman
remembers those years with some bitterness.

"Where I come from, in Fort Worth," he says, "they have
a big cattle industry. It's where the West begins, and where
life ends. I was playing there in a white place, I had a beard
and my hair was thicker than it is now, and this fellow came
up to me and says, 'Say, boy, you can really play saxophone.
I imagine where you come from they call you Mister, don't
they?' He couldn't see me with my hair and beard coming
from Texas, Negroes don't go around looking like that. So I
said, 'No, this is my home.' 'I want to shake your hand,' he
says, 'it's an honor to shake your hand because you're really

a saxophone player, but you're still a nigger to me.' That's how sick he was. There's no answer for that. That's insanity. Playing in a white place, I couldn't tell him what I wanted to tell him, because I would have been jeopardizing my life.

"Because of being a Negro, I've been in certain places and had certain kinds of sadness that would never bother you, that you could never conceive. Do you think some sadness surpasses a reason why you don't have to be sad?"

Coleman remembers that one man, who told him, "I got enough money to burn a wet elephant but I ain't gonna give it away," offered him three dollars a night to play from nine PM till two AM. "I can see," he says, "that someone who never had to worry about being something to someone, but someone always had to be something to him, how you can get like that. I thought that as long as they were white, they all had the same thing in common, to control and rule you." Nor were other working conditions all they could be. "During intermission," he recalls of one Texas club, "I'd have to go in the back and sit down like I was a porter. One night a drunken woman came right up in front of me and raised her dress over her head, and I was frightened.

"People in Texas," he sums up, "they're so wealthy, it's still like slavery. You had to be a servant. You had to be serving somebody to make some money. When I finished high school, all the kids I knew who'd been to college and came back, they had porter jobs. What's the reason of going to college? That's the reason I didn't go. You got to try to get a job teaching in the colored school system, or that's it. People been teaching there for fifty years, you have to wait for them to die. I didn't come from a poor family, I came from a *po'* family. Poorer than poor. Even the principal where I went to school worked in the summer at the hotel where I worked as a busboy. I saw him doing some things, I didn't have respect for him." The Texans, Coleman says, "thought I was just a mixed up, complex Negro."

In 1954, Coleman again went to Los Angeles, where he supported himself by working in a department store as a stock boy and elevator operator. He used to bring books on music theory to work with him, park the elevator, and read. Coleman, married by this time, lost his job when the store installed self-starting elevators.

Trumpeter Don Cherry and bassist Don Payne heard Coleman's music at sessions in Los Angeles and were impressed with it. One night in 1958, the well-known bassist Red Mitchell heard some of Coleman's music in Payne's apartment, and was also impressed. Mitchell, knowing that pick-up groups for recording dates are often at a loss for fresh material, suggested that Coleman might make some money by selling his pieces to Lester Koenig, who owns the Los Angeles jazz label, Contemporary.

Coleman went around to see Koenig, mentioning Mitchell's name. Koenig asked Coleman to play his music on the piano, but Coleman could not play the instrument that well. While Koenig was trying to figure out how he could hear the music, Coleman, who had his saxophone with him, took the horn out and began to play. The result was an album of Coleman's music, performed by the composer.

Coleman recorded two albums for Contemporary, and began to work intermittently. John Tynan mentioned him a couple of times in *Down Beat*. His change of luck came one· night when Payne brought the Modern Jazz Quartet's bassist, Percy Heath, to hear the saxophonist play. Heath, in turn, brought John Lewis, and things began to happen.

Acting on Lewis' recommendation, Nesuhi Ertegun of Atlantic Records signed Coleman, and paid for his scholarship at Lenox. While still in California, the first Ornette Coleman Quartet—Coleman, Cherry, bassist Charlie Haden and drummer Billy Higgins—recorded two Atlantic albums, and with the money advanced against record royalties, moved to New York. In November, 1959, the quartet opened at the Five

Spot for the first extended engagement Coleman had ever had, and the battle began.

Unfortunately, Coleman immediately became a scapegoat; critics used him as a shield behind which to take potshots at other critics. Two of Coleman's staunchest admirers were Nat Hentoff and Martin Williams, co-editors of *The Jazz Review*. The publisher of that magazine, Hsio Wen Shih, became Coleman's manager for a while. Some journalists began to see a Lenox-Atlantic-*Jazz Review* Establishment, forcing Coleman on the jazz world. There was talk of king makers determined to prove the typewriter more powerful than the ear, ignoring the obvious precept that even a Golem will not find an audience unless it can play. With such poison pellets in the air, reasoned comment on Coleman's music became nearly impossible.

Many writers found it handy to deride Coleman because he likes a plastic alto, white and smaller than the standard model. It looked like a toy, particularly when seen alongside Don Cherry's pocket Pakistani trumpet. But Charlie Parker had played such a saxophone at times, and Coleman, who had been using plastic altos since 1954, clearly explained his selection to Hentoff: "I needed a new horn badly but I didn't have much money. A man in the music store said he could sell me a new horn—a plastic model—for the price of a used Selmer. I didn't like it at first, but I figured it would be better to have a new horn anyway. Now I won't play any other. They're made in England, and I have to send for them. They're only good for a year the way I play them. The plastic horn is better for me because it responds more completely to the way I blow into it. There's less resistance than from metal. Also, the notes seem to come out detached, almost like you could see them. What I mean is that notes from a metal instrument include the sounds the metal itself makes when it vibrates. The notes from a plastic horn are purer. In addition, the body of the horn is made flat, like a flute

keyboard, whereas a regular horn is curved. On a flat keyboard, I can dig in more."

In the notes to Coleman's first Atlantic LP, Martin Williams wrote, "As several developments in the last few years
have shown, no one really needs to state all those chords
that nearly everyone uses . . . Someone had to break through
the walls that those harmonies have built and restore melody
. . . he breaks through the usual thirty-two, sixteen and
twelve bar forms both in his compositions and in his improvising . . . most jazz solos are not related to their theme-
melodies, but to the chords with which the themes are harmonized. Coleman and Cherry may relate to the emotion,
the pitch, the rhythm, the melody of a theme, without relating to 'chords' or bar divisions . . ." To this, Williams ap-
pended some remarks by composer-conductor Gunther
Schuller, which effectively outline both Coleman's techniques and the reasons why his adherents find them valuable: "Perhaps the most outstanding element in Ornette's
musical conception is an utter and complete freedom. His
musical inspiration operates in a world uncluttered by conventional bar lines, conventional chord changes, and conventional ways of blowing or fingering a saxophone. Such practical 'limitations' did not even have to be overcome in his
music; they somehow never existed for him. Despite this—
or more accurately, *because* of this—his playing has a deep
inner logic."

Coleman himself says, "I haven't read anyone yet who
wrote about my music. The only person I know that could
write about my music would be me. Writers can write about
the effects of it. Nobody's ever written about the music itself,
because nobody knows. It's beautiful for people to be interested and help me, but it's much more beautiful whenever
something exists, it doesn't have to be analyzed for symbolic
meaning, when it exists on its own. You know, they put all
kinds of stuff in toothpaste, but you don't try to go out and

find what it is. They might put anything in toothpaste. You don't worry about what they got in it. You use it, and that's it."

Coleman, as Charlie Mingus has pointed out, "is really an old-fashioned alto player. He is not as modern as Bird." He is concerned with duplicating the sounds and emotions of the human voice on his instrument, a goal that is present in the trumpet growls and trombone moans of the oldest jazz, as well as in the raucous harmonicas and twanging guitars of the most primitive bluesmen. Indeed, Coleman's most out-standing characteristic is his feel for the blues, present everywhere in his playing. He moans, he shrieks, he hollers, he laughs. In discussing his music, he uses the word "pitch" with an aura that recalls a political reformer exhorting his constituency to "move forward." He uses it because the word "note" is imprecise. Musical notation is a result of the mathe-matical formula of the well-tempered scale; the equivalent of the notes available on a piano. Both a vocalist and Cole-man on his alto can produce sounds which cannot be dupli-cated on a piano; the well-tempered scale, for Coleman, thus becomes a fiction of convenience.

While the whole of Coleman's music may seem anarchic, its parts obviously are not; they are, indeed, quite old-fashioned, as Mingus says. And Coleman himself does not claim that he plays with absolute freedom ("It was when I found out that I could make mistakes that I knew I was on to something.")

Many of Coleman's pieces have programmatic titles which attempt to convey a mood: *Lonely Woman, Congeniality, Peace.* While these pieces are not harmonized ("Chords are just names for sounds, which really need no names at all, as names are sometimes confusing"), the notes imply an area of sound, and the titles a mood for solos.

Whitney Balliett has written, "It is hard to think of any jazz musician, alive or dead, who has ever exhibited as much naked emotion as Coleman." This is apparent to anyone who has heard him, and may have more to do with the Coleman controversy than all the talk about form. Albert Goldman, who wrote in *The New Leader* that "Coleman's vision of the world is terrifying: bleak, cold, desolate, full of frightening violence and the lonely presence of death," may have discovered the true reason why people who do not even know what a chord is walk out of the room when Coleman plays.

There is general agreement that Coleman would be able to hold a performance together if only by the power of his individual emotion, his personality as expressed through his horn. Coming from the Southwest, much of his playing echoes not only the blues, but the Mexican and country music that he has heard, three traditions that come together most successfully in the remarkable piece called *Ramblin'*.

"I'm from the country," Coleman says. "I *do* play from memory of what I have felt and heard. One night I'd just gotten off work in Texas, and there was a white fellow standing on the corner by the bus stop, yodeling, and he was very sad. We started a conversation. He was a truckdriver, to New York and back, and he was married. One of his buddies at work had been makin' it with his old lady. He thought he was working to make his family happy, but he's away for three days, his wife gets lonely, and she found her man. Me and that man had nothing in common, but I can remember the whole feeling, the way he was singing, the tears in his eyes, everything about him. I can just think of that and recreate the kind of feeling. I felt sad for him, because he really had the blues. Lots of my playing is like that. I play just life, things that I encounter and experience, and what you hear, maybe I've been exposed to that."

Such a statement goes a long way toward explaining how Coleman can play as he does. But the tenuous adhesive of individual emotion is not enough for all players. Coleman's first trumpeter, Don Cherry, seemed to have worked out a distillation of Coleman's more overt mannerisms, and early in his career seemed to be attempting to substitute this for personal expression. Coleman may be referring to Cherry when he says, "I've been trying to find musicians who had a way of playing so that they wouldn't take what I was trying to do and say this is them, but take what I am doing and use it to better what they're doing." Just this seems to have happened with three of the finest contemporary saxophonists: Sonny Rollins, John Coltrane, and Jackie McLean; these players have been able to take elements of Coleman's approach while sacrificing none of the personal idiosyncrasies of their previously established styles.

It is even more notable that each of the three has used one or more rhythm players formerly employed by Coleman. Each has made some use of Coleman's notion of freeing melody from what has been melodramatically called "the chord prison," but it seems likely that Coleman's irrevocable contribution will be rhythmic. He has found, one after another, superb bassists and drummers, virtually unknown before working with him, who have since begun to attract wider attention. The drummers have included Billy Higgins, Ed Blackwell and Charles Moffet; the bassists, Charlie Haden, Jimmy Garrison, David Izenzon, and the late Scott LaFaro. Since Coleman first began to have impact, the number of remarkable new rhythm players to appear has been unusually high. Coleman explained in *Metronome* that "my music doesn't have any real time, no metric time. It has time, but not in the sense that you can time it. It's more like breathing, a natural, freer time. . . . I like spread rhythm, rhythm that has a lot of freedom in it, rather than the more conventional, *netted* rhythm. With spread rhythm, you might tap your feet awhile, then stop, then later start tapping again. That's what I like. Otherwise, you tap your feet so much, you forget what you hear. You just hear the rhythm."

As one drummer remarked, in onomatopoetic epitaph for

the conventional rhythm section, "Goodbye ching-chinga-ching."

But hello what? The most extreme indication so far has been an Atlantic album, *Free Jazz*, recorded by what Coleman calls a "Double Quartet" (two saxophones, two trumpets, two bases, two drums). By comparison, Coleman's own early recordings have Mozartean placidity. After a brief opening statement, "each man goes for himself": rhythmically, melodically, harmonically. As if to bear out the previous remarks, the bassists and drummers (Haden, LaFaro, Higgins, Blackwell) are superb, although it is interesting that during Coleman's solo the drummers are reduced to the dull rumbling figure (deedle, deedle, deedle) that, in this day of rhythmic freedom, seems regressive. The other horn-men (Eric Dolphy, Fredie Hubbard, Cherry) remind one of a remark of Coleman's which is not so self-evident as it might sound: "I think you have to hear something new to play something new." The trumpeters, especially Hubbard, hear music conventionally, and point up, by example, the terrors which await anyone not ready for freedom. Coleman finds snatches of lovely melody, but not the others. Since Cherry's replacement, Bobby Bradford, returned home to Texas, Coleman has worked with only bass and drums.

He has not worked often. In December 1962, Coleman played a Town Hall concert he had arranged for himself. It was his only job in about a year. A previous Double Quartet one-nighter in Cleveland, which ironically was to include saxophonist Steve Lacy, most harmonically oriented of musicians, never took place, and dissolved in legal wranglings. Not all of this is due to the widespread hostility to his music, nor is it traceable to publicity techniques like the lead-with-your-chin titles which record companies have given his albums: *Change Of The Century, Tomorrow Is The Question, The Shape of Jazz To Come*. Much of it is due to Coleman himself.

Whether or not he ever had the inner peace attributed to him, he does not have it now. A small, slight, bearded man, once a model of impeccability but now less carefully dressed, he speaks very softly and abstractly. He now seems more bitter about those who have aided him than about his enemies. "I haven't had anyone try to help me or not help me. It's just everyone's been going along with what's been happening, in their own mind. I have to say this. Everything that I've done musically has been part of some business transaction. I have a one-track way of thinking. I think of people as what they're doing. If they're doing something that will help me, that's good. If they don't, that's them. I wouldn't want to change my music for publicity men or booking agents." This essentially solipsistic view has led him through a rapid succession of personal managers, each of whom is replaced as Coleman feels the winds of a betrayal. He once hit trumpeter Don Cherry just as they were about to go onstage at a concert. The prices he asks for appearances are more in line with his publicity than his drawing power, and he has found no takers. In nearly solitary battle against a business establishment and fandom that regards him with increasing indifference, he left Atlantic Records and in 1963, announced he would form his own company, Fugue, and write a book which will contain his theory of music, all with the help of a new manager who was not a part of the music business.

It is by no means all his fault. In 1960, Martin Williams wrote accurately that "this is not a 'finished' music, nor is what one can hear now from the Coleman quartet 'finished' improvising, nor has anyone suggested that it is. Hearing this music now is like hearing Armstrong *before* Chicago or hearing Parker *in* Kansas City—perhaps not even like that, since what Coleman is working on represents in a sense an even more radical departure from established convention." But Armstrong, or at least Parker, at the comparable stages in

their careers, did go through something of what Coleman
has been experiencing.

Jazz requires heroes with much greater frequency than
they are likely to arrive, and a player who has a glimmer
of what might be new may find himself innovating in a fish-
bowl, with little opportunity to perfect his style under anything like normal circumstances, with no chance for privacy
when it is most needed. When Coleman first appeared at the
Five Spot, the audiences lined up along the bar were composed of curiosity-seekers, musicians waiting to be shown
(and fearful that they might be), the faithful, and critics,
unsure of Coleman, but fearful of being left standing flat-
footed while the next new development passed them by. To
which Coleman adds, "The first band I had was out of my
control, and that was some more pressure on me that I
couldn't really afford to have."

At a later date, he could look back on the furor with
greater equanimity. "To me, it's all kind of funny. There's
nothing but music, and if you need a class of people to
identify it, that's another thing. To me, people identify music
more than music identifies people. There's a law to what I'm
playing, but that law is a law that when you get tired of it,
you can change it. It's only a law because every time you
hear it, that same feeling is going to be there. It's not something you can break or change. All music is really like that.
When you play the blues, you could be using a thousand
changes, but because it's the blues itself, that's the law itself.
The effect it has, not the way it's put together. But by certain
people using a certain natural law that they hear, makes
what they're doing different than the other person. I don't
know much about words, but there are just a few words that
describe exactly what something is. Music has suffered from
that. People read something, and get an idea in their minds.
The only thing you can do for music is feel it and hear it."

Coleman can explain his own music, though, and tends to

be disarming about it, as when he told Whitney Balliett, "I know exactly what I'm doing. I'm beginning where Charlie Parker stopped. Parker's melodic lines were placed across ordinary chord progressions. My melodic approach is based on phrasing, and my phrasing is an extension of how I hear the intervals and pitch of the tunes I play. There is no end to pitch. You can play flat in tune and sharp in tune. It's a question of vibration. My phrasing is spontaneous, not a style. A style happens when your phrasing hardens. Jazz music is the only music in which the same note can be played night after night but different each time. It's the hidden things, the subconscious that lies in the body and lets you know: you feel this, you play this."

Albert Goldman countered, "it seems excessive to hail him as a master of that new asymmetric, discontinuous form all the hip critics are rooting for because he is not a creator of any kind of form. His playing is a welter of subjunctive expressionism so loose and unformed that he is unable to control or even anticipate it." In this connection, a remark of Don Heckman's in the *Saturday Review* on Coleman's music is especially interesting: "Like action painting, it is the very *act* of improvisation that becomes significant, with the tyranny of inspiration rejected in favor of a deep plumbing of spontaneous and immediate emotions." Coleman, who has become friendly with many of the abstract expressionist "East 10th Street" painters who frequented the Five Spot, might well agree with this.

Coleman has only twice recorded music not his own. The first instance was *Embraceable You*, which he ingenuously described as "the first standard that we have recorded and we played it the way standards are played and with as much spontaneity as we could." Although Coleman, like some other modernists, has never been comfortable in any group other than his own (once invited to sit in by Dizzy Gillespie, he insisted on using his own drummer), he participated in a recording of two Gunther Schuller works, and functioned well, although he once forgot when he was supposed to play.

His experience with more formal music has been frustrating. Thinking of writing larger works for larger groups, "I thought I'd take a few notation lessons from Gunther Schuller. But he doesn't notate the way I play it. So what's the sense of going? I can notate my own music. I don't write bar lines. When I write music down it doesn't have anything to do with how fast it can be played. The pitches of music have their own notation. When you speak, the meaning itself gives the speed to the word. The same thing happens in music. That's what I've been trying to tell these people, but they don't see that. Notation is a universal guide to notes, not to the way music is played. I think music is closer to notation than notation is to music. Like with words. I think punctuation should be for the idea itself, not the way you think about it. If you're going to punctuate something and get a different idea from what's there, why should it be there? When I write a letter, I very seldom put in periods or commas. There are some words that are much stronger than periods or commas."

Even Coleman's friends have not always helped. John Lewis has recorded two versions of *Lonely Woman*, one with the Modern Jazz Quartet and one with a violinist, and both refine away the raw passion of Coleman's vision, leaving a cold perfection that was noticeably absent from the original.

Coleman has gotten more and more fatalistic about such things. "You're born," he says, "you learn something to do, you work, and you die." Separated from his wife and son, and in the absence of regular employment, he has concentrated on writing. He is somewhat puzzled by the reception his music has met with ("That's the only thing in my life that makes me feel sad, when I know something that I'd like to explain but I can't"), but his conviction has not diminished: "There's nobody complete. If you met someone who could tell you what was going to happen to you forever, and you told them to write their name, they'd probably write it jagged. Say you wrote a word that wasn't in the dictionary. Would you expect me to worry about what it means if you proved your point?" The world, he adds, irrefutably, "ain't you writing, and it ain't me playing music."

By now, the voices of those who said that Coleman was *not* playing music have been mostly stilled. In a way, he has simply gone to the furthest reaches of what Gerry Mulligan implied when he formed his pianoless quartet (like Mulligan, Coleman has become an excellent amateur pianist). But his remark "I'd like to hear a difference between the tune and the improvising" has had wider implications than many will countenance. Insisting that "I know enough music and I know enough about the horn to know everything I'm doing," he returns over and over again to the theme of what is "natural." Admitting that he himself is not always "natural" ("My mind is like a vacuum cleaner, it picks up a lot of dirt, and it takes me a long time to get rid of it"), he says, "I think feeling is the only thing that is creative."

Early in his career, Coleman told Nat Hentoff, "I think one day music will be a lot freer. Then the pattern for a tune, for instance, will be forgotten and the tune itself will be the pattern, and won't have to be forced into conventional patterns." The remark turns out to have been what some general semanticists call a "self-fulfilling prophesy". It is happening, and Coleman has accomplished it. He is being followed already, by fakers, and by some of the most valuable musicians we have. He has, indeed, sparked the first major change in jazz since Parker. And he may have ruined his own career in doing so.

As the fifties in effect have been "Jazz Since Parker," it is conceivable that the sixties will be "Jazz Since Coleman". Once, speaking generally, Coleman made a statement that sums up his own career better than anything I have seen:

"Do you think it's possible for a kid to be brought up without being told how to do something and end up doing it? I believe that it's possible for a kid to pick up an instrument and play creative, and never know nothing about it. I think kids are very close to having a creative mind. I have a little boy, and if I had the power to get him and let him live with me, I would give him the opportunity to live with what his mind is made of. That's a quality that every person has, but we've lost it, that's the reason we go out and see people who haven't lost it. You see a person with a brilliant mind, it means he's been less touched by things than we have. I don't think that what anyone really wants to do has anything to do with destroying."

Selected Discography

The Shape of Jazz To Come, ATLANTIC 1317.
Change of The Century, ATLANTIC 1327.
Ornette!, ATLANTIC 1378.
Ornette On Tenor, ATLANTIC 1394.